BACKWARDS
IN HIGH HEELS

THE IMPOSSIBLE ART OF BEING FEMALE

BACKWARDS IN HIGH HEELS

THE IMPOSSIBLE ART OF BEING FEMALE

—

BY TANIA KINDERSLEY & SARAH VINE

FOURTH ESTATE · LONDON

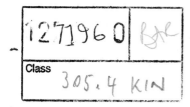
First published in Great Britain in 2009 by
Fourth Estate
An imprint of HarperCollinsPublishers
77–85 Fulham Palace Road
London W6 8JB
www.4thestate.co.uk

Visit our authors' blog: www.fifthestate.co.uk

9 8 7 6 5 4 3 2

A catalogue record for this book is available from the British Library

ISBN 978-0-00-727383-6

Typeset in GillSans by 'OMEDESIGN
Illustrations by Marta Munoz

Printed and bound by Arvato Print Italy

CONTENTS.

ONE ..... LOVE I

TWO ..... FOOD 32

THREE .... CAREER 50

FOUR ..... MEN 72

FIVE ..... HEALTH 96

SIX ..... POLITICS AND THE NEW
ORTHODOXY 122

SEVEN .... PHILOSOPHY OF LIFE,
SELF-ESTEEM AND THE
WHOLE DAMN THING 152

EIGHT .... DRESSING AND SHOPPING 172

NINE ..... MOTHERHOOD AND FAMILY .. 192

TEN ..... MONEY 234

ELEVEN .... GRIEF 254

TWELVE ... AGE 270

THIRTEEN .. BEAUTY 290

FOURTEEN .. SEX 312

FIFTEEN ... THE PRACTICAL CHAPTER 334

TO ALL THE GREAT WOMEN
(AND A FEW GREAT MEN).

INTRODUCTION.

There was a great indie pop tune not so very long ago which went: This is not a love, is not a love, is not a love, is not a love song.

This is not a self-help book. It is not a How To manual. There will be no easy ten-step life plans. If you want one of those, go immediately to another section of the bookshop. You will find no admonitory instructions about how to keep your man happy or make your hair glossy or lose weight. We may occasionally pass on something about life which we have learnt, or offer an illustrative anecdote, because we love an anecdote. Quite frankly, we are in absolutely no position to set down diamond-hard advice, because half the time we don't know what the hell we are doing. If this book is about anything, it is about figuring it out as you go along, about making up your own mind and trusting that mind, whatever the zeitgeist might be telling you.

It is the literary equivalent of the conversations that women have every day of the week. There might be a few more flights of fancy and moments of abstract thought; there will be more going off on tangents, because one of us is addicted to tangents. But the spirit of it is exactly the same as when you carefully put your friend back together after she has taken an existential bashing: you do the empathy, you make the jokes, you remind her that everyone gets a little bit crazy sometimes and there is no law against that.

We don't necessarily want to be correct; we want to make you feel that you are all right, in all your complexity, because there are entire industries out there devoted to insisting that you, as women, are somehow all wrong, and we've had enough of it. We are mad as hell and we're not going to take it any more.

Tania Kindersley and Sarah Vine

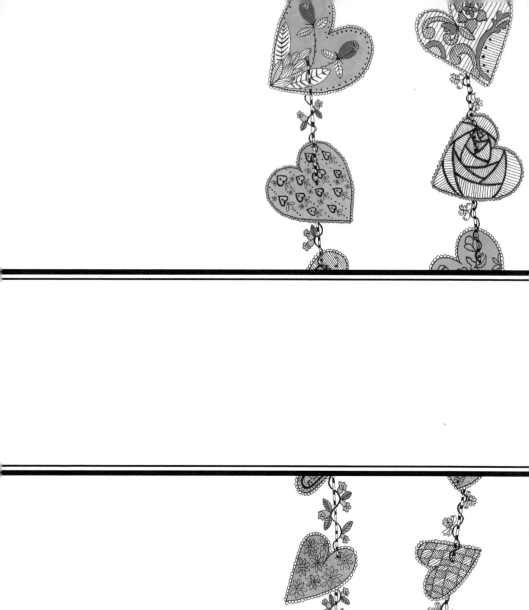

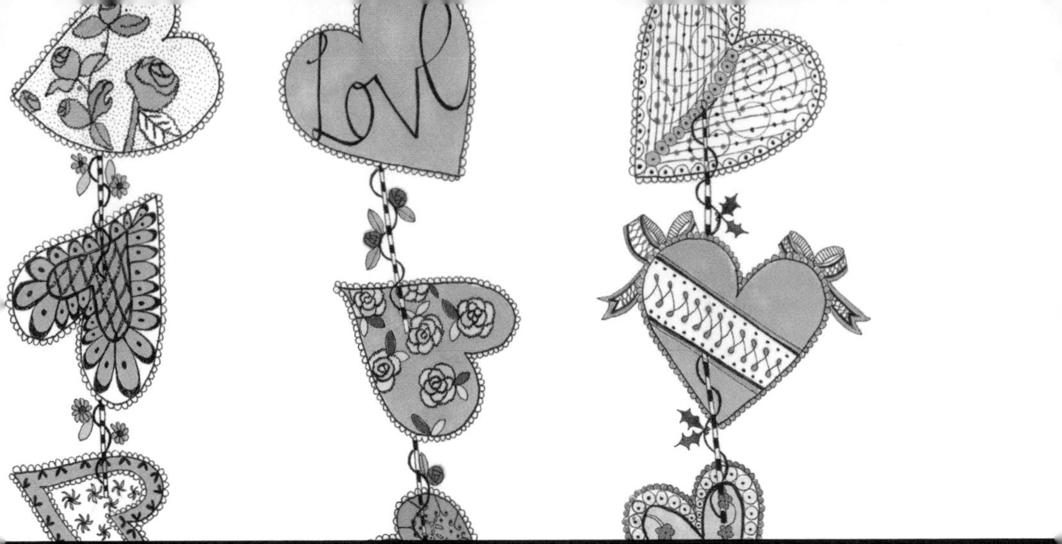

LOVE

–

CHAPTER ONE

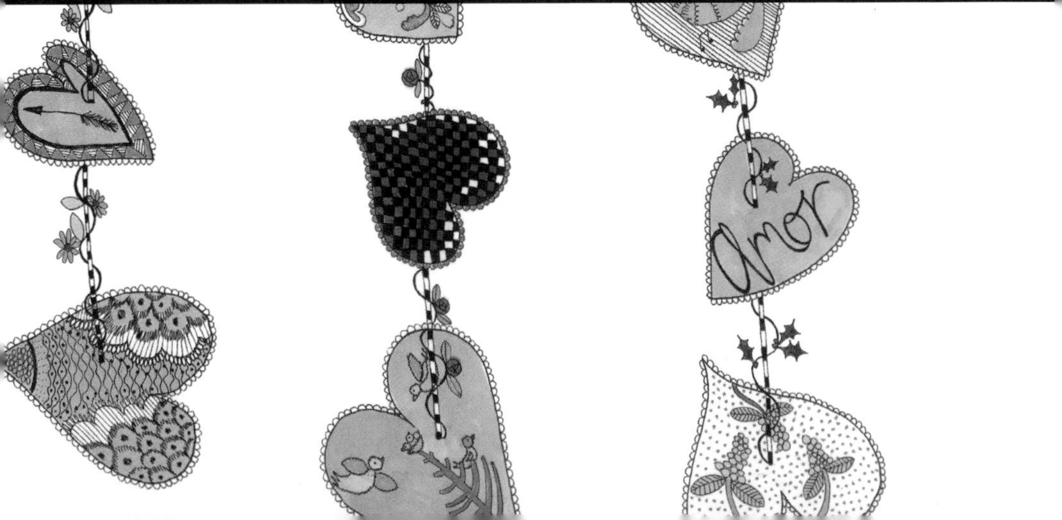
Amor

ROMANTIC LOVE.

There are twenty-one dictionary definitions for the word love. Every woman (or Everywoman, the heroine of this book) may come to a point in her middle life when she suspects she doesn't understand the first thing about any of these. Poets, philosophers, playwrights and pop singers from Socrates to Stevie Wonder have had a great deal to say about love. It is the sweetest thing; it is a red, red rose; it is a battlefield; it is a drug, a delusion, a lunacy. It is the answer, and the question. It is a balm, and a piercing arrow. H.L. Mencken compared it to perceptual anaesthesia; Keats wrote that it was his religion; Shakespeare called it a familiar, a devil, an ever-fixed mark, a smoke, a fire, a sea, a madness, a fever, a choking gall; it is like sunshine after rain, and does not bend.

Of the various loves, romantic love is the most complicated and inexplicable. It can come on when you least expect it (and with the most unsuitable person), it can cast you from the heights of ecstasy to the abyss of despair, it can roar in you one moment then dissipate as quickly

as breath on glass. It is what drives you to offer yourself to another human for the rest of your natural life, but only a few years later you may look back and have no memory at all of that initial ecstasy. Romantic love can be so confusing that sometimes you just want to give up on the whole thing and concentrate on the nature of dark matter, or macro-economics, or something else less tiring.

A little biology can be helpful here. In the first throes of romantic love you are under the influence of a powerful chemical cocktail: dopamine (which makes opiates look like aspirin) is rushing through your veins. As if that were not enough, a perfect mixture of vasopressin and oxytocin, the attachment hormones, are raging around your body. Much of this was discovered through extensive study of prairie voles, who mate for life, spend a great deal of time tenderly grooming each other and nesting together, and studiously avoid meeting other potential partners. If only all men were just like prairie voles, we say, but if wishes were horses we would all be Lady Godiva.

Aside from the chemical cosh, you also have the small brain problem. MRI scans have shown that falling in love involves only a very tiny part of the brain, a much smaller part than is used when, say, operating heavy machinery. Researchers at University College London have remarked wryly that it was fascinating to reflect that Helen of Troy could have launched a thousand ships through the agency of such a limited expanse of cortex.

It is vital, therefore, to bear in mind that when falling in love and choosing your mate you may be making a decision about the rest of your life based on only *a fraction of your cognitive function*. This limited section of the brain is also the exact same part that responds to the ingestion of cocaine, which means that you may select a partner for life, move to Anchorage and decide to make many babies, all based on the same area of the cortex which enjoys illegal substances that make you talk accelerated gibberish all night long.

Plato said that love is a mental disease. Modern researchers agree enthusiastically, categorising love as a form of madness and echoing what psychologists have been telling tearful patients for years. (There are certain shrinks who refuse to treat people in the early throes of love because they are too insane to do a thing with.) Currently, scientists are having a genteel academic squabble over whether love most closely resembles the manic phase of bi-polar disorder, or the characteristics seen in obsessive compulsive disorder.

There is also a school of thought that insists love is a cultural phenomenon. As the great French cynic La Rochefoucauld said, 'People would not fall in love if they had not heard love talked about'. The culture keeps up a rapid-fire bombardment of the power and the glory of romantic love, and yet it seems curious that so many of the Greatest Love Stories Ever Told – Cathy and Heathcliff, Tristan and Isolde, Heloise and Abelard, Lancelot and Guinevere – all end in disaster, if not death and unrestrained carnage. If we were being really sceptical, we might conclude that it is frankly delusional that 'in love' should be regarded as the greatest and most time-consuming aspiration of the modern female.

There is a highly dangerous literary subset to this, most vividly exemplified by Elizabeth Sharp's novel *By Grand Central Station I Sat Down And Wept*, which privileges true love over all other considerations. You can lay waste to families, other people – entire countries even – but it's all perfectly fine because you are doing it in the name of Love. If you ever find yourself leaning towards this point of view, we suggest that you have a strong cup of tea and read something enlightening about pig husbandry until the delusion has passed.

It is only when the insane chemical phase of love dies down that you can tell whether it is the real thing. If it is, it will shift into the deep steady love that gets you through rainy days and financial crises and the small quotidian tasks that make up a life. This is why couples who have been together for fifty years always talk about marrying their best friend.

The mysterious thing about this proper love is that it contains no trace of the early lunacy. It does not make you want to rip the beloved's clothes off at inappropriate moments; it is nothing to do with the wild urge to create a universe with only the two of you in it. Instead, it is the kind of profound affection that makes you smile at idiosyncrasies that anyone else would find irritating or pointless, or get the joke that nobody else will understand. This kind of love is built of the bricks of a hundred small memories and moments in time. It is the feeling you get when you read a story in the paper, or see a comical character in the street, or overhear a conversation, and know that there is only one person you have to call and tell. It has nothing to do with extravagant hotel suites, or watching the sun rise, or impetuous trips to distant cities. It is not what you see in the shuttered dark of a movie palace; it is finding romance in the unheralded, the mundane: a sudden surge of adoration because a certain person actually knows how to fix a dripping tap. It may not be the world well lost for love, or 'Shall I compare thee to a summer's day?', but it is less likely to leave your heart in shards on the floor.

Romantic love, however deranged, is still one of the great delights of life. It has given us sonnets and plays and entire sonatas; it has given us *The Great Gatsby*, *Pride and Prejudice* and *Doctor Zhivago*. It lent us Yeats' pilgrim soul and Herrick's sweet infanta, and Keats' bright star. The wild twist in the stomach at the mere sight of the adored one, the random smiling at strangers in the street, the sudden desire to swing from lampposts, all add vastly to the gaiety of nations. (It should be noted that all these symptoms are not just for the very young: the sensible, forty-

—

year-old female can just as easily become unhinged by the glimpse of a
delightful pair of green eyes.)

Love can be crazy, delicious, thrilling; it can make you feel as if every
atom in your body is dancing. It can bring back lost youth, make you
remember forgotten dreams, revive dashed hopes. It's just that it needs to
come with a caveat, a health warning, an unromantic but insistent voice of
reason. So, the next time you fall in love, you should bear in mind that in
those early days you are a little crazy, and it might be wise not to make
any sudden moves.

THE DANGER OF ROMANTIC LOVE.

We don't mean danger in the obvious heartbreak way – the cheap
betrayals, the easy lies, the broken promises – we mean the dark danger
that lurks when sensible, educated women fall for the dogmatic idea that
romantic love is the *ultimate goal* for the modern female.

This idea is a particular monster because although it is in fact quite
new, it feels old. Its phoney patina of age gives it an immutable quality. The
very few voices that qualify it, such as the great psychiatrist Anthony Storr
(read his book on solitude, we beg you), are so quiet that they get
entirely drowned out by the noise of the thousands of films, poems,
books and articles that shout for its dominant truth.

Its credentials are bolstered by ancient and unimpeachable sources: it was Plato who said that humans are like two sides of a flat fish, endlessly searching for their other half. And then there is Shakespeare, who still has the last word on everything even though he has been dead for 400 years, and who gave us the sonnets and *Much Ado* and *Antony and Cleopatra* – even though, admittedly, that last one did not turn out so well. Throw in Byron and Yeats, and even jaded old Auden, and the conclusion is that pure romantic love surely must be the highest human goal: the sources are irrefutable.

There are women who entertain the subversive notion, like an intellectual mouse scratching behind the skirting board, that perhaps this higher love is not *necessarily* the celestial highway to absolute happiness. Their empirical side kicks in, and they observe that couples who marry in a haze of adoration and sex are, ten years later, throwing china and fighting bitterly over who gets the dog. The divorced admit, quietly, that the overriding emotion after a marriage cracks is shame, because they once had romantic love, they stood up in a church or register office to prove it, they promised faithfully in front of a crowd of hats that only death would part them, and now they must admit that they were wrong.

But the women who notice these contradictions are often afraid to speak them in case they should be labelled cynics. Only the most jaded and damaged would challenge the orthodoxy of romantic love. The received wisdom goes that there is not something wrong with the modern idea of sexual love as ultimate panacea, but that if you don't get it, there is something wrong with *you*. You freak, go back and read the label.

The most potent contemporary distillation of this is The Look. There is a moment in every single film that deals with love between a man and a woman (you know the one, you have seen it so many times that it is as familiar as your own face) when the hero gives the heroine The Look. The

Look is so devastating that it can make perfectly rational women fall into lachrymose despair because their secret terror, which they can hardly admit even to themselves, is that no one will ever come along and give them that look. The Look says: you are the most magical, mysterious, unique creature I have ever seen in my life and if I can't have you now I shall surely *die*.

It does not help that The Look is always delivered by handsome actors with melty eyes and a great lighting director. George Clooney is the reigning King of The Look, but there are honourable pretenders to the throne: Ralph Fiennes gave Kristin Scott Thomas The Look in *The English Patient*, and Andie Macdowell got it from Gérard Depardieu in *Green Card* and James Spader in *Sex, Lies and Videotape*. Colin Firth became a household name after giving Jennifer Ehle The Look whilst wearing a wet shirt in *Pride and Prejudice*. Robert Redford made The Look his own when he was in his pomp in *The Way We Were* and *Out of Africa*. There are certain women who have never quite recovered from the moment when Omar Sharif gave Julie Christie The Look in *Doctor Zhivago*.

The Look is the very crucible of the dogma of romantic love: it kills the single and the married, both. Women on their own, however much they may pride themselves on their independence and their refusal to fall for fairy tales, think: no one will ever look at me like that. The married woman, proud of her ability to compromise and face reality, suddenly loses all her reason and wonders why her husband never gives her that look any more; in her darker moments she wonders if he ever did, or whether she imagined the whole thing.

And then comes the massive category error. Even the most highly educated woman will not wonder, as she ought, whether the entire thing is an invention of the zeitgeist, a cultural farrago, a malicious invention to make her feel sad. She will think: What is wrong with *me*?

We say: absolutely nothing. Of course it is very heaven to find a handsome gentleman who will give you The Look from time to time, and we would never deny the sheer exhilaration found in the hurly burly of the chaise longue, as Mrs Patrick Campbell liked to put it. But the privileging of romantic love over all others, the insistence that it is the one essential, incontrovertible element of human happiness, traced all the way back to the caves, is a trap and a snare. The idea that every human heart, since the invention of the wheel, was yearning for its other half, is a myth.

The interesting psychologist Oliver James has observed that all those old sonnets and plays and operas and haikus and novels lauding romantic love to the skies were written by a minuscule minority of the thinking and leisured classes. In fact, far from being obsessed with the joys of sexual love, the mass of humanity was too busy trying to stay alive. There was no time for mooning about over a pair of pretty eyes; the ordinary person was occupied with tilling the soil and tending the livestock and keeping warm. It was only in the twentieth century, when almost everyone had the sort of labour-saving devices unimagined two generations ago, and people could buy food from a shop instead of having to go and dig it up in a field, that ordinary people could develop the space to contemplate the mysteries of the human heart, previously the province of a tiny elite.

The old, unchallenged idea is that love is a force of nature. It just is. It is inscrutable, mystical, stitched into the universal human heart and the collective unconscious as irrevocably as the twisting strands of DNA that make up the genome. You can't fight it; you must have it; it is, in fact, what makes you human. It is better to have loved and lost, as every schoolgirl knows. The suspicion that romantic love might be a societal construct is a peculiar form of heresy, only entertained by the terminally sceptical and the entirely mad.

Yet concepts of love have varied wildly according to time, place and culture. Consider the love of children, regarded as visceral and profound and incontrovertible as romantic love: this too has shifted radically throughout history. Until very recently in human evolution, a child's life was a fragile and uncertain thing. Parents could not afford to fall in love with their children as women do now, because they would have been incapacitated by grief if, and when, they died in infancy. Queen Anne famously went through eighteen pregnancies and suffered numerous miscarriages in the mad race to produce an heir to the British throne. Twelve of her children were stillborn, three lived only for a single day, two died before their second birthday, and Prince William, after years of ill health, finally succumbed to smallpox at the age of eleven. Such a litany of grief would derange any contemporary woman; it is an article of modern faith that people never get over the death of a single child. And yet Queen Anne carried on, grumpy, fat, but coherent and alive; she did not resort to morphia or strong drink or just walk into the Thames on a foggy day.

There are a hundred other examples of the way in which love for children has shifted through the centuries. The Victorian climbing boys sent up chimneys until their knees bled, the tiny factory girls of the late eighteenth century, the young boys sent off to serve in Nelson's navy

—

'CHAINS DO NOT HOLD A MARRIAGE TOGETHER. IT IS THREADS, HUNDREDS OF TINY THREADS, WHICH SEW PEOPLE TOGETHER THROUGH THE YEARS.'

Simone Signoret

'WHEN TWO PEOPLE ARE UNDER THE INFLUENCE OF THE MOST VIOLENT, MOST INSANE, MOST DELUSIVE, AND MOST TRANSIENT OF PASSIONS, THEY ARE REQUIRED TO SWEAR THAT THEY WILL REMAIN IN THAT EXCITED, ABNORMAL, AND EXHAUSTING CONDITION CONTINUOUSLY UNTIL DEATH DO THEM PART.'

George Bernard Shaw

might not exactly have felt bathed in pure parental adoration. Spare the rod and spoil the child, said stern schoolmasters, as they made lavish use of the strap and the birch. The imperial classes shipped their children back to Blighty when they were old enough to walk, and often did not see them again for years. Among the affluent, the habit of abandoning a newborn baby for a long restorative sea cruise was a favourite tendency right up until the end of the 1960s.

None of this means that love, for children, for husbands, for wives, did not exist: love is a human constant; it is the interpretation of it, the *meaning* given to it, that changes. The way that love has been expressed, its significance in daily life, and its central properties, have never been immutable or constant. The different kinds of love and what they signify are not fixed, whatever the traditionalists might like to tell you.

So the modern idea that romantic love is a woman's highest calling, that she is somehow only half a person without it, that if she questions it she is going against all human history, does not stand up to scrutiny. It is not an imperative carved in stone; it is a human idea, and humans are frail and suggestible, and sometimes get the wrong end of the stick.

MARITAL LOVE.

Firstly, and incontrovertibly, there is no such thing as the perfect marriage. It does not exist. What there can be is a successful marriage: a sexual and intellectual partnership where neither party is subsumed by the other, where the needs of the individual are at least in part satisfied by the needs of the whole, and vice versa; and where one of you occasionally remembers that suitcases do not pack themselves.

Being married can be a thing of wonder and delight. It is exciting and heartening to journey through life knowing that there is someone with you who is always on your side, but it can also be complicated, difficult and unremittingly mundane. It is no coincidence that all the great love stories are about courtship, and very few about the actual marriage. All dutiful screenwriters learn the device of UST – unresolved sexual tension – once the couple get together, the story is over.

There are a few ingredients that are, experience shows, vital for keeping the complex stew that is a marriage from congealing. Because marriage is mostly the outcome of the craziness that is romantic love, you will, unless you place yourself permanently on hardcore medication, find yourself at some point coming down from an almighty high. It is easy, in the excitement and frenzy of wedding preparations, of choosing a dress and deciding on the flowers and drawing up the wedding list, to forget that when all the speeches have been made, the cheap champagne drunk, and the honeymoon sex indulged in, you are going to have to get on with the rest of your lives – together. How you do this is not always entirely obvious.

The absolute first principle is respect. Essentially this means you do not allow yourself to be taken for granted, either as a woman, mother or

unofficial towel monitor. This goes for men, too. It is just as rude to expect a man to do all the drilling and driving and bread-winning as it is to expect the ladies to have the slightest interest in knowing where the clean shirts are hiding.

Good manners are crucial. It may sound old-fashioned, but maintaining a basic level of civility will get you through even the toughest of times. It is sometimes permissible to be rude about your spouse – although you should never do this in mixed company, such as a party or family gathering, not even if the outcome might be gales of laughter (this is called Having a Joke at His Expense, which is not conducive to harmony) – but you may (and should) have a medicinal moan over a glass of wine or a telephone to a dear and discreet friend who will offer useful words of comfort and advice.

Meanwhile, on the ground, basic manners will provide a useful brake and will stop a spat developing into a full-blown domestic. Once you've actually called someone a useless fat fuckwit, it's a long way back to any semblance of bliss. But that is not all there is to civility. Remembering to put the loo seat down is a cliché, but actually doing it does make a difference. Marriage is an ancient and honourable institution (even if it was invented by people who were lucky to live to forty-five), and attention should be paid. If you ignore this basic tenet, it means that, in some way, however banal or benign, you have become so used to each other's presence that you have developed a lack of consideration for each other's needs. And that is a very slippery slope.

Second to respect, but also integral to it, is acceptance. Accept the person you have married. A perennial danger is to marry a man thinking that, once you've got him all sorted and settled in a house with babies and a front garden, he will miraculously transform into your dream prince. He won't. A frog is a frog is a frog. He will remain the same person he was the day you married him, only with progressively fewer hairs on his head and alarmingly more emerging from his ears. All you will do is exhaust yourself trying to shove a round peg into a square hole, and make him hate you with your incessant nagging.

So, if you are the sort of person who falls in love with dashing war correspondents with unkempt hair and sweat-drenched shirts, do not even in your wildest dreams entertain the thought of him settling contentedly to a life in the suburbs, remembering your birthday, and spending happy hours doing interesting things with Play-Doh to amuse the children. Do, however, expect him to suddenly race off on a very important assignment the second your first child needs its nappy changing, pausing only briefly to buy you an entirely inappropriate set of lingerie from Agent Provocateur with the promise of making it up to you on his return.

For this reason, it is very important to think about what it is you want from marriage before embarking on it. It sounds hideously unromantic, but a vast part of marriage is the managing of expectations. (There is a school of psychology which insists that false expectations are the number one enemy of happiness.) If you see yourself in five years' time in a giant house with hot and cold running staff, marry someone with a decent chance of helping you achieve that – whether because he works for Goldman Sachs and has a winning way with a hedge, or because he's likely to facilitate your own stellar career. Do not marry someone who wants to live on a beach in Ibiza, however appealing that fantasy may seem after six strong cocktails.

Linked to expectation is compromise: no marriage can succeed without it. Selfish stubbornness is the enemy of marital harmony, since it breeds resentment and one-upmanship. The ability – and the desire – to compromise represents a concrete demonstration of love, even if it is simply a question of whose favourite restaurant you are going to eat at.

Knowing when to compromise says: I am backing down on something I care about in order to make you happy because your happiness is what I care about most. If you want everything perfectly your own way and just so, you should probably think about getting a dog.

Assuming you do, by some happy miracle of luck and good judgement, marry someone whom you actually like and love: don't rest on your laurels. A successful marriage is like a beautiful but draughty stately home: it requires constant maintenance. You'll find that no sooner have you fixed the metaphorical leak in the roof, another will appear in the kitchen. This can be exhausting, but it is inevitable, and makes it all the more important that you enjoy the good times. In other words, don't just appreciate the cornicing when you're up a ladder fixing it: take time to gaze lovingly at it for no reason other than that it is there.

Two women we know recently had the following conversation:

Mrs A: *'Do you know anyone who is happy in their marriage?'*

Mrs B: *'Let me think.'* Pause. *'No.'*

Both these women were in their early forties. They desperately cast about among their friends and acquaintances, trying to think of one couple that exemplified the love and joy that marriage is supposed to offer. All they could come up with were people fretting over money, fighting over long hours, desperately trying to reconcile children and work. Everyone was tired; no one had enough time. The very idea of romance was a hollow joke.

We think this is because marriage is now presented, like romantic love, as the cure for *everything*. You get hitched and all your needs will be met. You will have someone on your side for ever and ever. You will never feel lonely again. Your life will be a carnival of sex and jokes. And when that does not happen, you are not prepared for it, and you want your money

'FRIENDSHIP MARKS A LIFE EVEN MORE DEEPLY THAN LOVE.'

Elie Wiesel

back. You are sold the fantasy, and the reality can be a jarring shock.

In the war against inflated expectation, get out the cynic's dictionary. Think of Disraeli, who said that it destroyed the nerves to be amiable to the same person every day, or Rita Rudner, who joked that what she loved about marriage was that she got someone to annoy for the rest of her life. Once you accept that sometimes it is hard, and baffling, occasionally lonely (Chekhov said that if you are afraid of loneliness, you should not marry), that there will be misunderstandings and hurt feelings, the whole thing becomes much easier. Someone, stupidly, did promise you a rose garden, but you know better.

We have a personal theory that all marriages go through a test of fire during the baby and ambition years. Once the children are older and the career is more settled, there will be time, there will be, miraculously, sleep, there will be a moment to remember, with a falling feeling of relief, why you fell in love with each other in the first place. You might have to grit your teeth and hold on for a while, but if you have chosen well, it will be worth it.

LOVE OF FEMALE FRIENDS.

Unlike the insanity of romantic love, or the fraught complications of married love, love of friends can look like the absolute real deal – it's just that it has never had the press. If love were a brand, friendship would hover somewhere between a Skoda and white goods: quite useful to have about the house, but definitely not aspirational.

Bizarrely, even when the most successful sitcom of all time was actually written about friendship, was actually called *Friends* (huge clue right there in the title), the major water cooler conversation was whether two of the characters would get together or not. Oh, and the hair, of course.

There is a complicated zeitgeisty thing going on with female friendship. There is the cultural shift that views a night out with the girls as quite an amusing diversion for a Friday. (Just think for a moment about that phrasing – a night out with the girls – the merest shade of derision, a subtle twist of less than. No one ever talks about a night out with the women.) But then there are all the newspapers that delight in running gleeful articles about women stealing each other's husbands, or denying each other promotions at work. There are the women's magazines, who should know better, regularly publishing pieces on How to Delete your Toxic Friends, or how to recognise the so-called friends who are in fact in the business of denigrating, belittling, and sucking the emotional life out of you (before they run off with your husband).

The subtext is that really women are faking it when it comes to friendship: they might look all smiley and supportive and spilling over with empathy and sympathy and we're all in it together, but in fact they are secretly plotting to ruin your nice life. This is one of those bizarre gaps between perception and reality; rather like people insisting that we are living in a feral society despite crime statistics going down year after year.

The feminist conspiracy theorists among us might suspect that there is still something threatening about any kind of female solidarity – just too much crazy oestrogen floating around for comfort – so it's safer for the consensus to be that, despite all evidence to the contrary, women are too much in competition with each other for their friendships to be uncontaminated.

We would like to come out of the closet and declare that a true friendship with another woman is possibly the greatest love of all. The stereotypes do, of course, still exist. There is the woman who drops everything when a man appears, or the one who tells you maliciously that you really do look seductive in yellow, or the one who drones on endlessly about her own problems and never, *ever*, asks you about your own. These can be baffling, because the temptation is to think that all

THE SCIENCE OF FRIENDSHIP.

A fascinating study from the University of California in Los Angeles, discovered that men and women have radically different reactions to stress. With men, it's fight and flight; with women, it's what the researchers call tend and befriend. This revelation came after two female scientists at the university noticed that when the women who worked there were under pressure, they came into the lab, made coffee and bonded with each other, while the stressed men disappeared into their offices and did not speak to anyone. The fact that women turn to their friends in moments of high tension is partly due to the effect of oestrogen, and may explain why women live longer than men. Friendship produces physiological reactions in the body, lowering blood pressure, heart rate and cholesterol, so the hormone most routinely mocked in women ('that time of the month again?') is actually *saving your life*.

Another study by the Harvard Medical School found the physical benefits of friendship so significant that it concluded that not having close friends was as detrimental to health as smoking or obesity.

So it's not just sentiment when you wonder what you would do without your girlfriends; it's cold, hard science.

women friends are equal (i.e. perfect and fabulous in every way). This is called the Pitfall of High Expectations, and is a kind of reverse sexism, where you assume that just because someone is female, she automatically has a hotline to kindness and goodness and the gentler arts.

But if you weed out the duds, you will find you have a hard core worth more than diamonds. No one will ever have written sonnets about them, but you will almost certainly feel like doing so, because they make you laugh so much you can't see straight, and they don't judge you, and they adore you because of your flaws and not in spite of them, which Balzac said was the truest form of love. You can ring them after midnight when you are so muddled and frenzied that you don't know what your name is, and they will carefully piece you back together like an intricate jigsaw. They remember the tiny things, things so small and pointless that you hardly remember them yourself – your hatred of kidney beans, the song you loved most when you were seventeen, your incoherent rage over dangling modifiers, your odd obsession with Napoleon. They will drop everything and drive halfway across the country when you are in trouble, without having to be asked. They will send you flowers on your birthday, make you soup when you are sad, and take you out for martinis when you are happy. They know, better than anyone, how to listen.

None of this is especially sexy, or glamorous, or newsworthy, but it's real and true and *contra mundum*. Sometimes we think that the deepest human desire of all is to be understood, to be *got*, and a great woman friend will get you like no one else.

So when you form a till death us do part friendship, don't just call it 'like'. Don't take it as read and think that all relationships go in that profound and seamless way. Treasure it, and celebrate it, and call it by its name, which is Love. And maybe write a sonnet about it after all, in the privacy of your own boudoir.

LOVE OF HETEROSEXUAL MALE FRIENDS.

Sometimes a film comes along and puts the last word on a random aspect of life. So when, some time in the late eighties, Billy Crystal told Meg Ryan that men and women could never be friends, that was the *When Harry Met Sally* stamp on that subject, and no one has raised it since. We think this is absolute and utter buggery bollocks: it was just a great line, that was all. Sometimes a line is just a line, and not in fact a Universal Verity.

There are some men that you will never, ever, want to sleep with. This is not an insult, because you know perfectly well that you have leapt into bed with humans whom otherwise you would rationally cross the road to avoid (that old dopamine rush again, how can you forget it?). But it is possible not to fancy someone and still adore them unconditionally.

Having a platonic male friend means you can indulge in your affection for those character traits which, whilst extremely dangerous in a lover, are vastly diverting in a buddy – impetuousness, recklessness, a fondness for fast cars, gambling, guns, hard drinking, being in a rock band. If you are pathologically attracted to dark-eyed poets with faraway eyes and self-indulgent souls, you can have an adorable Byronesque friend without ever having to worry about him wandering off with some accommodating blonde who can suck the chrome off a trailer hitch.

The male friend is great on advice (he really does love to be asked, it makes him feel virile and needed). He can give you the masculine perspective, which is especially useful when you have absolutely no idea why your latest crush has not called you back. The faithful male friend will not, unlike your female friends, make soothing noises and tell you it will be all right and that lack of contact is surely due to a freak lightning strike or the gentleman being immobilised under a heavy piece of furniture. The male friend will inform you that the Crush has not called you because he is Just Not That Into You. (There is actually an entire book on this very subject, which we highly recommend.)

He will add that the idiot is not worth losing any sleep over, anyway, because anyone who insists on listening to trance music after the age of twenty-five is deep in the throes of an ugly Peter Pan complex. The male friend will not sugar-coat this; but, oh, the relief of a little straight-talk from the horse's mouth.

Even if they are card-carrying metrosexuals, your male friends will be far more brutal than your women friends, and far less inclined to the tactful white lie. This is a valuable kind of love, so butch up and take it. Sometimes you need someone to tell you when to cut your losses, declare your latest haircut an unadulterated disaster, bully you out of a dead-end job, or say things like, 'He's an absolute arse,' about the man you worship.

This is strong medicine. But it is love, for all that.

There can come a time when you suddenly look at one of your favourite men friends and wonder why you don't just sleep with him. The night is dark with rain and your last relationship has crashed in flames, and he knows you so well, and has been on your side for so long, and you long for the press of human flesh. You are both sentient adults, you have been around the block, you know that sometimes sex is just sex. Why not do the wild thing?

If you have exceptionally strong boundaries and no illusions, you might be able to get away with this. You may be able to turn an enduring male friend into what the Americans call a fuck buddy, and the British, rather more delicately, call an arrangement. We know one woman who spent her twenties going to bed with one of her very close friends whenever they were both single; he is married now, and they are still good friends, with a lot of happy and risqué memories.

The problem is that when you are no longer in your twenties, you tend to want more than a few jokes and a night without strings. You start to find (whisper it) that you want a proper ocean-going, five-star love affair, and an arrangement doesn't quite cut it. And there is the danger that once sex comes into the equation the delicate balance of the friendship is shifted, and it may never shift back. What may have been wonderfully simple when you were twenty-nine can become labyrinthine when you are thirty-nine.

If you want to take a nice straightforward friendship and complicate the hell out of it by throwing sex into the mix, just go ahead – but you should remember that, unless you are very lucky, it will get convoluted. If you yearn for the simple life, but still want a little comfort sex to get you through a dank Sunday night, you might be wiser to go out and find yourself a lovely, unequivocal one-night stand.

LOVE OF GAY MALE FRIENDS.

Now we are wading deep into cliché territory.

It's the most popular saw of the last twenty years: a woman is not a woman without her Gay Best Friend. The trite idea goes that every woman needs a man in touch with his female side, who loves interior decorating and listens to Judy Garland records and gives great make-up tips. Because *everyone knows* that a gay man cannot be really gay unless he listens to show tunes, and a woman cannot really be a woman unless she is fascinated by soft furnishings. Even now, there is a subterranean suggestion that this is all that gay men and straight women are capable of. Sometimes we are surprised that they have not all given up and formed a society of Stepford Wives.

The heart of this particular friendship is none of those things. There are two great things that gay men and straight women have in common, and these have nothing to do with Barbra Streisand or interior design. One is that they both want to go to bed with other men, which is a tremendous leveller; the other is that they understand very well what it is to have been reduced to stereotypes for the last many hundreds of years. They know how it feels to be shut out of power, to be pushed to the sidelines. They know all about the assumptions and the sideways looks. There is something deeply and oddly touching about this mutual understanding.

Even after all these years, as they walk tall in more enlightened times, the straight women and the gay men do not ever quite forget those dark days, although they put a very good face on it, because no one likes a bore. So a friendship with your gay friend is not only the usual camaraderie of old jokes, or shared experience, or all the other imponderables of which friendship is made; it is something more profound than that.

And yet, some of the clichés are true. These are worth celebrating, because all love has a pinch of cliché in it.

So, let us admit that the camp thing is very heaven. Even the gay men who do not have an inch of camp in them can still talk about emotions in a way that would make many straight men blush. There is not even a batsqueak of sexuality between you, which is astonishingly liberating. There is no echo of competition, because you are going after different men – 'is he one of mine or is he one of yours?' Yet, at the same time, there is equal fascination in excavating the imponderable depths of the male psyche.

Most crucially, for the women who have decided to follow a different drummer and not do the marriage and children dance, the gay best friend will understand better than anyone else what it is not to join the mainstream. (There's that *contra mundum* again, the very engine of love.) He will also make a great date for weddings, birthdays, and New Year's Eve, the loneliest night of the year for the single woman.

There are gay men who prefer football to musicals, who cannot tell the difference between Bobbi Brown and James Brown, who would rather die than exfoliate, but for some reason, they are still the ones who notice that you really do look like a bit of a fox in your new black satin pencil skirt, and when they do, you know there is not one single ulterior motive, just heartfelt admiration from the barricades.

It is a Great Love. There really should be sonnets about this one, too. There should be entire *operas* about this one.

LOVE OF THINGS (BY WHICH WE MEAN ANYTHING FROM POETRY TO PLACE; FROM FOOD TO FROCKS).

Say the word love and everyone sighs and assumes *Romeo and Juliet*, or *Casablanca*, or some doomed affair on a blasted heath with a soaring soundtrack, heavy on the string section. But to apply love only to the romantic version seems absurdly reductive, stupidly limited. We say: bring on the loves that don't get the swoony poetry and the high prose; stand up tall and proud and salute the loves that dare not speak their name.

There are women who get a pulling twist in their chest every time they hear a song by Neil Sedaka, or finish a fiendishly complicated knitting pattern, or peel a perfectly ripe avocado, or plant a winter-flowering cherry. These are not the things that dreams are made on. Forget sonnets, these unglamorous unfashionable loves would not even merit a haiku.

We think that perhaps we should look to the Eskimos, with their twenty-seven different words for snow, and invent a myriad of names for love.

There are the higher loves in this category which might stretch to the sublime. A line from Prufrock, the sea at dawn, the beginning of a Mozart sonata, the first glimpse you get of that wild rearing Stubbs horse as you walk into the National Gallery – all these might comfortably slot into the canon of higher love. These are the loves that bring you out of yourself, that speak to your deep heart, that, in a secular age, bring you close to some imponderable spiritual sense, which some people call God, and some people do not. The love of great beauty is a soul thing, and it should be cherished and prized when the news brings daily ugliness.

The love of food, which so many women fight because it has become twisted up with ideals of thin and corrupted by the diet industry, is one. Good food, made with love, eaten with love, is one of the greatest and truest loves of all.

The love of place, warped by insane notions of jingoism and nationalism, is another that should be purified and reclaimed. Place, which does not mean where you were born, or which tribe you come from, but rather where you choose to belong, can move you so much with a sense of coming home that it is like an affair. We know one woman who fell in love with a country as one would with a man, so she moved 600 miles from her old life on a sudden unexpected imperative, and every time she crosses the border to her adopted home, she sheds actual tears of recognition and gratitude.

The love of nature can lead to those oceanic universal moments that take you out of the world and make you part of it at the same time – the feeling you get when you look up at the night sky, littered with stars, and think that Joni Mitchell was exactly right when she said we are all stardust.

You can look at a wild blue mountain range and know that those old hills were here for a million years before you were even invented and will be here for another million after you have gone, and feel perspective and peace fall on you like snow on a windless day. You can watch swallows nesting in a tumbledown old shed, and know that they have come all the way from Africa right back to your front door, and get a little arrow of awe and wonder straight to your beaten-up heart.

But there are the small pointless loves, too, which the poets and the playwrights never really talk about. You don't have to save the word love for special occasions.

Life is earnest, life is real, but sometimes you have to admit, even if only to yourself, that you really, really love the smell of new leather, or the moment in *The Big Chill* when everybody except for Jeff Goldblum is having sex, or a pristine set of playing cards, or the way that Karen Carpenter sang about interplanetary craft.

Maybe what we really mean is: honour your passions, however bizarre and flaky they are. You don't always have to admit to them in public.

LOVE OF SELF.

This is the really tricky one. It's all very well admitting that you in fact do really love The Carpenters, but loving yourself? Oh, too shameless, too self-help section, too damn *difficult*.

Loving yourself is, we hate to admit, a life's work. Whatever glib self-improvement manuals tell you, it takes more than standing in front of the looking glass saying 'I am a Worthwhile Human Being'. In technical terms, it means embracing your shadow side, unravelling all those wrong constructions from your dysfunctional childhood, possibly even unpicking your mother introject. (You need a good dark room for this, and no interruptions, and maybe some strong liquor.) You might even have to understand something about archetypes and societal expectation; it could involve a close reading of Adler and years on the couch. The hard-liners will tell you that you cannot even begin to love another until you love yourself.

Before you go into primal scream at the very thought, there are a couple of quite useful shortcuts. These do not work for all of the people all of the time, but we have found them quite astonishingly efficient in moments of crisis.

The first is, every so often, conjure a picture of your six-year-old self. There you were, small, hopeful, filled with antic hopes and absurd laughter. How can you not love that small optimistic person? You are smiling now, just at the thought of her. It sounds madly shrinkish, all that getting in touch with your inner child, but just try it when your critical voices come and you feel there is no hope in you. Your six-year-old is still there, and she is heaven. She can't balance a chequebook any more than you can, but you would never, ever blame her for that.

The second, in the same spirit, is if you are in a spiral of self-recrimination, imagine you are talking to your best friend, the one who makes you laugh, the one that you love the most. You do not have to do this out loud or anything shaming like that, you can do it in the bath, or in the car, or in the kitchen, silently; you can do it in the privacy of your own head.

You know exactly what you would say if she were with you now. You would tell her that you don't want her to be flawless, you don't care about her career prospects or her ability to do the right thing, you love her just *because*. Now try saying those things to yourself. It sounds absurd, but give it a shot; you may be surprised. You know what they say: you can't necessarily change things, but you can change how you think about them. We think they are right.

So go on, be vulgar. Love yourself madly, for all your faults.

If, on the other hand, you really can't face it, you could always get a dog. A dog will love you forever: when you sing in the bath, it will truly believe you are Nina Simone; when you smile at it, it will be sincerely convinced that you are Grace Kelly. And all you have to do in return is give it some food, walk it twice a day and rub its stomach every so often. That's one hell of a bargain.

THE DARK SIDE OF LOVE.

You didn't think you were going to get away with it altogether, did you? In the words of the late, great Dorothy Parker:

Oh, life is a glorious cycle of song,
A medley of extemporanea;
And love is a thing that can never go wrong;
And I am Marie of Roumania.

Dotty, we salute you and all who sailed in you.

In the dark side of love, you will get your hopes and dreams shattered, your illusions ripped up, your very core shaken. Your heart will break. You know this because it has been broken before, but even in the high drama of heartache, there are some things that can help. They are:

WRITING IT DOWN.

Even if it does not make a novel, anguish put down on the page can relieve a battered heart. Do some nice little ritual burning of the piece of paper afterwards, if the fancy takes you. This can be fantastically cathartic. Otherwise, save it and read it back to yourself later, when the trauma is long forgotten. It can make hilarious reading.

TIME.

We know it's an ancient chestnut, but time does slide along and do its thing.

CHOCOLATE AND RED WINE.

Sometimes the old therapies are the good therapies.

PRIDE AND FURY.
Really, actually, fuck him.

PLEASE YOURSELF.
A new frock can help, if applied at the right time. Or, occasionally, a bit of judiciously meaningless sex, just to show you can. And you can.

WORK.
Slightly obsessively, if you need to, until the worst is over.

SLOW DOWN.
Conversely, you may need to go gently. You are in the emotional equivalent of post-traumatic stress disorder, so take small, slow steps. Imagine yourself as an Edwardian invalid: lie quietly on the sofa and take a little beef tea.

FISH IN THE SEA.
Count them. The idea that there is only one great love for each person is an evil canard invented by sexists.

SLEEP.
On good linen, if you have it. In pyjamas. With a hot water bottle.

BE BRAVE.
Try to remember not to be afraid of being alone: single is not a dirty word. It is better always to be on your own than trapped in a silent, loveless relationship.

MUSIC.
Of course, *of course*, the songs of Leonard Cohen.

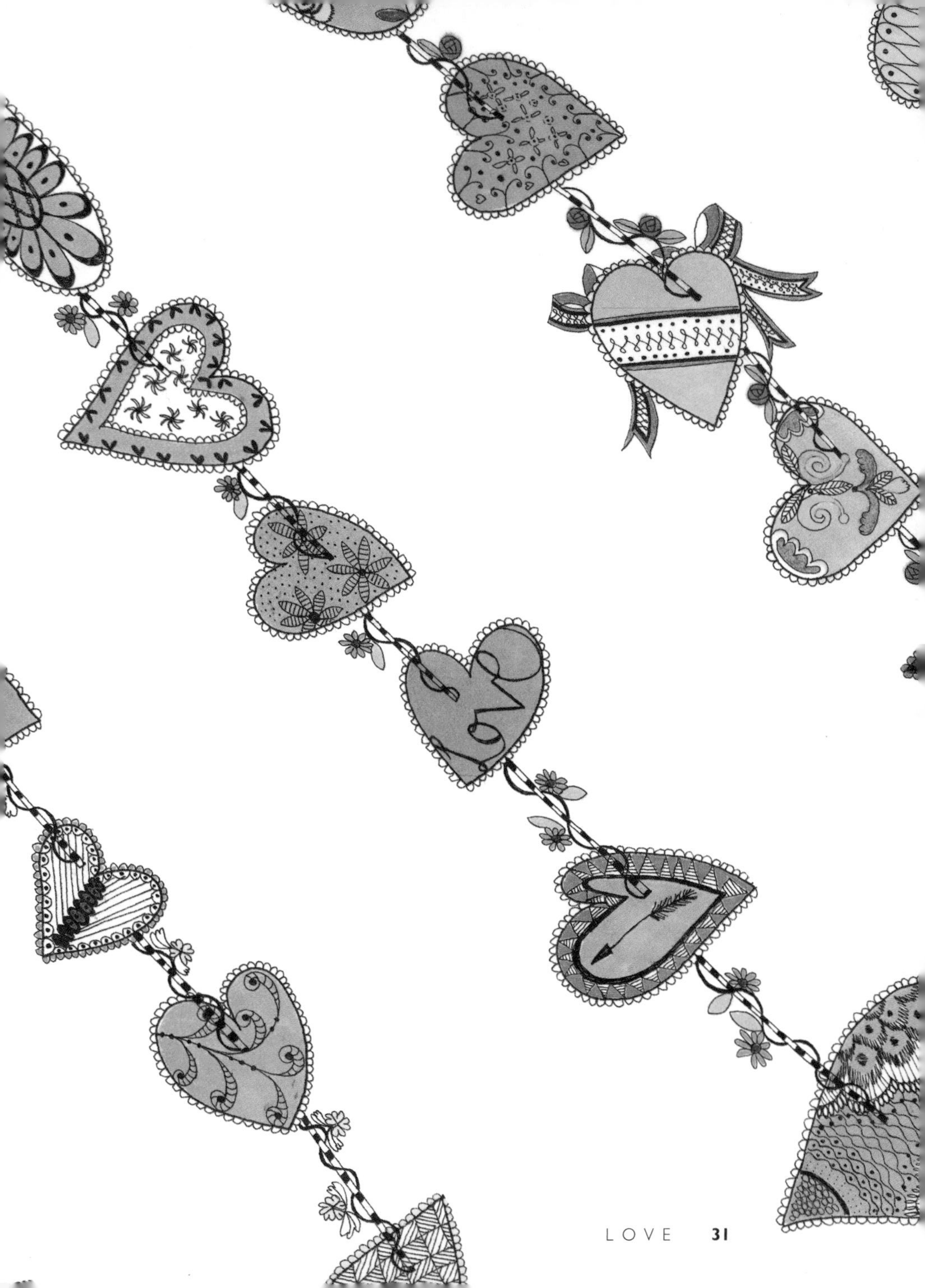
Love

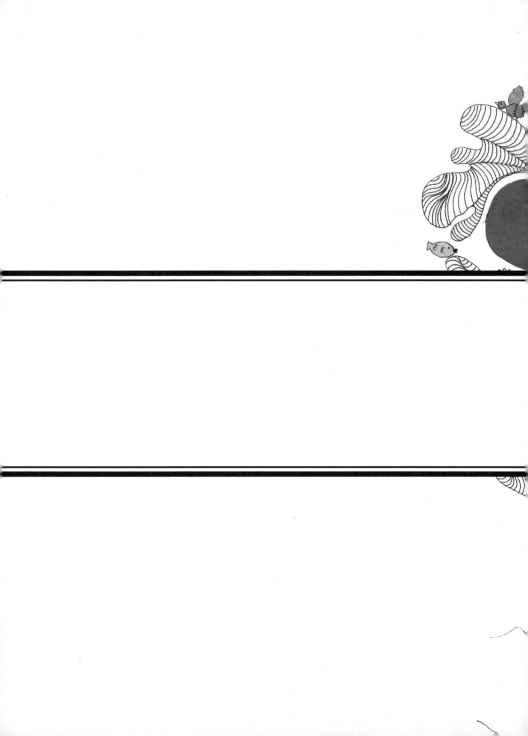

FOOD

–

CHAPTER TWO

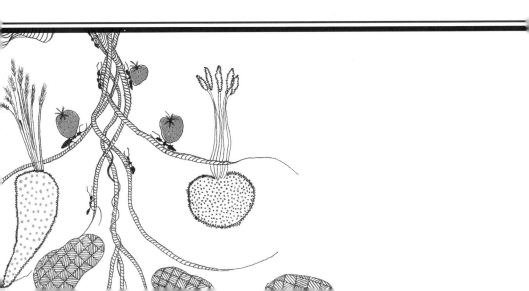

'THERE IS NO LOVE SINCERER THAN THE LOVE OF FOOD.'

George Bernard Shaw

THE TRUE WONDER OF FOOD.

Food is one of the great, unalloyed pleasures in life. Did we say pleasure? So sorry, we must have accidentally slipped into a parallel universe where invented allergies, the outlawing of carbohydrates and Size Zero never happened.

At its most basic level, food is fuel – purely for keeping the good body going – but it also performs many diverse and wonderful functions. Protein makes your muscles grow; oily fish charges up the brain; eggs, mangoes and shellfish make your hair glossy; garlic cleanses the blood; olive oil and avocados plump the skin. Chillies and dark chocolate act directly on the pleasure centres of the brain in the same way as sex, and are so much easier and less tiring to obtain.

Food also sustains the mind: it has powerful psychological effects. We, like the Jewish mothers of myth and reality, truly do believe that a bowl of chicken soup can cure most ills. In times of strain and fret, a soft-boiled egg with soldiers will transport you back to the safe, simple days of

childhood; the spicy, clean taste of gazpacho or the cool, green flavour of cucumber salad is summer on a plate; a proper Irish stew with pearl barley is the very essence of winter.

Food is a sensual delight; the way it looks on the plate, the feel of it in the mouth, the very texture of it. Good cooking, done for those closest to you, with care and attention, is one of the great acts of love.

THE THERAPEUTIC POWER OF FOOD.

Apart from chicken soup, which is, of course, the universal Platonic gold standard, everyone has a personal comfort food. For some, it is as simple as a bar of good chocolate, or even a packet of Quavers. (We are not food snobs, we have nothing against a lovely cheesy snack.) For others, it is taking the time to assemble a delicate and complicated dish: the very act of concentration calms the harried mind.

The power of food to comfort has obvious basic roots: when you were a baby and you cried, your mother fed you, then as an older child you were given a lollipop after a visit to the doctor – a little something sweet to distract you from the pain.

This is fine in infancy. In adulthood the danger is that comfort can be confused with obliteration: make the bad feelings go away by stuffing yourself with toast or crisps. If you find yourself mindlessly eating an entire cake after a career crash, you are not comfort eating, you are seeking oblivion and you might want to think seriously about the ramifications of oral fixation. The mark of dangerous eating is that you feel horrible about yourself afterwards, which is not the point at all.

On a physiological level, it is no coincidence that this compulsive kind of eating involves sugar and starch. These elements are un-evolved, but crafty. Their effect is radical and straightforward at the time of eating: a blunting of emotion, followed by a serotonin rush that leads to a spurious feeling of well-being. They work, but they make you pay for it: your blood sugar, which has been raised exponentially, crashes, leaving you tired and querulous and vulnerable to the horrid voices in your head, which are now clamouring for your attention – yelling that no sane adult woman would actually eat five iced buns in a row, rhetorically asking what kind of person you actually *think you are*. (A fat, greedy one is the usual unkind answer.)

True comfort food has nothing to do with any of this, it is more comprehensive, more subtle; it bolsters, not undermines. The secret is to make it yourself, or allow someone you love to make it for you. Love is a basic ingredient of comfort food. Even if it is just a toasted cheese sandwich, it should be prepared with attention and care: good cheese, cut at just the right thickness, lovely fresh bread, perhaps a dash of mustard.

Proper comfort food is also, by definition, slow food. If the rain won't stop, the news is all bad, you are assailed by the Sunday night blues, the very act of making your own favourite comfort dish is a kind of healing. The slow, careful stirring of a risotto is almost meditative; the softening of onions until they are translucent and sweet for the base of a great soup is in itself a calmative. You are demonstrating a profound psychological truth: that you love and care for yourself enough to take a little time and trouble.

The small things become symbolic: adding a few saffron strands to a hot chickpea mash just to give it that certain *je ne sais quoi*, chopping up springing verdant parsley to scatter over a steaming spaghetti *alle vongole*. You could not bother: both dishes are perfectly fine without, but it is in the bothering that the true comfort lies. It is the epicurean equivalent of putting a vase of flowers by the bed when a friend comes to stay; it is a tiny, telling act of thought and affection. A strand of saffron will not change the world, or make up for the fact that your father left when you were seven, but the aromatic, indefinable flavour of it in your chosen comfort dish will remind you that you have the capacity and imagination to soothe yourself, which is one of the defining marks of being a functioning adult.

THE INTELLECTUAL AND MORAL ASPECTS OF FOOD.

The intellectual power of food is often overlooked. You define yourself in some way by the food you eat. 'Oh, I'm just a meat and potatoes kind of girl,' is a way of signalling lack of pretentiousness; 'I'll eat anything,' can denote an open mind; 'I always eat fish on Fridays,' obviously means that you are a devout Catholic. The stupid old line about lunch being for wimps still has some currency — the current fad for eating on the run is a way of showing importance: just look how busy and important I am, too vital to the corporation even to eat. From the gastronome to the vegan, everyone presents an image through what they decide to put in their mouths.

There are class ramifications, too. Certain foods are still associated with ideas of status. The upper classes, traditionally tied to great estates, are thought to know exactly how to tackle a grouse or a woodcock, while it is the harried middle classes who go organic and fret about food miles and additives. What the government now pleases to term the Underclass is officially consigned to McDonald's and other nasty fast-food outlets. In an ironic twist, the classic foods of the old working class — tripe, oxtail, offal, and the cheap cuts that through judicious cooking could be rendered thriftily delicious – have been rediscovered by grand London chefs and are now being offered to the chic metropolitan rich at £30 a plate.

On top of all this, there is the constant lecturing and hectoring about food. As obesity levels rise, food has taken on a curiously Manichean aspect: certain foods are labelled 'bad', according to prevailing fashion; fatwas are imposed on entire food groups. Currently, simple starches are the demons of our day, the evil carbohydrates that will lead everyone into temptation. It used to be fats: in the 1980s everyone went out and dutifully bought soulless low-fat spreads, the revolting name reflecting with uncanny accuracy the revolting taste. Then it was discovered that they were made using a process called hydrogenation, which produces trans fats. Trans fats are fabulously unhealthy, possibly even carcinogenic, so, suddenly, butter was rehabilitated and another food had to be nominated for the Enemy of the Month club.

Foods are not only proclaimed good or bad depending on their physiological effects. If you are eating chocolate made by downtrodden farmers in Third-World countries, then clearly you never got the memo. You must embrace Fairtrade; you must buy responsibly if you are to hold your head up in public. The simple act of shopping has become a moral swamp. Is your selfish decision to stock up conveniently at Tesco destroying small businesses, screwing down the profits of beleaguered farmers and leaving the high streets of small towns inhabited only by tumbleweed? Do you really need asparagus in February, when it has to be air-freighted all the way from Peru, blowing another hole in the fragile ozone layer? Or is it in fact your duty to purchase it, as a good citizen of the world, if only to ensure that adorable baby Peruvians don't die of starvation?

These arguments are always presented in their most reductive tabloid form. Of course ethical arguments about food should be waged, but amid the clamour it is easy to forget that the affluent West is vastly privileged to have such choice and abundance. How many other cultures can afford to be so precious about which kind of foods they buy?

Supermarkets are not intrinsically evil. They are single-minded in their pursuit of profit (and personally we think there is absolutely no call for fifty-seven different types of breakfast cereal). They can be unsympathetic to the travails of small producers, and their insistence on placing piles of sweets at checkouts is actively unhelpful both to the problem of national obesity and harried mothers on the verge of being pestered to death by small children. But to someone brought up in Soviet Russia, Sainsbury's is a veritable palace of pleasures.

It is easy to get romantic about the poor little local shops being driven out of business by grasping corporations, but many of those traditional shops were sitting lazily on captive markets. People had nowhere else to go, so it was easy to stock shelves with dispiriting collections of tinned custard and ageing vegetables. Conversely, anyone who lives in a village with a really fine butcher, of the sort who can tell you where each lamb came from (and probably its name), knows that it takes more than a branch of Asda to get rid of such a business. The market, while never perfect, works quite well in this regard. The current vogue for farmers' markets and organic box schemes and co-operative ventures shows that the consumer does not have to be a victim of crushing capitalist forces.

There is one aspect of modern food that we really do hate (apart from battery farming of course, which goes without saying). This is the Ready Meal. The very name makes our hearts plummet to our boots. Soulless dinners served up in plastic containers, put together in factories, laced with E-numbers and arcane preservatives, sold at exorbitant prices, are not our idea of a good time. We know that contemporary women are starved of time and convenience is king and it is fabulously tempting to buy a packet of chicken nuggets on your way home from a fraught day at the office, but it does only take five minutes to bash a chicken breast with a rolling pin, coat it in polenta flour (you do not even have to go through the egg and breadcrumb stage, polenta will give you the crispiness you crave), and fry it in olive oil, perhaps with a scattering of oregano or thyme. How much more lovely that is than an artificial orange thing out of a packet.

There is a final, twisted moral complication to food: greed. A newspaper interview with Nigella Lawson in the autumn of 2007 reported: 'Nigella refers to herself as greedy, a word most women fear.' The Lawson phenomenon is telling: every single article ever written about her refers to her figure, her cleavage, her unapologetic voluptuousness, as if astonished that she can go on getting away with it. What she does with food is in many ways profound: she shows that it is intimately associated with a sense of home, of comfort, of continuity, of normality. Her recipes are all about simple pleasures. Many of them are handed down from her mother and grandmother – a potent reminder of food as part of the ties that bind, of happy family associations, the passing on of wisdom. And yet the media constantly focuses on the dark side: the greed that women must fear, because it might make them (you, us) fat. And it's no longer voluptuous and amusing, but just another lonely woman sitting on her sofa, mindlessly filling her face.

We say, boldly, that in the context of food we are unabashed Gordon Geckos: greed is good. Twenty stone and chafing thighs is not much fun, but you have to eat a lot of seriously nasty food to get to that stage. A healthy size 14 and an appetite, on the other hand, is so much more life-enhancing than counting every calorie and staring bleakly at the scales each morning. Becoming obsessed with thinness is to see food as the enemy, and there is a profound human sorrow in that.

Also (and we hate to be vulgar about this), if a man takes you to dinner and you play with a salad and one sardine, he is not going to look at you and imagine how wonderfully insatiable your sexual appetite is. He will almost certainly remember that he has a pressing 6 a.m. conference call and go home early.

THE TRUE MORAL AXIS OF WOMEN AND FOOD.

It is absolutely not right that extreme thinness has become the Holy Grail for women. Famous women in the public spotlight grow thinner and thinner. It is like an old-fashioned freak show: 'Roll up, roll up, see the lady vanish before your very eyes!' The inescapable implication is that success and achievement for women translate into irredeemable skinniness. The exclamation, 'Oh, you've lost weight' is offered to women with more passionate congratulation than any other; you would hardly get the same level of admiration had you won the Nobel Peace Prize.

At the same time, elements of the media collude in a devilish conspiracy to make women fear food, with a scattergun bombardment of scare stories and nutritional fables. If you want to see a truly depraved business, forget the supermarkets – look at the diet industry. Disgusting shakes, soulless meal replacements, bogus teas and potentially dangerous pills are marketed like silver bullets, at inflated prices, dressed up with spurious science and shameless lies.

It has become an unchallenged truism that all women want to lose weight, that they think constantly about calories, that pretty much all of them are on some kind of diet. There is a bizarre consensus that most women entertain a low-level hatred of their own bodies. Highly intelligent females will state frankly that they loathe their thighs, as if this is merely part of the usual discourse.

There is *nothing* normal about any of this; it is not a profound human truth but a societal construct, and you have the power to fight it. You can just say No. You can stand up tall and challenge the accepted wisdom.

Babies come into the world as little fat dimpled things: it is their very chubbiness that makes them so adorable. As they reach adulthood, the slavering jaws of social expectation grab them and they spend the rest of their lives fearing the very thing that once made them so lovable. There is a surrealist absurdity about this: the body, which performs so many unnoticed daily miracles, becomes something to be hated. Those thighs are what enable you to walk and run and jump; that bottom, which you are encouraged to disparage, is what makes it possible for you to sit down comfortably. (Also, crucially, it stops your trousers falling down.)

Thinness is not intrinsically good. It is emphatically *not* a moral goal. There is something repulsive about affluent First-World women torturing their bodies into simulacra of starvation, when there are actually women who do not have anything to eat because of poverty or drought or famine, or the fact that their country is being run by some lunatic despot with gold taps and the planet's biggest collection of Rolls-Royces.

Occasionally, popular women's magazines run articles about how scary it is when the starlet *du jour* gets too bony, but the messages are impossibly mixed. Increasingly, these articles are just an excuse to publish gruesome pictures of the beleaguered model/actress/whatever's emaciated frame – drooling voyeurism dressed up as concern. The same magazines that celebrate the refusal of Kate Winslet to diet away her 'curves', invariably present her as being on the larger end of the scale. Well, we once saw Kate Winslet in the street, and she is tiny. If she is

considered representative of the curvaceous woman, anyone over a size 8 must be beyond the pale and might as well go and sit in a box for the duration and ponder her lack of self-control.

There is a reason that the Incredible Shrinking Women are a growing cohort: they are the ones that get the big bucks. A Hollywood actress or a fashion model can earn more in an hour than most women dream of in a month. And so the message is perpetuated: when it comes to women, thin is success. Thin is *cash*. The less of you there is, the more you are worth.

Paradoxically, the rise in obesity is partly a consequence of this emphasis on the skeletal. The actress/model level of skinniness is only possible if you take laxatives, eat little more than a yoghurt a day, and live with a constant feeling of hunger (that's success for you), or if you are rich enough to have a personal trainer and a chef who makes you five tiny meals of sashimi and poached chicken and salad without oil. As Julia Roberts said in *Notting Hill*, when playing the actress Anna Scott: 'I've been on a diet every day since I was nineteen, which basically means I've been hungry for a decade.'

For the normal woman, these images of so-called perfection are as beyond reach as a castle in Spain. Baffled by her inability to fit into this season's skinny jeans, she may easily give up and go to the opposite extreme – punishing herself for her perceived failure by obsessively overeating.

The immovable Thin is Good paradigm also provides fertile ground for anorexia and bulimia. These serious mental disorders have as much to do with control and feelings of powerlessness as food itself (you can no more order an anorexic to eat than command a horse to dance a minuet), but they arise from a context. The brilliant Susie Orbach (psychoanalyst and author of *Fat is a Feminist Issue*) has pointed out that there are developing countries where anorexia was absolutely unknown before the rise of advertising and the spread of television. Eating disorders do not spring up from nowhere: you do not become anorexic overnight. It is a gradual process, fostered by a culture which insists that if you are a very thin woman you can conquer the world.

The other danger of this obsession with size is that it leads to narcissism and solipsism. Punishing your body into some random ideal is a full-time job. If you did decide that you wanted to look like Madonna, you would have to spend four hours a day in the gym to do so. This means that you will never have time to read *War and Peace*. You are in severe danger of no longer being able to make amusing conversation, or develop informed opinions, because you have spent more time thinking about your abdominal muscles than what the Neo-Cons are up to with their crazy old domino theories. You may be able to list accurately the exact calorific content of any given comestible, but can you recite the poems of Yeats? If you are hungry all the time, you are not going to have much energy for making jokes.

The Size Zero obsession is the sickest and most inexplicable element of women and food. How is it possible, after all the effort women have made to be equal, free and in charge of their own lives, that they have arrived at a situation where they ACTUALLY ASPIRE TO BE ZEROS? Of all the numbers to signify female perfection, why choose zero? Nothing, zilch, nada, negligible, devoid of value, empty. Even worse is size double-zero. Even more worthless. *Double* nothing.

The Pankhursts were too busy battling for emancipation to worry about the evils of a cream cake. If Virginia Woolf had expended all her mental energy wondering whether she should really eat that crumpet she would have not had time to write *A Room of One's Own*. Vanessa Redgrave did not become a theatrical genius by shunning bread. No great woman from any era, from Nina Simone to Dorothy Parker, Elizabeth I to Rosa

Parks, Marie Curie to Marie Stopes, is now remembered and celebrated for something so insignificant as her size; they are remembered because of who they were and what they did. Sarah Bernhardt had a wooden leg, for God's sake, and still managed to be the finest actress of her age.

Imagine your own obituary. Would you like it to read: She wonderfully never went above a size 8, knew exactly the calorific value of celery, and had a shining talent for refusing potatoes of any variety? At your funeral, those who love you will not weep because they will never again see your perfect figure. They will cry because they are going to miss your left-field sense of humour, your habit of singing out of tune, your ability to listen, your good heart. They will mourn the fact that they will never again get to eat chocolate cake exactly the way you made it. This much we can guarantee.

We want to stand up and say: Stop the Insanity. Why not go ahead and set the children free? Show your daughters that they do not have to grow up to be victims of some random cultural diktat; regard the ability to savour the delights of food as a truly revolutionary act; take delight in proving that not all women are obsessed with diets, because they have twenty-seven more important things to think about before breakfast. By taking pleasure in real, good food you are flying the flag of liberation. You have nothing to lose but your scales.

DEVELOPING AN INSTINCTIVE RELATIONSHIP WITH COOKING.

When it comes to cooking, it is vital to know yourself. If you are the kind of person who finds reassurance in rules and parameters, you should go at once to Delia Smith, who will inform you firmly of the exact measures and techniques necessary for success. Some women, on the other hand, feel constrained by the dictatorial nature of recipes but are uncertain how to do without them.

We are of the instinctive dash-of-this, touch-of-that school. It can be a high-risk strategy. There will be some magnificent disasters (our own include the exploding microwave egg and the Chernobyl Christmas turkey). You need to accept that sometimes you will just have to hurl whatever suppurating mass you have mistakenly concocted in the dustbin, telephone at once for a takeaway, and learn from the experience. Conversely, a mistake will often turn out to be a fabulous new recipe: the thing does not rise, remains liquid when it should be solid, is patently not what you started out to make; it may be utterly delicious, for all that.

Learning to be an instinctive cook means being prepared for failure. But if you persevere, cooking becomes second nature and food turns into a familiar friend. Your confidence grows until, eventually, you become the sort of person who really can conjure up a feast using three eggs and some elderly Parma ham. You will genuinely have no fear (if we were only slightly more flaky than we actually are, we would quite seriously believe that food, like horses, can sense fear). Confidence and conviction are as fundamental to good cooking as any amount of technical knowledge.

The other aspect to instinctive cooking is thought. Before you start, you need to imagine exactly what tastes and textures you want. Invention should not be confused with slapdash: just because you are not slavishly following a given recipe does not indicate a lack of care. Attention is the foundation of good cooking: it is not a mysterious talent that only a few can develop, it is the loving taking of pains. Go slowly, keep tasting, allow yourself to wonder what if – a little more of that, a tiny pinch of the other – and marvellous things will happen.

THE SIGNATURE DISH.

No woman *has* to have a signature dish, any more than she must have a signature style or a signature scent, but it does bring many various pleasures. Having a signature dish means that you no longer have to be baffled by myriad cookery books, food magazines, recipe websites: you are not just following someone else's ideas and tastes, but expressing something of your very own self. It does not have to be grand or complicated, or even a complete course (one of our own signature dishes is known only as Special Green Sauce, so humble that it does not have a proper name, yet such a shameless crowd-pleaser that if we serve a leg of lamb without the little verdant pots of delight people ask for their money back).

The key to the signature dish is that it is something you have developed yourself – perhaps even by taking a well-known recipe and adding a little of this and a little of that until it is your very own. It might be your very special way of roasting a chicken, or the secret ingredient you add to an omelette, or the idiosyncratic manner in which you make a soup, but the core of it is simplicity and individuality. It is yours, and people will come to ask for it, and love you for it.

The relief of a signature dish lies in the tacit acceptance that you will never be able to master all aspects of cooking. It can be tremendously liberating to admit that, however hard you try, you just do not have the talent for making mayonnaise, or that you will never be known for your sourdough bread or béarnaise sauce. There is a lovely freedom in identifying your strengths in the kitchen and playing to them.

The signature dish also comes from your own inclinations. If you love slow cooking, become famous for your Irish stew or Scotch broth; if you are the kind of person who likes throwing everything into the oven, you may become renowned for your Spanish chicken with olives and bay leaves, or your particular genius for roasted vegetables.

The deep joy of the signature dish lies in finding something that you can make again and again, relying on bare instinct instead of complicated recipes, in the sure knowledge that it will give pleasure every time.

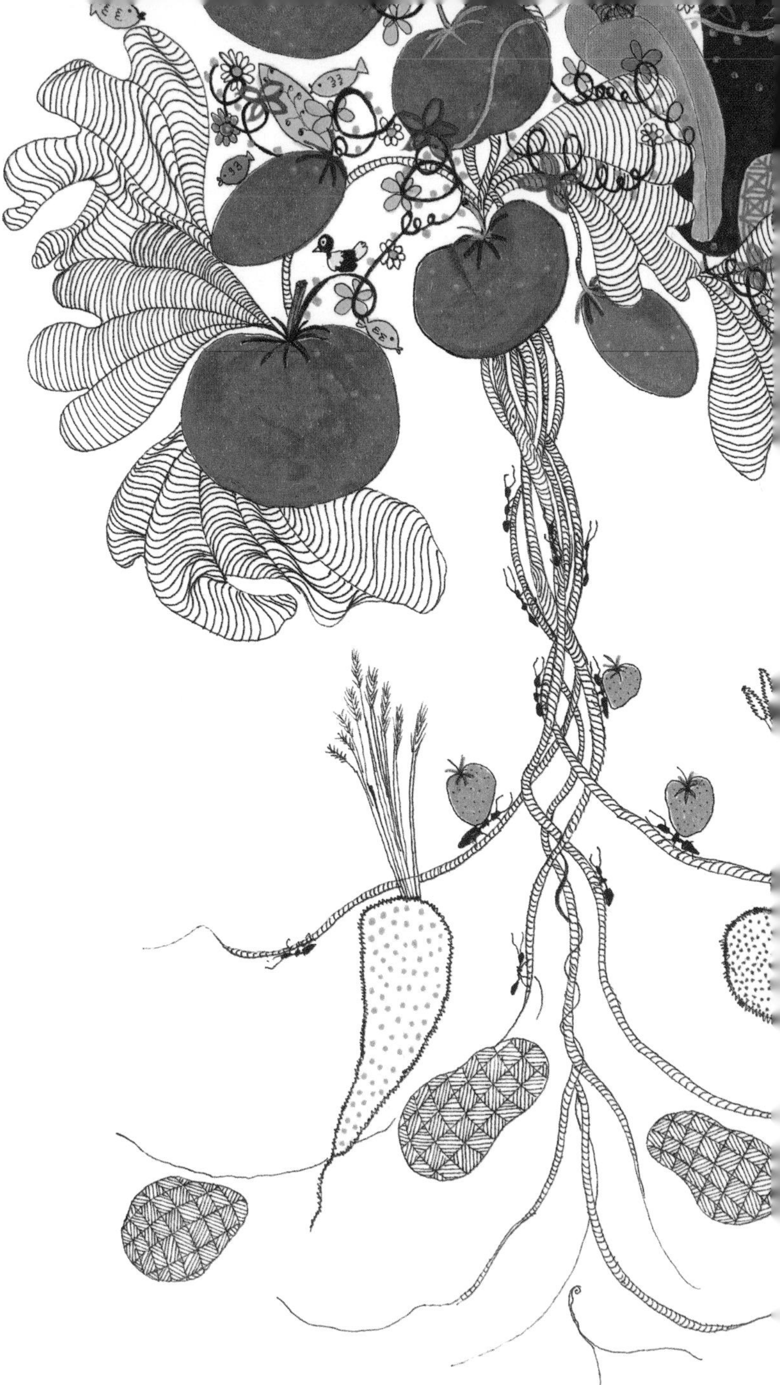

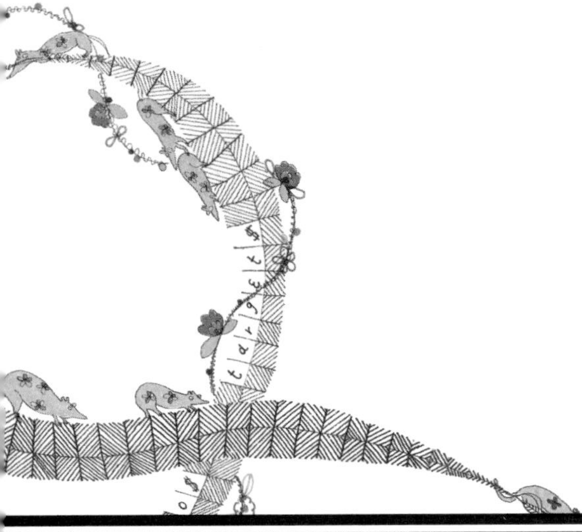
target

CAREER

—

CHAPTER THREE

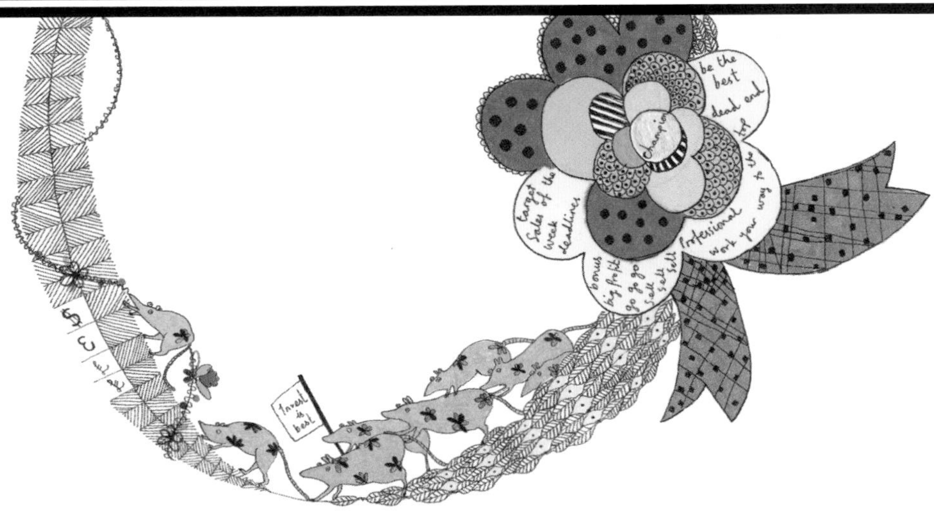
be the best
dead end
top
Champion
target
Sales of the week
deadlines
Professional
work your way to the
bonus
big profit
go go go
Sell Sell Sell
Invest is best

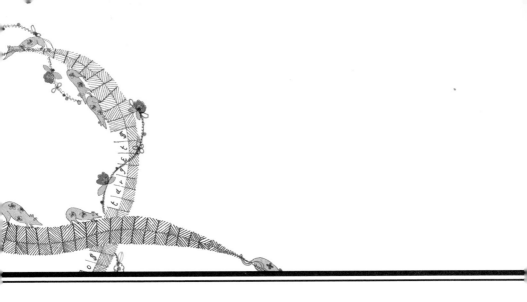

'I HAVE YET TO HEAR A MAN ASK FOR ADVICE ON HOW TO COMBINE MARRIAGE AND A CAREER.'

Gloria Steinem

THE REAL NATURE OF WORK AND WOMEN.

Work, once you get to thinking about it, is so fantastically contradictory that it can make your head shoot right off your neck and into the street. It can be the thing that defines you, or what confines you. It can be an act of defiance or submission. It can spring from a puritan work ethic, or raw greed. It is the way that people judge you, on initial acquaintance, but at the same time it can be a mere fraction of what you are: you might be a computer programmer who dreams of climbing Everest, or a managing director who secretly sees herself as a farmer of rare breeds.

For women especially, the world of work is fraught with complication and unexpected tiger traps. Even in the liberated shining First World, there is a subterranean lode of antediluvian thought that it is not quite seemly for the ladies to put on spike heels and invade the boardroom. It's not only the obvious things: the glass ceiling, the lack of females at the top of every single visible profession, the mad hours that mitigate against family life. It's not just the pay gap, which our friend the tycoon insists is invented by

company heads in the men's lavatories. (We *think* he is joking.) It's the low hum of the culture itself, an almost indecipherable static which insists, through articles in the media and unchallenged assumptions, in lingering attitudes and crude jokes, that somehow you have to justify yourself. It's the bloody old double standard which says that if a woman is hard-nosed in business she is a ball-breaker (just think about the ramifications of that particular expression for a moment), while if a man acts in the same way, he is a buccaneer, driving all before him as nature intended.

Proud feminists that we are, even we are loath to complain too much about this. At least we are allowed to go to work, and walk in the street unchaperoned, and have our own money, which is not the case for all the women of the world. Playing the victim is disempowering and deadly dull. Sing another song, girls, because this one has grown old and bitter. But if we read one more article in a mainstream newspaper insinuating that working women are somehow undermining the very fabric of society, we think we really will have to punch someone in the nose.

'Having It All' – that great mad promise of the modern world – has become insinuated into some kind of ruthless imperative. It's not so much having it all, as Being It All. The covert suggestion is that if women will insist on going out and pursuing a high-powered career, they have to prove that they can still hone all their female faculties: they must also perfect their cooking skills, be ideal mothers and loving wives, and, you know, look pretty. There is no such imperative for men. In the twisty little firestarter of the zeitgeist, once a man is good at his job, that's it. He does not also have to be marvellous at gardening or interpreting the works of Aristotle; he does not have to style his hair and choose his suits with care. For a working man to be judged a good father, he just has to show up.

All right. All right. We're not bitter, really. Maybe a little, in our darker hours. All we are saying is that it is still complicated for the women. You have stout walking boots, you can tackle the incline, it's just that we really would like someone to give the ladies a little credit for having to walk uphill against the prevailing wind. That's all.

AMBITION.

Ambition is fraught with contradiction. It is a brilliant human device to foster achievement; it is what pushes you to leaps of the imagination and a higher level of invention; it can bring you cash and praise, which is a pretty potent combination. On the other hand, there is a moment in the middle of your life where you may suddenly take a stern look at ambition and find yourself revolted by it: it is competitive, narcissistic, even ruthless. It is saying, shamelessly: 'Look at me, see how brilliant I am.'

Some women see ambition as a dirty word, possibly because of the old cultural expectation that it is men who are built for glory. It is not quite seemly for the ladies: too much associated with sharp elbows and raw egotism. The *Harvard Business Review* echoed this subliminal fear when it published articles titled: 'Nice Girls Don't Ask', and 'Do Women Lack Ambition?' (Our answer: NO. But they have learnt to keep quiet about it.)

Yet without ambition, the human mammal would still be wandering vaguely about the savannah saying: 'Fire: it will never catch on.' The most lunatic, pointless striving follows the law of unintended consequences. If the ancient Egyptians had not been so crazily ambitious about achieving a high place in the next world, the moderns would have no pyramids to gaze on, no magnificent tombs and temples to visit, no totemic Tutankhamen sarcophagus to admire. The Romans destroyed their own empire through vaunting ambition, but they left the marvels of the

Coliseum and the Pont du Gard and amphitheatre at Arles. The ambitions of these old cracked civilisations did not, in the end, do themselves much good, but they left a soaring beauty for the generations that came afterwards.

More focused ambition has produced everything from electricity to aqueducts. It was what unravelled the mystery of DNA and illuminated dark matter. If Shakespeare had not been ambitious enough to try to map all human life in his little wooden O, there would be no Lear or Hamlet.

The tragic paradox is that, historically, those most driven by ambition – the ones who achieved remarkable things, who struck out into the unknown – did not draw much personal happiness from it. The story of invention and high beauty is littered with drunks and suicides and the terminally insane; from John Nash to Hemingway, Byron to Alan Turing. The driving ambition that propels people to build up vast business empires can result in a different kind of madness: a loss of reality, a rampant megalomania and a shattering of any moral compass, which leads them to prop up repulsive regimes and influence governments and have secretive meetings in Davos to carve up the world between them (if you believe the conspiracy theorists, which occasionally we do, when the light is coming from the right direction).

But there is something wildly exciting about chasing a high ambition. It is reaching for the stars rather than moping about in the foothills. Whatever the culture has to say about it, you should never have to apologise for your dreams, however outlandish. Ambition can remain benign as long as it is constantly examined; if not, you may find yourself lost in it, and one morning you wake up and do not recognise your reflection in the glass, which can be disconcerting. It can be salutary to step back from your own chugging aspiration and ask it a few hard questions. Mostly: so now what? And: at what cost? You may reach the pinnacle of your profession and suddenly discover that you do not like the view.

When channelled exclusively into work, ambition can be a narrow thing. We like the idea of a broader striving: not merely to be successful in what you do, but in what you are. In absurdly reductive terms, don't end up running the company but having no friends and no time to read a book and coming home to find your husband asking: who is that strange woman? Once you acknowledge the dangers, you can let your ambition rip – and don't let anyone tell you different. You can be a nice girl, and still ask for anything you want.

THE HARD ART OF BALANCING WORK AND LIFE.

Oh, the hoary old work–life balance. Sometimes we think we will do something foolish if we ever hear that expression again. For some reason, the media is entirely obsessed with it and runs endless dictatorial articles about how to find the magical fulcrum between duty and pleasure. The implication is that you have almost certainly got it wrong.

Alongside this goes the insidious vogue for articles about people who have thrown up their jobs in the city and gone to farm sheep in Northumberland, or spent a year trekking up Annapurna, or meditating in Nepal, usually illustrated by photographs of smug individuals wearing questionable footwear. The reality is that hardly anyone can afford, in financial or practical terms, to go off and live in a yurt, however joyful that might make them. So we don't really know why some feature writers seem determined to hold this up as a new nirvana.

Dictating to people how they should live and work can seem both patronising and simplistic. It goes back to the perennial habit of putting people into nice comfortable little niches, complete with clearly written labels: observe here the suited career woman, while in the other corner is the domestic goddess, wafting about in her velvet skirt. The balance is fantastically hard to find, and only you know how to do it. Do not let the culture make you feel guilty because you are not following the prescribed rules or conforming to the sketched stereotypes.

We think that there is only one profound psychological way of checking your balance, which is to imagine yourself at eighty, looking back on your life. Try to cast yourself into the future and conjure up which decisions and compromises you might regret. The old saw goes that no one lies on their death bed thinking: 'Oh, I *wish* I had spent more time at the office', but if you end up being the nearly woman, you might wish that you had put in a few more hours at your desk. It's a question of how you want to be remembered, which is a little melancholy perhaps, but a hard dose of perspective. We know one woman who very much wants to be remembered for having planted many trees. She runs a business and paints pictures, but her idea of a legacy is a fabulous canopy of verdant beeches and limes which future generations can stand under, not knowing whom they should thank for it. It was this revelation, which came to her in her mid-forties, which made her realise that there was no point in killing herself for her business, because it was not her defining feature.

In the same way, you might like to imagine what your children, should you have them, will feel proud of you for. It seems that criticising working mothers has become a national reflex, but it may be that your offspring will want to remember you for more than singing 'The Wheels on the Bus' for the fortieth time. By building up something in the world of work, you are leaving them a valuable bequest, not just in terms of a family enterprise perhaps to carry on – a farm, a shop, a book-binding business – but also in the more nebulous sense of showing them what is possible through graft and application. You can show them that one puny individual can leave a mark on the wide world, often in the most unexpected ways.

FAILURE.

It is at this moment we find ourselves falling into a platitude attack: into every life a little failure must fall. What is astonishing is that human beings seem to persist in the odd belief that they can cheat failure, that it is not necessary, that it is something that happens to other people. Just as Thoreau said never to trust any enterprise that requires new clothes, you might consider nothing to be worth doing that does not involve the risk of failure. If you do not crash and burn once in a while, you are not doing it right.

But failure has become oddly unfashionable. There used to be the affectionate idea of the noble failure, which ran along with the old British habit of loving the underdog. Now, there are schools which have banned any competitive games and entirely changed their marking systems, because the delicate small pupils must not be scarred for life by actually losing. This is not some made-up the-world-is-going-to-the-dogs urban myth, but actually true – we have proof. The insanity of it is that when the children come out of the charmed confines of a school where all shall have prizes, they have absolutely no armour to protect them from a world where some of them will not win anything.

At this point: a small anecdote involving ponies. (Go with it. Really.) We know a woman who spent her childhood showing ponies. One year, she qualified for Peterborough (the Cup Final of the Show-Pony world), and after all the work and hopes and anticipation, she was eliminated after three refusals at a jump with a spooky ditch of blue water under it. Her brave steed took one look at the water and said No. She can still remember the humiliation and tears as they trotted dejectedly from the ring.

Did she give up? Did she, hell. She took her pony home and spent the next year putting him through every kind of water: she walked him along shallow rivers and rode him patiently through fords, she set up a difficult course in her back field and schooled the pony over it three times a day. She went for extra riding lessons with an expert to improve her own skills. (She was eleven years old at this stage.)

A year on, she qualified for Peterborough again, and when she went into the ring, facing those enormous fences, she could almost feel the atoms of her body reconfiguring themselves into a single point of determination. She talked to her pony all the way round, whispering in his ear: 'Come on, come *on*, we can *do* this.' They flew the course, in a mad ecstasy of achievement. They did not win the class, not even close, but for the rest of her life, she could say to herself: I got round Peterborough.

Years afterwards, when she hit a near-terminal patch in her career and came close to giving up, she recalled that childish comeback; she would grit her teeth and summon up the memory of that time, and think that if she had got round Peterborough on a difficult wayward pony, she damn well could put her career back on track. And, reader, she did.

It's easy to laugh at the little pony girls, to write them off as spoiled and pampered – with their grooming and plaiting and oiling of hooves, their silly rosettes and pointless competitions, their obsessive getting up at six to muck out and their endless making of bran mashes – but, as you can see from this small parable, they are learning a vital lesson in life.

The main thing we take from this story is that failure should not be feared. It sounds very pretty on paper to say that there are profound lessons to be drawn from a complete rout, but we think it really is true. Failure is what exposes your core of steel; it throws you back on elemental principles and gives you the chance to discover inner resources you never knew you had. It allows you the opportunity to star in your very own comeback movie: you too can be plucky little Erin Brockovich in a tiny skirt fighting against the might of a multi-national corporation.

It is no coincidence that some of the most successful films ever made are about gutsy characters fighting back against all the odds. In the screenwriting manuals, the strict advice goes that at the end of the second act there must be a plot-point where it seems that *all is lost*. It is one of the enduring elements in all human storytelling: the ugly duckling turning into a swan, poor downtrodden Cinderella getting her Prince.

Failure tells you that you have a choice. You can accept it and let the waters close over your head (no movie in *that*) or you can dust yourself off and realise that you still have all your arms and legs and your undeniable sense of rhythm, and you are categorically not going to let the buggers get you down. You are going to show the lot of them.

So much for the theory. It's a good theory, but it's still just abstract, nice words on the page. In actual life, here is what failure is like: bloody awful. You will almost certainly feel it physically, as if someone has laid about you with a blunt instrument. When it first happens, it can come as a terrible jarring shock. Like all people in shock, you may be stunned into brain freeze, unable to make sense of the world. Your grasp of reality will flicker on and off like a faulty circuit. You will be covered in a haze of shame, certain that people are pointing and laughing. Some people *will* point and laugh, although you should understand that this is a nervous reaction: they are terrified that it will one day happen to them, and are so relieved that it has caught someone else that they cannot remember how to behave in a reasonable manner.

Fail, and there is a militant sorting of the sheep and the goats. The interesting thing is that the people who love you most will not laugh, or point. Oddly, even though you are suddenly yesterday's woman, they will appear to love you more. This can seem so counter-intuitive that it takes a while to accept that it is real. Surely they should all be running away screaming? Or at least pity you a little, or give you the sympathy look, or something? Your precious business has gone down the tubes, your great English novel has been rejected, your definitive molecular theory has collapsed, and your nearest and dearest are persisting, bizarrely, in regarding you as exactly the same person.

Just as you may be startled by the reaction of those closest to you when you fail, you may find yourself even more astonished by their

attitude when you pull yourself out of it and get a new contract, win a better job, return in triumph from the wilderness. When you ring up to tell them, expecting exclamations of frank disbelief, you may find that, while delighted, they are not surprised. *You* are surprised, because for all your backbone and gritted teeth, there was a part of you that thought maybe you would always remain the forgotten woman. The ones who love you did not think this: they had faith. They had more faith in you than you had in yourself.

So, for all the hurt and the shame, failure offers you two lodes of pure gold: it shows you the stuff of which you are made (which is, of course, *of course,* the Right Stuff) and it reveals to you how much affection and belief you inspire in those who love you well.

A lovely side-effect of this is the cessation of pain equalling pleasure. If you are afraid of flying, landing in a foreign airport induces a disproportionate euphoria simply because you have cheated certain death in a massive fireball. In the exact same way, success after failure has an intense savour to it which would not come if your career had merely been a smooth linear progress from one triumph to the next. You have got your groove back, and, my God, it is sweet this time around.

THE ART OF RECONCILING THE FANTASY WORLD OF WORK PAINTED FOR YOUR YOUNGER SELF WITH THE MUNDANE AND OFTEN ALARMING ADULT REALITY.

Sometimes we think that by the time you get to forty your career can feel like that great Talking Heads song: 'this is not my beautiful house, this is not my beautiful wife, how did I get here?' You may, through a quirk of luck or fate or sheer brilliance, find yourself in the job which entirely suits your personality, stretches your imagination, and illuminates all your strengths. Or, you may not.

People go into jobs for all kinds of complicated reasons. You may be living out the unfulfilled dreams of your parents, or simply following tradition or the swell of the crowd; you might be caught up in a money trap, or tangled in a web of low expectations. We are leery of the bossy life-coach school, which insists on giving you strict checklists to assess your career priorities and wants you to make sudden earth-shifting decisions and radical swerves in direction. You may simply not have the time or energy to transform your entire life in Ten Easy Steps. There is the small, but potent, question of what is realistic.

There is no doubt that your middle life is the time when you are confronted, often brutally, with the gap between the dreams you had when you were young and invulnerable, and the actuality of your adult nine-to-five. You once dreamed of being an intrepid investigative reporter, and now you are an accountant, and it can feel as if something in you has died.

There are some things you can do about this, without having to follow ten easy steps, or resorting to industrial amounts of brandy. The first is to examine closely those youthful dreams. We know a woman who held a cherished childhood fantasy of having her own shop. Finally, in her forties, she opened one. It looked gorgeous, filled with enchanting and esoteric objects, just as she had always imagined it. But then she discovered all the aspects that were not in the dream: margins, VAT, health and safety regulations, finding reliable help. She ran up against the granite fact that most small businesses do not make any profit for the first four years. The shop, far from being the pinnacle of her youthful dream, became a fat millstone round her poor slender neck.

We hate to dismantle dreams: it is the existential equivalent of pulling the wings off flies. But sometimes a fantasy should remain just a fantasy: it is what you would do, in a parallel universe, if you were in fact a completely different kind of person. Once you learn to tell the difference between something that is heavenly in your head but would not work in reality, and something which would fulfil all your unmet yearnings, then you put yourself in a stronger position to make radical decisions.

A useful psychological exercise is to work out whether your choice of job is working with your character. If you find yourself oddly drained by work which seems good on paper, which other people seem to manage quite easily, it may not be merely that you are not getting enough iron in your diet, but that you are running against your own nature.

The simplest way to work this out is to discover whether you are an introvert or an extrovert. These terms are commonly misunderstood as shy versus gregarious, but they are more complex than that. You do not have to fill in a detailed questionnaire to find your type; there are two basic questions you need to ask yourself. Is the internal world of thoughts and dreams more interesting and comfortable to you than the external

world of actions? And: is your greatest fear that your mental world will disintegrate, or that you will be left entirely alone? If you answer yes to the first of both these questions, you are naturally introverted; if you choose the second answer, you are an extrovert. Part of the reason these get muddled is that natural introverts can have highly developed social skills, making them appear extroverted – they crack jokes and are perfect guests at parties – while an extrovert can sometimes appear taciturn and shy.

If you are an introvert doing a job that is suited to an extrovert, you will use up vast reserves of energy: it is as if you are using your left hand to write when you are naturally right-handed. You may perfect the art so that no one ever notices, but it will take a great deal of study and effort. An introvert who is doing a job where she must deal with people all day, give lectures and presentations, constantly be on show, is having to call on something which rubs against the grain of her nature. If an extrovert becomes a writer, the sitting in a silent room and living inside her head will be more tiring than it would be for someone who is instinctively introverted. The rewards that you get from a job which goes against your inner nature can be worth so much that the extra striving required is absolutely worth it. But it is instructive to do a quick mental check: it may explain why it is that your perfect job is quite so enervating. Knowledge really is power in this case: it means that you are not making decisions in the dark.

An added shaft of elucidation can come from doing a sharp audit on your pain–pleasure ratio. All jobs, however wonderful, involve some strain and sacrifice. There will be colleagues who drive you demented, hackwork that makes you feel demeaned, hours that stretch you to breaking; but as long as the pleasure outweighs the pain, then it is surely worthwhile. The pleasure can be simple and ruthlessly practical: you really *do* want the money; or it can be complex and nebulous: it fulfils your sense of self. (If you secretly see yourself as a crusading humanitarian, it is as well not to end up as a lawyer defending heartless corporations against pollution charges.) If the pain–pleasure ratio is seriously out of whack, you might want to consider a change.

Change: another of those words that is absurdly easy to write, and incredibly hard to act on. This is why we are so grumpy about all those self-help books, with their facile life plans. Change, especially in your middle life, when you are getting a little set in your ways and easy with your comfortable habits, can induce a state of rank terror. The nasty voices in your head charge up, delighted to have a moment in the sun, and start chattering about how you are simply not equipped for it, and what makes you think you can do something entirely else? It is so much easier to stick with what you know, even though it is not making you tremendously happy and you get a slightly sick, sinking feeling in your gut when the alarm goes off in the morning. There probably are ten magical steps for this, although we have never found them. The best way to discover the courage to change is to consult the people who know and love you most. Even this can be quite scary: what if they laugh and scoff at your secret idea? Well, what if? You can quickly turn it into a joke. But chances are, they will put their heads back and say, 'At last, at last, this is what we have been waiting for.' You can get so lost in the tangle of doubt that sometimes you cannot see your own talents clearly, whereas those around you can see them like flashing beacons. 'Yes, yes', they will say, 'of course you should give up the city and write a cookery book; you were made,' they will state with authority, 'to breed rare goats instead of crunching numbers.'

There is only one small caveat to this. We all have friends who are, how shall we say, a little *definitive* in their opinions. Do not let yourself be bullied into anything, just because they have decided it is a fabulous idea.

Be very clear that it is purely a consultative exercise, you are canvassing opinion, and you will take all their notions under consideration. Then, trust your instincts, close your eyes, and jump.

Or not.

NOT WORKING AT ALL.

We know. Have you just dropped your gin all over the carpet? Not working? Are we *mad*?

The odd thing is that only two generations ago, women did not work unless they had to. The majority of jobs for women were strictly working class: factory work, domestic service, clerical work, various badly paid menial jobs which now are taken by eager Eastern Europeans. Today, it is so taken for granted that all but a very few eccentric rich ladies go out and earn money that it is easy to forget what an extraordinary revolution has occurred in the last fifty years. Even as late as the 1960s, reflexively thought of as a decade of liberation and mad change, most middle-class women still got married and did something gentle with a charity of their choice.

This revolution is, of course, an undeniably Good Thing. It is a miracle that, apart from All-in Wrestling and being a sperm donor, there is no career path that is closed to females. It is a source of awe and wonder that vast swathes of women who were, only a few short decades ago, spending their days getting their hair done and pondering whether to buy brisket or fillet for dinner are now flying aeroplanes and practising heart surgery and unravelling the mysteries of the human genome. The twenty-first century is one of choice and freedom, except in one strange regard: should you choose not to work, you will be thought of as so peculiar and subversive that people may dismiss you as ill or insane.

We are not talking about women who decide to stay at home and look after their children (although this carries controversies of its own – it is still work, just of the unpaid, unsung variety. Some clever policy wonk once worked out that the work done by women in the home saves the economy £739 billion a year); we are talking about the kind of woman who is in a position to do absolutely nothing. There are no children, or the children have gone; there is, miraculously, the money. She might have built up a business from nothing and sold it for millions, or had the great luck to have a parent who patented some vital widget which is used in space exploration; she might have hit the numbers on the lottery. We are not talking about the mistress of one of the new Russian billionaires, because being a kept woman is a job all of its own, we mean a Woman of Independent Means. Imagine that you found yourself in such a position. (You may be in it, even as you read this.) Chances are that you would feel some urge, like a dull pressure in the back of your head, as if a cultural imperative is leaning on your very brain, to be seen to do a job, because choosing not to is so unimaginable in this modern commercial world that the very act of having to explain your decision might feel like work in itself.

It is so accepted that work is ubiquitous, and *good,* and necessary for any sense of self, that no one questions it. There are discussions about the length of the hours and the meagreness of the pay, with a few clichés about job satisfaction thrown into the soup, but no one stops to ask whether work itself has actual intrinsic value. If you are a physicist who can see the raging beauty of the universe, or a mathematician for whom the Fibonacci numbers carry the aesthetic delight of a sonnet, or a writer enduringly fascinated with the human condition and enchanted by the very *nature* of the semi-colon, then your work is so stitched into your heart that it is hard to know where it ends and you begin. If you are in a vocational job – saving lives, defending human rights, comforting the old and the sick – there is never a question that it is worth it. But for many people, work is a necessity rather than a joy.

If you take a step back and actually examine what it is you are achieving, the answer might be: not much. The reply might be: acting as a slave to the bourgeois work ethic. You must work not because it adds to human happiness, or illuminates human truths, or fills your heart with delight, but because you would be considered crazed and feckless not to. It becomes a negative imperative. Work is regarded as so necessary to the human spirit that single mothers are hustled into a job, *any* job, by government dictat. A housing minister recently threatened to evict people who refused to take job offers. The newspapers love to print stories about how this Lotto winner or that pools millionaire is still doing the same old job that they had before their windfall. The implication is not only that this is a perfectly marvellous example of the phlegmatic character of the British worker, whose sensible head remains unturned by filthy cash, but also that the very fact of working is a universal good.

We wonder. We sometimes secretly dream of a life that has nothing to do with salaries and deadlines and worldly achievement. What if, as someone once said (we can't remember who), the rat race has to survive with one less rat?

Could it be that, if circumstances made it possible, choosing not to work is in fact a radical blow against the heedless, unthinking speed of modern life? Imagine not having to rush from your bed the moment the alarm sounds, head already filled with lists, dashing to catch the train, worrying already about leaves on the line or the wrong kind of snow. Imagine no office politics or schmoozing of potential clients. Imagine no *meetings*. Think

of no more weak coffee, bad lighting, hideous office furniture, soulless desk lunches. Why would a life in which there was time for reading Proust, smelling the roses and watching the sun set be of a lower value? Imagine the luxury of time, and bringing living itself to a high art.

The unquestioned wisdom is that those who do not work are risking death by boredom, but what could be more dull than the inevitability of the same old drone, the same old commute, the same old office conversations. You are trapped in a relationship with people you would normally pay to avoid. You could be taking the time to make a mushroom omelette and a pot of proper coffee for breakfast instead of eating a disgusting cereal bar on the bus; you have the leisure to listen to your friends and take your godchildren to the park and oh, we don't know, see the latest exhibition at the Royal Academy. You could knit socks or learn decoupage or master the trick of sourdough bread. You could think *thoughts*. You could move slowly.

You, alone, could prove that the entire commercial imperative is a huge con trick, engineered to stop people examining the real nature of things too closely. By refusing to fall for it, you are carrying out your very own one-woman revolution.

Or, you are just fabulously lazy and want to lie on the sofa all day eating Turkish delight.

We're just wondering, that's all.

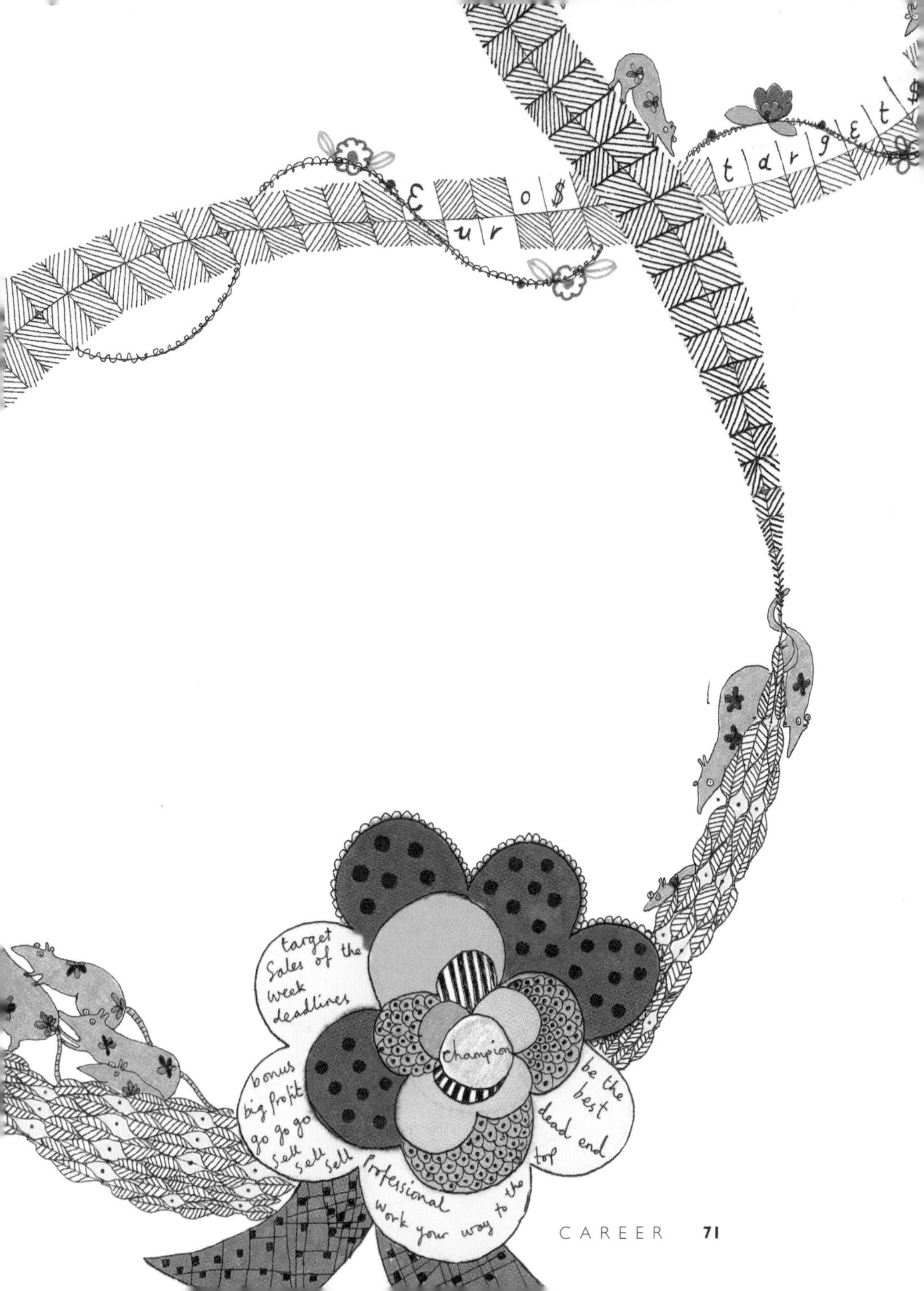
target
Sales of the
week
deadlines
bonus
big profit
go go go
sell sell sell
Professional
work your way to the top
champion
be the
best
dead end

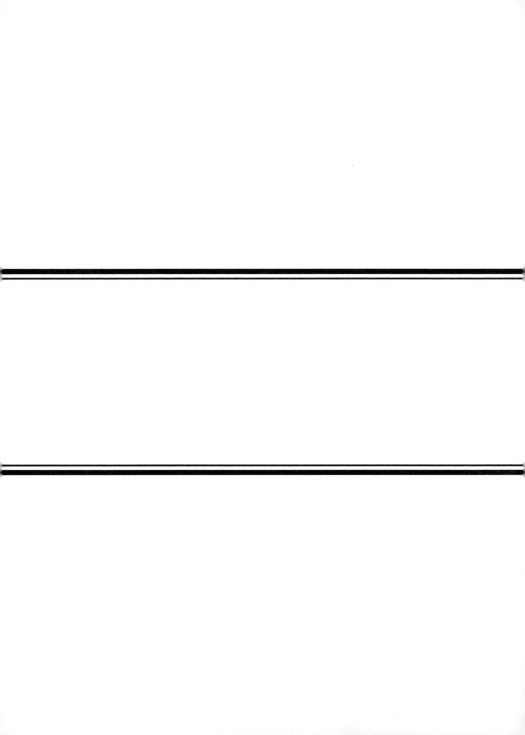

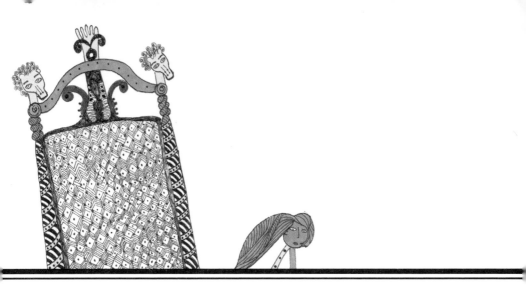

MEN

–

CHAPTER FOUR

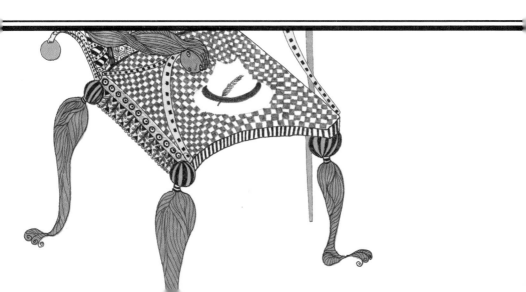

WHY YOU LOVE THEM, EVEN THOUGH YOU DON'T LIKE IT VERY MUCH WHEN THEY GET ILL OR DON'T RETURN YOUR TELEPHONE CALLS.

You know all the quirky reasons why you love the men in your life – the sense of humour, the sudden kindness, the ability to chop wood. You forgive the blatant male failings – like the enduring belief in the Laundry Fairy, which spirits away their dirty clothes and returns them pristine and fresh, or the inexplicable habit of disappearing utterly whenever any kind of food is on the table. The love is all of these things, but on a more profound level it is to do with a desire for the other. This is slightly paradoxical, because humans are frightened of the other, alarmed by difference, and yet they also crave it. It is some ancient Darwinian imperative. Women, with their soft, smooth skin and deep capacity for empathy, are drawn towards men, with their hairy muscular bodies and advanced spatial awareness. Of course this is an absurd generalisation, you only have to look at a female triathlete compared to a gentle male North London liberal, but the general point holds.

Simon Baron-Cohen, the professor of psychopathology at Cambridge,

has done some fascinating work demonstrating the essential difference between the male and female brain, which echoes the more nebulous Jungian idea of the animus and the anima. Although these tend to run on a continuum (so that a woman may have many male attributes, and vice versa), they do show that there really is a difference. A boy child of even the most progressive, gender-defying parents will somehow find a way to fashion a gun, even if he has to do it out of recycled hemp or a spare crevice nozzle; girl children, on the other hand, are more drawn to what is termed, rather horribly, co-operative and nurturing play. Even as newborns, boys will focus more on a mechanical object and girls will stare in fascination at faces. It used to be feared that observation of such diversity was a sort of confirming sexism: as if the system-oriented brain that men most commonly show was somehow superior to the empathetic female brain. At its most simple, this means that men tend to be good at reading blueprints and women are good at reading people. There is no value judgement here: both talents are vital to human discourse.

It is this siren call of difference that leads to some confusion between the sexes. The rise and fall of the metrosexual is a case in point. There was a period in the late nineties when some men really got in touch with their female side — staying at home to look after the children while the women ran the company, going out to do the shopping, ostentatiously carrying babies about in papooses, pondering over fabric swatches. At first the women were delighted: a newly sensitive, malleable male — what a triumph for evolution. But then the whole thing got a little worrying. It was a relief not to have so much chest-beating, but was this new breed going too far in the other direction?

The television series *Sex and the City* did a brilliant riff on this phenomenon in an episode where one of the characters started dating a sensitive pastry chef who had impeccable taste in placemats. At first she assumed he was gay. Then they had perfectly marvellous sex. After some discussion with her friends, it was decided that he was a gay straight man – every woman's dream. But when he squealed like a girl at the sight of a mouse in her kitchen, she realised that, despite the perfect-on-paper aspect of this new genus, it was just not quite manly enough for her. Reader, she dumped him.

'THE OBVIOUS AND FAIR SOLUTION TO THE HOUSEWORK PROBLEM IS TO LET MEN DO THE HOUSEWORK FOR, SAY, THE NEXT 6,000 YEARS, TO EVEN THINGS UP. THE TROUBLE IS THAT MEN HAVE, OVER THE YEARS, DEVELOPED AN INFLATED NOTION OF THE IMPORTANCE OF EVERYTHING THEY DO, SO THAT BEFORE LONG THEY WOULD TURN HOUSEWORK INTO JUST AS MUCH OF A CHARADE AS BUSINESS IS NOW. THEY WOULD HIRE SECRETARIES AND BUY COMPUTERS AND FLY OFF TO HOUSEWORK CONFERENCES IN BERMUDA, BUT THEY'D NEVER CLEAN ANYTHING.'

Dave Barry

The modern woman does ask a great deal of a man: she wants him to be strong yet sensitive, decisive yet open-minded, gentle yet determined. There must be the Good Sense Of Humour. A little sartorial flair and the ability to dance are optional extras, but devoutly to be wished. Men sometimes complain about this, but personally, we think they should take it as a compliment: these high expectations are a sign that women believe that men are in fact complex and evolved creatures, instead of paper-thin stereotypes.

As well as the allure of the other, there is another profound reason for the enduring love women have for men. It is not just the bare fact that you can give birth to them – they are your sons and brothers, your fathers and friends – it is also the mystery. We suspect that however many books women read, or sociological and anthropological studies they pore over, they will always find something about men a little baffling. There is a part of the male psyche that is a challenge, with its inexplicable thought processes and arcane habits. One day, the women think – determined not to be beaten – they will discover the secret. It's like a fabulous mystery story, in real time. You've got to love that.

It is for all these reasons that women love men. It is not the 1950s: you no longer have to believe in the inherent perfection of the male; you can love him just the way he is, rather than subscribing to some bizarre culturally dictated cult of worship. Of course it drives you insane when he gets a little cough and acts as if he has a fatal case of pleurisy; of course you get furiously frustrated at the traditional male inability to call when he says he will; and you will never quite understand what it is that he absolutely *must* do in his shed. (We really do think that all men dream of having a shed. Even men who do not have a literal shed will construct a metaphorical one. We have no idea why this is.) But for all this, you love him still.

SOME COMMONLY OBSERVED TYPES.

THE WOMANISING MALE.

Here is an entirely unscientific theory about men (with absolutely no peer-reviewed studies to back it up): they are either hunting dogs, or they are not. Some men are, as they really do say in Texas, hard dogs to keep on the porch. These men generally do not change, although sometimes, after thirty years of womanising, they get tired of the dance, decide that there is something entirely novel and fascinating about embracing monogamy, and turn into model husbands. Warren Beatty famously did this when, after cutting a swathe through the most beautiful women in Hollywood, he settled down with Annette Bening. We think that there was something rather honourable about this: he did not, unlike more careless womanisers, get married until he had got all the other women out of his system.

The Womaniser is not intrinsically bad. He will tell you that he loves women, and he is not lying: it's just that he loves *all* women. He will be charming, paradoxically comfortable with intimacy, very good at sex, and prone to sudden romantic gestures. Sometimes it seems that he truly believes it would be rude not to share all these great qualities with as many women as possible. He adores the chase, and will woo you with a courtly determination. The problem is that sex is a matter of conquest for him, and once he has conquered, his job is done, and so he must move on.

There is an odd irony about the dogs and the non-dogs. It is often the men who are not so romantic and thoughtful who turn out to be wonderfully faithful, and never look at another woman; you are their one, and that's it. They might not bring you roses, but they will not make you cry.

If you want to have a season in the sun with a great womaniser, it is, as our friend the playwright says, amusing once. You will get a high level of care and attention – quite possibly trips to Venice and dinners at high-tone restaurants – and he will treat you like a princess, for as long as you have his attention. It can be intoxicating, but know that it will not last. Unless he has reached sixty and hung up his boots, his eye will go on roving. You will not be able to change him. He may really mean it when he says he loves you and he has never met anyone like you, but he will be equally sincere when he meets the next one. It's like a disease, that way.

THE ALPHA MALE.

The Alpha Male is easily confused with the Womaniser, but he is in fact a distinct species. The Womaniser, for all his dreams of conquest, can actually be in touch with his female side: very good at chatting, quite happy to talk about emotions, and fascinated by the twists of a woman's psyche. For the Alpha Male, such pursuits are not worth much. For him, it is all about his place in the hierarchy. He might not be a hunting dog, but he must be top dog. He is fabulously competitive, defines success in terms of money and status and conspicuous consumption, and does not understand anyone who doesn't. His opinions are cast in stone, and he will not hesitate to broadcast them. He is not frightened of women, although he may regard them as an alien species. He has a tendency to take a trophy wife – he will be tremendously generous in his treatment of her, loading her with jewels and couture clothes, but he will be far too busy to talk to her at any great length. The Alpha Male likes to discuss concrete things: politics, business, sport. He is not interested in the abstract and thinks that philosophy is for wimps. He can be very funny, although he has to be funnier than anyone else in the room, and he will sometimes use humour as a dominating device. He is terrified of death.

Personally, we find the Alpha Male quite tiring, but there are women who love him. He does not need much care and attention – like the Duracell bunny, you just wind him up and watch him go. Gaze in wonder as he orders bottles of £1000 Petrus in high-end bars, buys a racing yacht on a whim, takes over three companies before breakfast! He is like a force of nature. The only problem is, he may suddenly reach a moment in his late middle age when he looks up and realises that all this acquisition is worth precisely nothing, and that no matter how many empires he builds, prizes he wins and cash he accumulates, he is not immortal, and he has never taken the time to build up any inner resources to deal with this existential crisis.

At this point, he can easily snap like a brittle twig, and spend a year sitting in a dark room, unable to speak.

THE BASTARD.

Oddly, in these evolved enlightened times, this type of man does still exist. We don't really understand why he is still allowed to roam freely in the wild, when he should be locked up in a cage and exhibited as a cautionary tale for the credulous.

Anyone who lies to you, puts you down in public, fucks your best friend, constantly criticises your cooking, your dress sense and/or your intelligence, is a bastard and should not be entertained for a moment. Oh, sure, his mother was a drunk and his father walked out when he was three and he was bullied at school, but it's no excuse. Everyone has ancient griefs and childhood scars, everyone carries the secret wound of never quite getting all the unconditional love they needed, but not everyone goes around undermining people's very sense of self as some kind of twisted revenge.

The Bastard is categorically *not* in desperate need of the love of a good woman. It does not matter that he can sometimes be charming, or even give the appearance of vulnerability, or offer sudden apologies for some egregious act. He is a grown-up: he has choices. Mental cruelty, betrayal, bullying, withholding affection and other assorted controlling behaviours are not cries for help, they are just nakedly horrible and should never be tolerated for a moment. We hate to resort to cliché, but life is, in fact, too short. You might be able to save a wounded man, but you can't rescue a Bastard. We have watched people try. It never ends well. There are no magic wands for this one, so recognise him for what he is, and run for the hills.

THE SPORTING MALE.

Ah, the Sporting Male. What can we say? Not much, as it turns out. If you adore activity holidays, would rather go free-climbing than read a book, enjoy standing in the rain watching thirty hefty men chase after a rugby ball, have a fascination for statistics, and are willing to put up with vast amounts of indecipherable equipment in your hall, then he's the boy for you.

If not, then, well, not.

THE SENSITIVE MALE.

Yes, he does exist. Although in our darker moments we have imagined that he is so rare that we must stalk him through dangerous terrain (whilst doing the special whispery voice like David Attenborough), now we see that most rare sight, the lesser spotted Sensitive Male, in his own natural habitat.

The Sensitive Male often gets unfairly branded as a wimp. We think the opposite is true: it takes a certain mental toughness to survive in the world if you have a sensitive nature. The insensitive barge their way through life, untroubled by the miseries of the Congolese women or the melting of the ice-caps; the insensitive do not have to worry about hurting people's feelings or going through the demanding process of putting themselves in someone else's shoes. They are what they are, and the world is what it is, and that's all she wrote.

The Sensitive Male is not actually the worn stereotype of a bleeding heart, *Guardian*-reading, organic-carrot-eating vegan; he may in fact be built like a heavyweight boxer and enjoy the novels of Raymond Chandler. What he will do, whatever shape or size he comes in, is think about *your* feelings. He will telephone when he says he will, because he knows that it means something to you, and even if he is fantastically busy, he will call to say that he can't speak right now. He will notice when you are so tired that you don't know what your name is, and just go ahead and make the supper, without being asked. He will not mock your unreasonable terror of spiders, but calmly remove them from the bath. He will make an effort to get on with your mother, even though she is a domestic tyrant, because he knows it makes your life easier. He will understand that sometimes even you, with all your emotional fluency, don't want to talk about it, and not take it personally. Crucially, it is *not* all about him.

It is attention more than anything else that marks out the Sensitive Male. Do not be misled by ersatz displays of sentimentality: the man who cries easily while watching *The Sound of Music,* or is visibly moved by a Schubert quintet is quite capable of running off with someone else's wife. The truly sensitive man does not parade his tender feelings as if expecting some kind of award. He does two crucial things, neither of them obvious crowd-pleasers: he listens, and he notices. This enables him to read between the lines. So he knows that when you snap, it is not because you

are angry with him, but because your best friend has just been diagnosed with Hodgkins and you are absolutely terrified. He understands and accepts your mysterious moments of melancholy. He knows that sometimes you get crazy for no reason at all, and will categorically *not* say things like, 'Is it that time of the month?' He is not only emotionally literate, but emotionally generous. He will celebrate your triumphs as if they were his own, and curse your defeats in the same way. He is a bit of a miracle, like that.

He may quite possibly not be given to high romantic gestures. Unlike the womaniser, the Sensitive Male might not flatter you and spoil you with bouquets of flowers and impetuous trips to exotic places or luxurious hotels, but the many small unscreenworthy acts of attention that you get from the Sensitive Male are worth more than emeralds. He might not swagger around like the king of the world, but he will, unquestionably, make you feel like a queen.

THE USUAL MALE.

All of the above are extremes, of one kind or another. They are diverting to identify, but the vast majority of men cannot be fitted so easily into neat little boxes. Just as most women are a seething mass of contradictions and perfect encyclopaedias of complexity and mystery, so are men. Sometimes it is tempting to regard men as somehow more simplistic than the wonderful enigmatic complication that is Woman. But this is a mistake.

It is pretty much proven that there are fundamental biological differences between the male and female brain – the systematic versus empathetic that Professor Baron-Cohen has observed – along with an overlay of persisting cultural expectations, and you should not forget the

crucial role of testosterone, a driving hormone. It is this very difference
that keeps the engine of enduring fascination and attraction between men
and women revving. But for all that, there is as much that unites the sexes
as divides them.

Men may place a greater dividend on the gaining of respect than
women do; even the most enlightened of them have an oddly old-
fashioned desire to be a good provider. This is not because they think you
are a poor helpless little female who cannot do anything for yourself –
they understand perfectly well that you may earn more than they do,
know how to change a tyre and are a genius at figures – but a great part
of the male sense of self is tied up in a man's ability to provide. Most men
are much less interested in dissecting the minutiae of the emotional life
than women are. (We know one man who has to be tied to a chair in
order to talk about Feelings.) And yet, just like women, men pretty much
all want to love and be loved, persist in the search for happiness, and hope
that their lives may turn out to have some small significance. Which is a
very long, winding way of saying that if there is such a thing as the Usual
Male you may find that he is, in many ways, quite like you. Apart from the
thing with the shed, of course.

—

'SO IT IS NATURALLY WITH THE MALE AND THE FEMALE;
THE ONE IS SUPERIOR, THE OTHER INFERIOR; THE ONE
GOVERNS, THE OTHER IS GOVERNED; AND THE SAME RULE
MUST NECESSARILY HOLD GOOD WITH RESPECT TO ALL
MANKIND.'

Aristotle (One of the most timeless examples of the male ego in full flood.)

THE MALE EGO: ORIGINS AND MANIFESTATIONS OF.

The male ego is more complicated than is often allowed for. Sometimes it can seem that the whole affair is a massive dick thing, and women wonder why the men don't just put their penises on the table and measure them, and get it over with.

In evolutionary terms, humans are not so very far from the caves, it's just that there is a lot of groovy technology to hide the fact. Men may now be wandering around wearing sharp Dolce suits and talking into iPhones, but sometimes it seems that they might as well be covered in bearskins and daubing themselves with wode.

The competitive side of the male ego stems from an ancient imperative: it is the man who kills the most boar and spreads the most seed that wins. While the women were working out which herbs and berries were safe to eat and which would kill them, looking after the children, literally keeping the home fires burning, the men had one straightforward task: go out and hunt down that wildebeest. The evolutionary psychologists suspect that this is why women are excellent at doing several things at once, while men tend to focus absolutely on one thing at a time.

Somewhere along the line, the male ego drove men to decide that they had to rule the world. This great scam has somehow managed to hold sway for the last 10,000 years. No one really knows why this happened. There is a feminist theory that the very oldest societies were matriarchal, centring on the worship of Mother Earth and honouring the miraculous ability of women to give birth. (It's still a miracle to us, but that's a whole other story.) In these early communities, the belief was that babies came from the gods, or the ether, or just straight out of the sky, and had nothing to do with actual procreation. One day, some clever man took the day off from hunting and realised that there was a cause and effect thing going on, what with him having the sex and then, nine months later, a child appearing. The theory goes that this revelation led to such a sense of ownership, with its riders of jealousy and appropriation, that the patriarchal society was born.

We think that this is a fraction simplistic and leaves important questions unanswered, most crucially – why did women allow it for so long? But the fact remains that the male ego was powerful enough to drive the men to dominate women for a very long time.

And yet, and yet. Oddly, paradoxically, the male ego seems a very fragile thing. From our own entirely personal observation, we find that it is the women who bend and bruise and get twisted out of shape, but it is the men who crack. It is the little boys who break our hearts; we look at the young girls, who, for all their Barbies and love of pink and adorable little bunches, have a secret glint in their eye that hints at some unimagined inner steel, and know that they will be all right. This is an inchoate, emotional, possibly irrational feeling on our part, but there are statistics to back it up. Men die earlier than women, their rate of heart disease is much higher, they are far more likely to commit suicide. It seems more and more probable that their famous driving ego is nothing more than an urban myth, a miracle of spin. Somehow, they, or someone who likes them very much, has managed to put it about that women are the weaker sex, while the men just swagger around, surfing the wave of their own self-belief, drinking and whoring and duelling and invading places and, well, the devil can take the hindmost.

In our own limited survey, it is the men rather than the women who say things like: 'I am still getting away with it.' It is the men who have a great fear of being found out, of being exposed as phoneys. Their sense of achievement is much more intimately bound up with professional success than is that of the women. Women tend to define themselves in terms of their relationships; when professional failure comes, they don't like it, but they will console themselves with the thought of those who love them, and those they love. They will count the ways: good friend, great sister, loving wife, attentive girlfriend, perfect aunt. For men faced with redundancy, these are absolutely no consolation.

This is why you cannot console a man when he has just been laid off, or his business has failed, or his book has had stinking reviews. It does not matter to him, in that moment, that he is a good husband and a wonderful father and a kind brother; his ego is so bound up with worldly achievements that nothing you can do will make him feel better. All your words of comfort, all your intuition and wisdom, will only sound patronising to him. Your offers of help will make him feel emasculated. The only, awful, thing you can do at times like this is to leave him alone to work it out. Or buy him a shed.

The other defining feature of the male ego is that men pride themselves in their ability to fix things. You have seen this manifested a hundred times. A disaster strikes, and you turn to your best girlfriend: her immediate reaction is to say, 'Oh God, I know *just* what that feels like.' She will do a fast search of her own mental database to find a parallel; she will dredge up all the feelings of sickness and rage and terror that she had when faced with a similar situation. 'Of course,' she will say, 'I remember exactly, no, no you are not going insane, that's just what it bloody well feels like.'

The man you call in the same situation may be vastly sympathetic, but he will surely offer you a *solution*. This is the male ego in its most disinterested form: it is not solipsistic or self-serving; he hates to see you in distress, and he feels that he must do something about it. Even the most sensitive man does this; if he can't mend it, he feels that he has failed. All you want is someone to tell you that you are not a freak and you are not alone and the whole shooting match is completely shitty and unfair and plain wrong, and he will offer you a ten-point plan. So when you want to scream that you don't want any *sodding* plan, you might like to take a breath and remember that, really, he is doing his best.

WHY IT'S PERFECTLY FINE TO NOT NEED A MAN.

There used to be a great tradition of the single female, usually some slightly batty old bird who had spent her time living with distant tribes or healing the sick, or locked in an ivory tower of academe, who never had a thought for a husband. This was not because these women were living in enlightened times; they were often mocked as spinsters, and openly pitied, although some of them, like Gertrude Bell and Freya Stark, did become national treasures. It was mostly due to necessity: the Great War killed off a whole generation of men, and the women left behind had to face the fact that there was, literally, no one for them to marry.

Now, at the beginning of a brand new century, it is still considered odd or even perverse for a woman to choose not to be part of a couple. There are a few famous women who remain resolutely single – Diane Keaton, Gloria Steinem, Germaine Greer. Condoleeza Rice managed to become fluent in Russian and play classical piano and become Secretary of State (admittedly not a terribly good one) without a husband. But they are regarded as anomalies, if not outright freakish.

We say that there is absolutely nothing, apart from lazy cultural assumptions, which proves that marriage is the ideal state for a modern female. A really great man to live with and love is one of the highest pleasures of life, but it is not the only route to happiness and fulfilment. It is absolutely *not* the single silver bullet. If you should decide this is not your thing, then embrace your inner bat and hold your head up high. Take pleasure in demolishing the arguments that will be ranged against you. What about the sex? people will say. Well, what about the thousands of wives who are lucky to do the wild thing more than once a month (and that's a good month), you will graciously reply. The great secret which many married couples hide is that once the honeymoon years are over, and the daily demands of children and work and financial worries calcify into harry and habit, they hardly even touch each other; sex becomes a distant memory, something they did when they were young and energetic. More dispiriting still, even if sex is still part of the repertoire, it often degenerates into a mindless ten-minute routine. We have heard women compare it to a household task: do the washing, pay the bills, have sex with the husband.

Oh, but the solitude, the concerned will exclaim. Well, solitude never killed anyone. The great thing about deciding to stay single is that you know that being alone is part of the deal. You know that you will occasionally get a sudden yearning for a strong pair of arms to hold you, and you know that this too will pass, and it is the price you pay for your absolute freedom. What destroys married people is that they are promised a lifetime of companionship, of having someone in their corner. When that fails, and the love mysteriously withers and dies, they find themselves living in an atmosphere of careful silence, and they are not armed for it: the agony of being with someone and yet feeling alone is the bitterest pain of all. As the great American writer Djuna Barnes once wrote: 'I could never be lonely without a husband.'

The fantasy of marriage is a lifetime of laughter and shared troubles and sex on tap; you are in it together. When this dream comes true, and a really wonderful relationship works, it may be the highest pinnacle of human achievement. You have all seen those old couples who still laugh at the same secret jokes and hold hands and take care of each other's tender feelings after forty years. The mistake is to think that they are the norm. They are astonishing exceptions, and you should gaze at them in awe and wonder and give them flowers and prizes. Marriage is incredibly hard work, and, like anything complicated and demanding, can bring marvellous rewards if you put in the graft, but you may not have the talent for it – just as not everyone can play Bach cantatas or cultivate prize-winning delphiniums.

You may, instead, have a raging flair for living, happily, successfully, defiantly, on your own, and you should not be ashamed of that.

FUN THINGS YOU CAN DO WITH A MAN.

Drive across America. Have sex. Play canasta. Cook a celebratory feast. Walk in the rain. Watch old black-and-white movies on a cold Sunday afternoon. Discuss politics. Drink espresso at Bar Italia.

FUN THINGS YOU CAN DO WITHOUT A MAN.

Drive across America. Have sex (work it out). Play patience. Cook a celebratory feast. Walk in the rain. Watch old black-and-white movies on a cold Sunday afternoon. Discuss politics. Drink espresso at Bar Italia. Be a lesbian.

WHAT TO DO WHEN YOUR HUSBAND/BOYFRIEND/ LOVER RUNS OFF WITH A TALL BLONDE WHO IS HALF YOUR AGE AND DRESS SIZE – OR, BETRAYAL AND ALL ITS RAMIFICATIONS.

God knows that we – and the women we love – have been on the sharp end of betrayal often enough. You might have thought that by now we would have devised the perfect, satisfaction-guaranteed-or-your-money-back solution. Sadly, there is no five-star, set-in-stone magic formula. Collapsing in a heap, staying up too late, smoking too many cigarettes, reading old diaries and watching endless re-runs of *Casablanca* is our traditional resort in the first few days and weeks; but that cannot be recommended in the long term, besides being very bad for the complexion.

The problem with being left is that it is not a simple grief: the loss is compounded by massive feelings of humiliation, culpability and plain foolishness. You feel as if you are walking around in a great big dunce's hat and everyone is laughing and pointing. You are convinced that everybody knew (sometimes they did), and that they are talking behind their hands. You feel plain and pointless; you are convinced that you will certainly never have sex again.

You try to talk yourself out of it. You will surely be better off without the conniving, lying, double-dealing little *shit*, but then you find yourself remembering the good times, and you get a pain in your stomach as if someone has stuck a knife in there and is twisting it. You know that you are not living in North Korea and you try to number your blessings, but the pain is so bad that you wonder if you will survive it. Then you feel ashamed: the irrational shame that it should hurt so much when it's just a man, and you are a proud independent woman, and of course you will not go under. You didn't work this hard and get this far to be brought down by one unreliable male.

Just to make things worse, the world is suddenly full of couples: everywhere you go there are people carelessly walking around in a haze of love. You start to wonder if it was your fault. You play the horrible 'If only …' game: if only I were a little more glamorous, brilliant, incisive, thin, understanding, and on and on. It is particularly bad if you did not see it coming. How could I be so blind, so idiotically trusting, so wilfully stupid? As if the agony of being abandoned is not enough, you give yourself a good beating, just to make sure you are really hurting.

Quite often, you are so dismantled by the shock and hurt of lost love that you do stupid things, like taking his calls or leaving messages on his answering machine after you've had a few shots of that nice Polish vodka with the gold flecks in it, or indulging in break-up sex, hoping in the illogical part of your brain that if only you can show him what he is missing he will come crawling back. There is one thing we can guarantee, and that is that this NEVER WORKS. Just as the 'Let's be friends' thing never works until at least two years after the break-up, and only then if it was mutual. It is categorically *not* friendly to lie to someone and leave them.

You know that nobody died, but when someone you loved and trusted and revealed yourself to buggers off with another woman, he is striking at your very sense of self. Your heart is broken into a million shattered shards, and it takes a while to gather them all up and put the pieces back together. It is important to understand that you have suffered a profound blow and to allow yourself a decent period of mourning.

The one great advantage of age is that you have precedent. If you are over thirty, this will almost certainly have happened before. It does not lessen the hurt, but you do have the priceless knowledge that you got through this once and you will get through it again. The tunnel may seem very dark and long, and the light at the end of it very distant, but at least you know there *is* a light.

If we were rash enough to offer any prescription it would go something like this:

The first thing to do is to shut up the voices in your head – the ones that are shouting at you about how you are not good enough, and no wonder he ran away, and that you are an unholy mess of a girl and there is no health in you. You may also have the particularly insidious voice that insists that in fact you are not cut out for love, and you might as well give it all up and join a nunnery. These voices are not only unhelpful, but *wrong*. The best women get left all the time. One of the great mysteries in life is why certain men leave absolutely fabulous women and run off with someone frankly mediocre and second-rate. We can't quite explain it, but it happens.

Surround yourself with as much good love as you can get. It was Jane Austen who said that friendship is the finest balm for the pangs of despised love, and she was right. Let your girlfriends rally round. Do not be too proud to ask for help. Not only will every single one of your female friends have been through the exact same thing, but by allowing them to help you through it you will give them a saintly feeling of being useful.

Your male friends are also vital. They are able to help you decode the bizarre vagaries of the masculine psyche, will hug you with their manly arms, and may possibly offer to go round and horsewhip the bastard, which will make you laugh. And, of course, they will offer you the ten-point plan, which you might want to have to hand after all, just in case.

If at all possible, resist the temptation to go all Miss Haversham. You will frighten the children and the dogs and any other observant humans in the near vicinity; more importantly, it will only make you feel worse. This is definitely the moment for a sharp haircut and a foxy new dress and the extravagant purchasing of gratuitous cosmetics.

Listen to the gloomy songs, watch the weepy films. Shout and rage. Get it all out. Indulge in some proper dramatic expression. The stiff upper lip does you no good here.

Remember the bad times. He was *not* sodding perfect. There was the drunken late night rambling, the nasty socks, the unattractive parsimony, the absolute failure to appreciate what it was that you actually did for him. You may come to the delightful conclusion that the twenty-three-year-old bimbo is welcome to him.

The absolute lovely truth is that, although it will hurt like hell, it has a shelf life. What comes along and saves you most often is, oddly, boredom. You will wake up one morning and you will be so damn *bored* of thinking about him and missing him and feeling betrayed by him that if you have to do it for one more minute you will jump out of the window. You will just have to think about something more interesting. It is at this moment that you know you have survived.

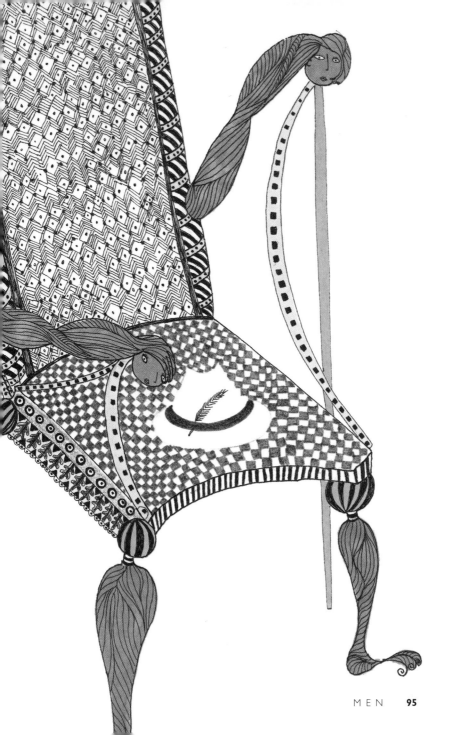

HEALTH

—

CHAPTER FIVE

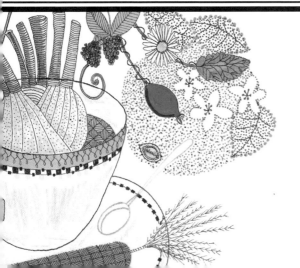

THE CONFUSIONS OF
HEALTHY EATING.

When it comes to food and health, every quack from here to California has a plan: you should not eat fruit after noon, dairy is evil, avoid the nightshade family on pain of death, yeast is the work of Satan. You must go macrobiotic at once because Gwyneth Paltrow has; you must eat according to your blood type like Elizabeth Hurley.

If you have a pressing desire to turn your body into a temple and nurse a deep fascination for the principles of nutrition, then there are a million books out there to tell you how to do it. However, if you, like us, fall into the normal range – you want to be healthy, but you adore strawberry tarts – there are a few simple precepts that will keep you on the right path and still enable you to go to dinner parties without taking a little bag of carrot sticks and three sheets of Nori and driving your hostess insane because you refuse to eat her perfect risotto.

THE FIRST AND DULLEST RULE IS MODERATION.

Have your cake and eat it for a real treat at Saturday tea, just don't buy one every day.

VARIETY IS EXCELLENT.

It is sometimes difficult, but cramming in as many different foods as possible, particularly vegetables, really does make the body very happy.

KEEP HYDRATED.

We know you are sick of being told to drink water. Two litres a day, yada yada yada; you are already dying of boredom. But it amazes us that such a simple free health aid is so often neglected. You don't have to spend a fortune on the fancy stuff extracted from abstruse mountain ranges by virgins; tap is fine. In case you are sceptical about the benefits of drinking water, it: keeps the kidneys and liver working, prevents fluid retention in the body, flushes out excess sodium and other toxins, aids the digestive process and stops constipation, and keeps your joints lubricated. The average brain is composed, astoundingly, of about 75 per cent water; you only need a low level of dehydration for your concentration levels to drop dramatically.

MASTICATE, MASTICATE, MASTICATE.

This is another incredibly simple and free health aid. Use those teeth. Bolting your meals puts a strain on the digestive system and means that you will not get the maximum nutritional value from the food you are eating. Also, the stomach takes about fifteen minutes to telegraph to the brain that it is full, so eating fast means that you will consistently eat too much. It is difficult to find time to sit down and savour your food, but if you can manage it, it makes a huge difference to your health. There are those who insist that you should sit very still for half an hour after eating, to allow the digestive process to do its thing. If you are running about, blood is diverted to the muscles, and the stomach and colon are left struggling at half speed. We know that, as they say in business, this is a big ask; we know you are busy; but it's worth bearing in mind.

TRY TO EAT A FEW PIECES OF RAW FOOD EACH DAY.

In Hollywood, where a new fad is born every day and twice on Sundays, the stars employ raw-food chefs and go to raw-food restaurants, and never know the profound delights of a lovely stew or a Sunday roast with all the trimmings or eggs on toast for breakfast. We would never advocate such a joyless regime, but uncooked fruits and vegetables are packed with vitamins and enzymes, so whether it's a couple of sticks of celery, a watercress salad, or half an avocado dressed with olive oil and lemon, something raw and fresh is a little nutritional present to your poor overworked body.

DON'T PANIC ABOUT THE LATEST SUPERFOOD.

Superfoods are like supermodels; there is always a new one on the catwalk. One moment it's blueberries and broccoli and wheatgrass, the next it's quinoa and goji berries and flax seeds. One website we found (we are not going to mention its household name, out of a sense of decency) even promises to 'take you through the latest celebrity superfoods', which is so fabulously stupid and vacuous that we stared at it in disbelief for a full thirty seconds before switching off the computer in outrage. It's enough to send you screaming to the nearest hot-dog stand. The truth is that there are so many foods that have fantastic nutritional properties that if you spent all your time chasing them down, you would never have time to do an actual job. Our theory is plain and realistic: find your very own list of superfoods – the ones that you love, understand how to cook, and know are good for you. Unless you are a film star or a yogi, it is simply not practical to live on green tea and acai berries.

Our own list of the loveliest and easiest superfoods, readily available, not too expensive, and simply incorporated into the diet of a regular working woman, includes:

WATERCRESS.

This delightful peppery leaf is packed with iron, vitamin C, beta-carotene, and antioxidants. A recent study by the University of Ulster showed that watercress protects against cancer by cutting DNA damage to white blood cells, which sounds pretty super to us.

GARLIC.

There is considerable scientific data to demonstrate that garlic is a potent antioxidant, particularly protective against toxins that build up in the liver. It prevents hardening of the arteries and lowers blood pressure. Populations that traditionally eat a lot of garlic suffer a much lower incidence of heart disease than those that do not.

CHILLIES.

Controlled studies have suggested that chillies can do everything from raise the metabolism to alleviate the pain of arthritis. The University of Tasmania has claimed, slightly unexpectedly, that chilli peppers may help you get a good night's sleep. They contain high doses of vitamins A and C, along with a good amount of potassium and iron, and they also stimulate the production of endorphins, which essentially make you feel happy.

OLIVE OIL.

Of all the foods with extravagant health claims, this is easily the one with the most rock-solid, ten-carat, double-blind evidence to back it up. At the moment, scientists are investigating suggestions that olive oil may be useful in the treatment of ailments as various as arthritis, diabetes, osteoporosis and even asthma. What is known for sure is that it has an almost miraculously protective effect on the heart. This is clearly seen in populations where risk factors for heart disease, such as smoking, are high, yet the incidence of the disease is much lower than in countries that do not use olive oil in their diet – Mediterranean countries versus America, most obviously. This claim is backed up by extensive medical literature. So hurrah for olive oil: delicious, versatile, incredibly easy to use, and a fabulous little dose of heart health in a bottle right there on your kitchen table.

APPLES.

Not obscure, or expensive, or much favoured by celebrities, the humble apple is loaded with free-radical-busting antioxidants. We talk a lot about these, but they really do a hell of a job as they rush around the body stopping the destruction of healthy cells. A study at Cornell University even found that phytochemicals found in apples can protect against degenerative brain disorders such as Alzheimer's. The pectin in the apple's skin is associated with lowering cholesterol.

TOMATOES.

The lovely ubiquitous tomato is filled with vitamin C and lycopene, an antioxidant associated with lowering the risk of certain cancers. Lycopene is more easily absorbed by the body when the tomato is cooked, so that's one in the eye for the raw-food zealots.

LEMONS.

Again, packed with antioxidants, vitamin C, and some studies even suggest they have an antibacterial effect. We use lemon juice for everything: in salad dressings, in fish stews, to perk up any green vegetable soup, on squid and spicy prawns, and for delightful homemade lemonade when we are playing at being domestic goddesses.

DARK CHOCOLATE.

We are not actually joking. In 2007, the BBC reported on a study by Dr Norman Hollenberg, an American scientist who had been studying the Kuna people of Panama. The Kuna drink up to 40 cups of cocoa per week. Their rates of stroke, heart disease and cancer are less than 10 per cent, they live longer than other Panama inhabitants, and they do not get dementia or suffer from high blood pressure. Dr Hollenberg suspects that this may be linked to the high levels of epicatechin found in cocoa, the effects of which he has been investigating for the last fifteen years. The study is slightly controversial, especially because Dr Hollenberg works for Mars confectionery. A wonderfully phlegmatic cardiac nurse at the British Heart Foundation responded to the claim saying that, despite it being 'an interesting observation' (oh, that lovely cutting British understatement), she would not advise that people here take up drinking cocoa in high quantities. Still, we salute the Kuna people, and think they might be onto something. Dark chocolate contains copper, iron, magnesium and those antioxidants again. Unfortunately, much as we would love to declare chocolate a health food, even the best brands do contain fat and sugar, which is why we recommend eating only three or four squares of the finest chocolate of 70 per cent cocoa that money can buy. We especially love Green and Black's 85 per cent proof.

THE CRUCIAL IMPORTANCE OF BLOOD SUGAR.

Maintaining steady blood sugar levels is one of the fundamentals of health. There are many complicated tables out there about the Glycaemic Index which can make your head spin so much that you feel like giving up on the whole thing and eating an entire loaf of bread in despairing defiance.

There is one very simple way of keeping your energy levels stable, without resorting to tables or complex calculation, and that is *never* to eat any carbohydrate on its own. So if you want a slice of bread, have a little bit of ham with it, or an egg, or peanut butter. Simple starches like potatoes, bread, pasta or rice turn almost immediately to sugar in the body; insulin is produced at a rush, which over-compensates, bringing your blood sugar too low. This is why if you have toast and coffee for breakfast you will feel weak and tired by eleven.

The three keys to stop the spike in insulin and subsequent sugar crash are protein, fibre and fat. This is why a rice cake, presented as a health food, is actually dangerous: the very fact that it is low-fat means that its starch is released without let or hindrance into the body, and you get the sugar high followed by the corresponding sugar low. It is also why cutting out all oils and butter from your diet is not a good thing.

Insulin tells the body to store fat, and if you are constantly producing too much of it, it does not matter how much low-fat nonsense you eat, you will put on weight. Bread itself is not the dark force it has lately been painted; it's just that you need to have it with a nice chicken breast and a good green salad with plenty of olive oil.

The Food Standards Agency is currently urging people to eat more starchy foods. We can only assume that this is a reaction to the fad for high-protein diets, but if you take that advice at face value, you will be in danger of falling into the blood sugar trap. Any starchy food should always be balanced by fibre and protein. Even a healthy, slow-releasing carbohydrate like porridge will mess with your blood sugar if it is eaten without anything else, especially if you have it with honey.

But here's some dietary good news:

Pulses, mocked for so long as the province of hairy hippies, are an absolute miracle with regard to maintaining steady levels of blood sugar, because they are a perfect combination of protein, carbohydrate and fibre, all in one unassuming little bean. Lentils do not have to be dull or earnest: the nutty Puy variety are delicious cooked in chicken stock with garlic and perhaps a hint of chilli and a dash of olive oil, the yellow and red kind can be spiced with cumin and cardamom and made into marvellous soupy dal. They also provide a good dose of iron and B vitamins, including folic acid.

Split peas, another legume usually consigned to dusty shelves in health-food shops, should also be taken out of the shadows and given a parade of their very own. High in fibre, with a perfect balance of protein and carbohydrate (like lentils), they are packed with potassium, which helps lower high blood pressure, and tryptophan, which produces serotonin, the neurotransmitter which helps maintain a good mood and regular sleep patterns. (All this from one minute pea.) They also contain the impossible-to-pronounce trace mineral molybdenum, which is a potent detoxifier. Split peas come in yellow and green, and both make wonderful winter soups, cooked slowly with a little onion and garlic. Yellow pea soup is lovely with saffron and chilli, while green pea soup is raised to ambrosial levels with the addition of a ham hock during cooking.

Chickpeas are another nutritional powerhouse, perfect for keeping blood sugar levels regular, fabulous in soups and stews, lovely as a mash.

IRON AND SALT.

Most women are deficient in iron. This is not only because modern women eat less red meat than they used to, but also because many people do not realise that in order for iron to be absorbed by the body, it needs to be aided by vitamin C. So, steak and chips will not do you much good, instead you should always try to have watercress or spinach or some other vitamin-C-rich food when you eat a fillet of beef or a lamb chop.

Iron is particularly important to avoid low-level anaemia, which makes you feel tired and grumpy. If you can't face a great big sirloin, then a bottle of Floradix iron tonic, available from any good chemist, is a brilliant standby. It is quite natural and has no preservatives, so you need to keep it in the fridge. It does make you feel like Popeye on a good day, and is pretty strong stuff, so you should always take it after food and with a full glass of water, or it can give you stomach gripes.

Then there's the salt myth. We have seen otherwise perfectly sensible people refuse to add salt to food because they are so spooked by scare stories about too much salt causing their hearts to seize up on the spot. The recommended daily salt intake is 6 grams. We once measured out this amount of Malden salt and found it was enough to fill an egg cup. We are generous with salt in our cooking, but even we took four days to get through that amount.

What you want to watch out for is known as hidden salt, which lurks not only in the obvious things like processed foods and ready meals, but also, oddly, in breakfast cereals. But if you are cooking from scratch with good natural ingredients, you do not need to be afraid of adding salt. We are quite strict about only using the best sea salt because it has a lovely flavour and texture and is strong enough so that you do not need much.

So-called table salt has added chemicals and a nasty bitter taste and is not worth the candle.

THE IMPORTANCE OF CALCIUM, AND THE DANGERS OF OSTEOPOROSIS.

Dairy products are a consistent demon in the pantheon of vilified foods. Oh, they are full of fat and clog the body with mucus and you are probably allergic to them and they will make you *die*. A very few people are lactose intolerant, and an excess of milk and cheese and butter will not do you any good, but it is worth bearing in mind the horrible female propensity to develop osteoporosis in later life. This is not a high-profile disease and does not get that much press; most people associate it with poor old ladies with a bit of a comedy hump. In reality, it is a horror of pain and incapacity. You can break your back by *opening a drawer*. We have seen this up close and this is why we are passionate about it.

It is vital to keep your calcium levels up and do some exercise in order to build up good strong bones so that you can skip around in purple hats and opera capes in later life. So a little mozzarella and a pot of yoghurt and a splash of milk in your coffee are actually your friends.

Other good sources of calcium are salmon, leafy green vegetables, almonds and brazil nuts. Almonds and salmon also contain magnesium, which is important to have in tandem with your calcium for optimum bone health. There is some evidence that the reason Americans are suffering from increased osteoporosis, despite their high intake of dairy products, is that their magnesium levels have fallen by 50 per cent over the last 100 years. Magnesium is also found in pumpkin and sunflower seeds, spinach and, rather oddly, halibut. We don't hear much about halibut these days; it is a resolutely unfashionable fish, but there it is, quietly battling against brittle bones.

It is also important to get a good supply of vitamin D, so go out into the sunshine for fifteen minutes a day. And jump up and down for another fifteen minutes (literally; you do not need to go to an expensive gym, just jump about in the comfort of your own home) to build up your bone density.

VITAMINS AND SUPPLEMENTS.

There is a rabid debate about taking supplements which shows no sign of calming down any time soon. The evangelicals insist on massive doses of vitamin C and niacin, injections of B12, handfuls of spirulina. The antis scoff that you get everything you need from a balanced diet, and all those pills just get excreted from the body, so you end up with very expensive pee.

As usual, we find ourselves somewhere in the middle. In a harried modern life, it can sometimes be difficult to get a fully balanced diet every day. There is considerable evidence that intensive farming techniques have leeched many vitamins, and especially minerals, from the soil, so that selenium, for example, which used to be naturally present in bread, is now only found in minute quantities. Even the staid Food Standards Agency has warned against worryingly low levels of selenium, and it takes quite a lot for them to get excited about anything.

So we freely admit that we err on the side of safety by taking a few pills. Besides, it gives us an ersatz Valley of the Dolls feeling in the morning.

Here are the ones we find most useful:

A good multi-vitamin.

Floradix iron tonic (as mentioned on page 114).

Turmeric. This has so many wonderful properties that we can't even be bothered to list them, but the healthiest man we know, who has studied nutrition all over the world and is actually a Minister of Wheatgrass in the state of California, says that if he were to take one single supplement, this would be it.

A fish-oil supplement. We are not crazy for salmon, now that it is farmed and flabby, and can only take so much mackerel, so we get our fish oils in capsule form. It really is good for the brain and sometimes we think that our brains are all we have.

Soya isoflavones. We first started taking these when we discovered that they have a miraculous effect on skin prone to blemishes; it's to do with balancing over-production of testosterone which leads to excess sebum. We kept on taking it when we found out that women in Japan do not get the same dramatic symptoms of menopause as Western women. They do not even have a *word* for hot flushes. Their incidence of breast cancer is also much lower than that of women in the developed West. This is almost certainly because they eat tofu every day for breakfast. Even if there is a grain of truth in this, we reckon it is worth going on taking the soya supplements. Or you could eat the tofu every day, if you are brave enough.

A vitamin-B complex. Good for the nerves.

Milk thistle. One of the few supplements that has some real evidence to back it up. It supports the liver, which is labouring under attack from pollutants, smoking, drinking, stress, fatty foods, and quite probably political correctness gone mad. We think anything that supports the poor beleaguered liver is worth the money.

Then there are the not necessary, but amusing, ones:

Blue green algae. It's from some 10,000-year-old lake and it's got more nutrients than twenty bags of spinach. We have no idea if this is true or not, but sometimes we give it the benefit of the doubt and buy a pot.

Green tea tablets. More antioxidants than an entire fruit and vegetable stand. Or something. Worth it on the off-chance.

Aloe vera. Sometimes we think we take it just because we like the name. Although people do say it has a wonderfully calming effect on the digestive system.

Guarana. The people of the Amazon rainforest swear by it, and we find it really is quite good for parties. Especially the kind in those little glass vials that you can swig like some illegal drug in the ladies' lav. It doesn't make you speedy, but you suddenly find your conversation is just that bit more sparkling.

MENTAL HEALTH.

There is an odd idea that physical health should be rigorously pursued —
all the gyms, supplements, shakes, superfoods and other paraphernalia —
while mental health is neglected, only really noticed when it breaks down.
The general expectation is that the psyche just keeps on working, until it
doesn't. Often, when it doesn't, this is blamed on outside agencies, beyond
your control — chemical reactions in the brain, traumatic events, reckless
abuse of drugs and alcohol stemming from an addictive personality,
genetic predilections.

Serious work on the mind by taking it weekly to a shrink is often
regarded as the province of the pampered rich or utterly neurotic. I don't
have time for that, people say; all that indulgent solipsism is not for me.
The Socratic idea that the unexamined life is not worth living is resolutely
out of fashion.

Yet, just as there are simple ways to keep the body healthy, so there
are small and straightforward ways to keep the mind sane. If there is one
single notion to think of, it is balance. The great psychiatrist Carl Jung is not
much read now; most people could probably not tell you what his
essential ideas are; yet every time you talk of introverts and extroverts, or
remark on someone's dark side, you are referencing Jung. He had many
fascinating ideas — about the collective unconscious, the meaning of
symbols and the nature of dreams — but his most useful notion was his
interest in opposites. He believed that the psyche is made up of a series of
opposing forces, like the yin and yang of Eastern philosophies. So there is,
within all of us, the male and female, which Jung called animus and anima,
the introvert and extrovert, the thinking function and the intuitive function.

His great idea was that these opposing forces must be brought,
consciously, into balance. Just as in physics an action produces an equal

and opposite reaction, so the mind will compensate if it leans too much one way. If this is not done consciously, in a positive way, the mind will do it in a negative way.

On a crude but instructive level, you can see this in the classic example of a mighty company director who pays a prostitute to beat him or pee on him or perform some other hackneyed act of humiliation. In his daily life, the director is all animus: he is in charge, giving orders, engaged with the outer world of action rather than the inner world of feeling. There is no room for the anima; he never consciously allows himself to be still or related, to receive rather than to impose. He sees the attributes of the anima as weakness. The feminine principle, denied and derided in him, struggles to find an outlet, and instead of coming out pure and vital, becomes twisted, so that he must go to Miss Whiplash, and, in a sterile transaction, pay a stranger to make him feel powerless. Instead of embracing the positive feminine of calm passivity, he finds himself in the extreme of absolute impotence, as the contrast to his outer manifestation of suited power.

In an interesting irony, many modern women have fallen out of balance by veering too much towards their animus, or inner masculine. The animus is vital for men and women both: in its simplest terms, it is the part of you that gets you out of bed in the morning. It is the anima, however, which allows you to pause and smile at the shafts of sunlight coming through the window as you wake. If you are too much in your animus, you do not have time to greet the rising sun; you are already up and thinking, your head filled with the lists of the things that must be done that day.

It is not just that women seem so busy now, no time to stand and stare, but also that in many professions they are bashing into the inner sancta of traditional boys' clubs. In order to take on the men at their own game, to hide any hint of feminine frailty, they dress in stern suits and learn to swagger and swear like the boys, laugh at the dirty humour, even go to strip clubs. To prove themselves on traditionally masculine territory, they may have to be more mannish than the men themselves, madly overcompensating for the sin of having ovaries. They must ruthlessly conceal anything that hints at the female: any sign of hormonal shift, tearfulness, emotion, will be seen as proof of suspect instability.

This life of frantic activity is what Jungians call doing rather than being. Fervid Western society rewards and admires doing: what do you *do*? is the first question you will be asked at any social occasion, and the one most freighted with judgement. You must have a good answer to it. If you were, rashly, to say, 'Today, Gerald, call me crazy, I am simply being,' you would surely never be invited out again.

Because the masculine idea of action is so garlanded, the feminine principle of stillness is often derided and misunderstood. It is seen as passive. In fact, the anima is profoundly powerful. As Jung explained it, it is the side of the psyche that is concerned with love, relatedness, softness, receptivity. To allow yourself to be open is not the passive choice of a wimp, but the courageous act of tigress. Think how terrifying it is when you first fall in love after an agonising break-up: you must lay yourself open again to possible hurts, which you remember so vividly from the last time. In the same way, to step back for a moment from your frenetic rushing about, your getting things done can be alarming, because you have time to feel all the emotions that you may have, literally, been running away from.

In all the great myths, the sun represents the masculine principle, while the moon stands for the feminine. The moon casts a fainter light, but its delicate beauty and profound symbolism are no less powerful for that. While the sun dazzles and overwhelms, the moon invites direct contemplation: you can stare at it, and trace all its mysterious fascination. An unexpected glimpse of a fat, amber hunter's moon, lying low in the sky on a clear autumn night, can feel like a spiritual revelation.

Oddly, on the very day that we started writing this section, we heard a perfect example of Jungian integration. Right there on the bathroom radio, talking to the *Today* programme, was a warrior poet; a gentle, articulate man who had survived the fire of Iraq and come out with a volume of poems that he had written in the heart of war. When asked what they were about he said: love and suffering. (What else is there?, we thought.) Just as the fighter can balance his bellicosity with poetry, find a solace from the horrors of dismembered bodies and bloody battles in creating a work of the imagination, so love and suffering form an inevitable axis. Even our own dear Queen once observed that pain is the price we pay for love.

There is a current hope that you can do without the pain and just have the love – a yearning for fast fixes, pills, food, fags, sex, anything to stuff down the fear and loathing. It's a worn trope that an allergy to pain is a twenty-first-century disease, to be countered with Codeine and Vicodin and Prozac, but actually humans have always tried to drive off existential agony by any means possible.

If there is one thing that women can do to guard their mental health in the same way that they pursue physical fitness, it is to think of this idea of Jungian balance. And, wonderfully, it can be done in the smallest and simplest of ways. If, like us, you find that you tend to get out of whack by leaning towards your masculine principle – busy busy busy, with your forty-seven things to do each day – you can bring your anima into focus by simply sitting for five minutes and actually breathing. Proper deep breaths – no little paltry shallow things. You may be amazed by the effect. It is no coincidence that the Eastern philosophies put so much emphasis on the metaphorical and literal importance of the breath.

You can find the feminine principle everywhere, once you start looking for it: listening to Mozart's *Gran Partita*, reading *The Love Song of J. Alfred Prufrock*, and, of course, staring at the moon. Open your eyes, your heart, your lungs; breathe and see and listen. This is the anima in her purest form. She will keep you sane, if you let her.

If, conversely, you find that your animus is withering – you are so mesmerised by gazing at the sky and listening to Bach's French Suites that you cannot keep organised, bills go unpaid and jobs are left undone – you need a galvanising dose of the male principle. Imagine him up, that vital active part of yourself. Take some time to bring yourself out of the dreamy world of love and feeling and contemplation, and spend a few minutes every day building up your male muscle. If you tend to wander when you walk, march; get the forensic, intellectual part of your mind fired up by reading the political section of the paper or doing a cryptic crossword; make lists and attack them as a marshal going into battle. Listen to Holst instead of Scriabin.

Perhaps the most important thing to remember is that the balance will never be perfectly achieved. It is an aspiration. Jung said that the journey, with its lessons learnt along the way, is more important than the destination. To embrace and accept, and even come to laugh at your human flaws and frailties instead of relentlessly fighting and denying them, is possibly the most complete prescription for a gentle sense of sanity.

MEN WHO ARE CLEARLY NOT IN TOUCH WITH THEIR FEMALE SIDE.

Muhammed Abdel-Al, leader of the Palestinian Popular Resistance Committees:
'If I meet these whores I will be the first one to have the honour to cut the heads off Madonna and Britney Spears if they will keep spreading their Satanic culture against Islam.'

(We especially like that peevish 'if they *will* keep spreading their Satanic culture.')

He added: *'If these two prostitutes keep doing what they are doing, we will of course punish them. A prostitute woman must be stoned or must be hit eighty times with a belt.'*

Glad we got that one cleared up.

The Reverend Pat Robertson: *'The Feminist agenda is not about equal rights for women. It is a socialist, anti-family, political movement that encourages women to leave their husbands, kill their children, practice witchcraft, destroy capitalism and become lesbians.'*

So, *now* we know.

George W. Bush gets more than one quote, because even we can't resist an open goal:
'We're kicking ass.' (On Iraq, 2007)
'I'm the Decider.' (2006)
'I'm the commander guy.' (2007)
'Success is not no violence.' (2007)
'Some people look at me and see a certain swagger, which in Texas is called walking.' (2004)
'I would say the best moment of all was when I caught a 7.5 pound largemouth bass in my lake.' (When asked in 2006 about the highlight of his time in office.)
'If this were a dictatorship it would be a heck of a lot easier, just so long as I'm the dictator.' (2000)
'I'm the commander – see, I don't need to explain – I do not need to explain why I say things. That's the interesting thing about being president.' (To Bob Woodward, 2006)

WOMEN WHO ARE NOT IN TOUCH
WITH THEIR FEMALE SIDE.

Ann Coulter, in her syndicated column: *'I think the government should be spying on all Arabs, engaging in torture as a televised spectator sport, dropping daisy cutters wantonly through the Middle East and sending liberals to Guantanamo.'*

We had to look this up in its proper context to make sure she was not quoting someone parodying her, or just being ironic. She wasn't.

Lady Macbeth: *'Come, you vile spirits that tend on mortal thoughts, unsex me here, and fill me from the crown to the toe top-full of direst cruelty.'*

Camille Paglia: *'Let's get rid of Infirmary Feminism, with its Bedlam of bellyachers, anorexics, bulimics, depressives, rape victims and incest survivors. Feminism has become a catch-all vegetable drawer where bunches of clingy sob sisters can store their mouldy neuroses.'*

A SMALL ASIDE ON SOCRATES.

Socrates was the son of a sculptor and a midwife. What a lovely example of Jungian balance: two absolute opposites, the man working with inanimate stone to produce beauty, the woman bringing actual breathing life into the world. And yet, as always with the yin and the yang, there is a synthesis in these two apparent contradictions. Both reveal something. Michelangelo said of sculpture that he was bringing out of the block of stone what was always in it, literally liberating the form of the statue from the surrounding mass. Just as sculpting is about revealing the creation within, so midwifery is revealing the life hidden in the womb. Socrates too was all about revelation. He saw himself as a midwife like his mother, only, in his case, to the truth.

ANOTHER SMALL ASIDE, ON JUNGIAN INTEGRATION.

On the morning we started writing about the idea of balancing the different parts of the psyche, a new copy of *Vanity Fair* arrived in the post. On the front was a photograph of Nicole Kidman, dressed up as a jaunty sailor, with her shirt open to show a white bra. If we had not been contemplating Jung that day, we would certainly have looked at the picture and found all our feminist fury roused like a sleeping lion. How *could* such an intelligent actress allow herself to be pictured looking like a floozy?, we would have thought. We would have hurled the magazine aside and felt another illusion dashed, and would certainly have been in a bad temper for the rest of the day.

As it was, we peered at it and thought: Nicole, you are a genius. It was a perfect illustration of Jungian integration. Here was an actress famous for choosing difficult, challenging, serious roles – Virginia Woolf in *The Hours*, Diane Arbus in *Fur* – showing her playful, feminine, teasing side.

The great paradox of successful film actresses is that although they are, on the surface, presenting themselves as tremendously feminine – dressing up for premieres, posing for photographs, all hair and make-up and diet regimes – in order to succeed in the unforgiving climate of Hollywood they have to be tough, calculating, organised, even ruthless: all attributes of the animus. Kidman has produced films, as well as acting in them, and, being Australian, must feel a little like an outsider in America, where she mostly works; to achieve the kind of success she has, she would have had to draw greatly on her male side. So the photograph, so girlish and frivolous, was a brilliant demonstration that she has not allowed herself to fall out of balance.

EXERCISE.

It is too boring and obvious for words, but whatever you do, however or how often you do it, exercise is vital. Human bodies were designed for activity and movement; without it they droop, become uneven, collapse under their own weight. They ache: neglected muscles cannot support the skeleton properly, and so the body compensates in disastrous ways. Joints wear thin with overwork; muscles endure painful spasms. Without exercise, the heart and internal organs grow sluggish; even worse, you never experience the euphoria brought about by the release of the body's own happy drugs, endorphins. The organism becomes its own worst enemy.

When it comes to exercise, we are like Jack and Mrs Sprat. One of us believes that a daily walk in the fresh air in the company of a pair of questing canines is more than enough, and quite possibly overdoing it (she finds the gym inexpressibly demoralising). The other is a veteran of almost every exercise regime on the planet, with the possible exception of 'boxercise', which she has shunned purely on grounds of good taste. She has spent a small fortune on personal trainers, participated in a variety of gruelling and frankly peculiar keep-fit classes, including spin (cycling on the spot to very loud disco music), circuit training, aerobics (classic and water) and that perennial favourite, bootcamp. In matters yogic she is familiar with most of the common varieties (hatha, inyegar, ashtanga) as well as the more exotic interpretations (Jivamukti, Bikram), and has practised all. And finally, at the end of it all, she has reached the conclusion that there is only one exercise regime that can be attempted by all ages and all levels of fitness and which produces tremendous results: pilates.

It's an entirely subjective view. Some would argue strongly the case for yoga, with that slightly fanatical gleam in the eye that yoga people often carry, but the trouble with yoga is that you can, in the heat of the moment, overstretch yourself and do more hurt than good. And for all those runners, riders, cyclists, sailors, netball players and footballers out there, we're not suggesting it as a substitute; but if you are searching for a type of exercise that will repair and re-educate tired or worn-out muscles, that will stretch sinews and relieve tensions, try the pilates.

For women, pilates is particularly miraculous because it strengthens the core, which is often the weakest part of the female anatomy: the pelvic floor and all the smaller, but equally vital, muscles that hold together and balance the pelvic area. Any woman who has given birth knows how destructive the deterioration of these can be, not just from an aesthetic point of view, but also in terms of general quality of life. Pilates fights back pain and bad posture, and steers the body away from that most ageing and ugly of afflictions, the dowager's hump.

Do not let yourself be cast down by the exercise zealots, who want to make you feel guilty and second-rate for your own shoddy habits. Whether you choose to walk, do pilates, bounce around on a trampoline, or perform arabesques in the bathroom on a Monday morning, as long as you are moving around a bit for twenty minutes a day, you will be fine. You don't need expensive equipment or hideous rip-off training shoes or ugly lycra: find a form of movement which you like and do it, and sod what anyone else has to say about it.

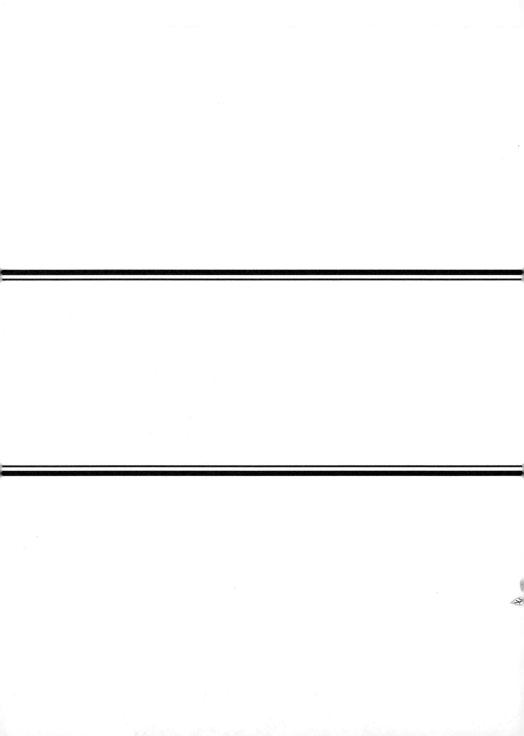

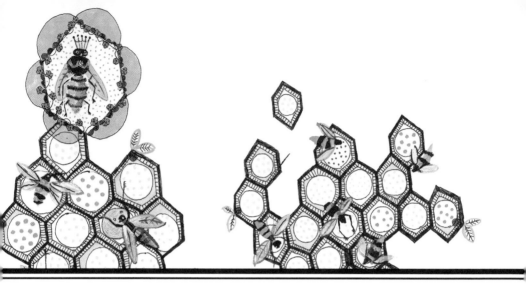

POLITICS AND THE NEW ORTHODOXY; OR, THE GENERAL CRAZINESS OF IT ALL

–

CHAPTER SIX

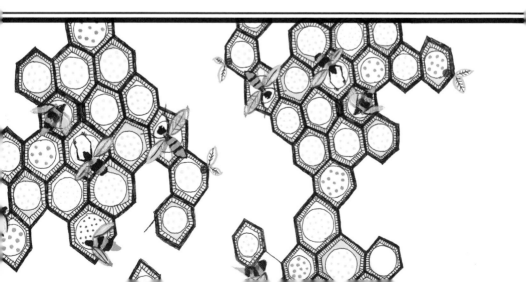

POLITICS, AND WHY IT MATTERS.

Politics, not so long ago the preserve of upright men in frock coats, is now, wonderfully, open to All. (Even the ladies may mark their ballots, although not if they live in Saudi Arabia, obviously.) Downing Street has gone bravely interactive, and there was great excitement in the press in the spring of 2008 when it was revealed that Gordon Brown had taken to telephoning actual voters early in the morning. At the same time, across the Atlantic, Barack Obama was drawing the kind of crowds that rock stars usually expect. Western democracy had surely reached its crest and peak.

Yet the line goes that Britain is a nation mired in political apathy. No one cares any more, politicians are all the same, it's nothing to do with me, guv. In an age of galloping globalisation, there is a suspicion that politicians may be entirely irrelevant. The vast multi-national conglomerates are the ones who really rule the world: Unocal and Monsanto and Halliburton are in charge, and some dusty backbencher is

not going to put a dent in *that* action. Politicians may talk nicely of the environment and healthcare and pensions, but the oilmen and the pharmaceutical companies and the hedge funds have the last word.

Paradoxically, at the exact same time, the public seems to expect these pointless political operatives to fix all that ails the nation. MPs must prevent floods, convert the creaking NHS to a tuned racing car of excellence, eliminate juvenile delinquency, and solve the international credit crisis, preferably before dinner. The citizenry thinks of them as idiots, and yet demands that they cure deprivation and inner city dystopia, eradicate criminality, slash red tape, and put everyone into work. They must guard the children and provide for the old.

Beyond all these confusions, there is a suspicion among the righteous that the political class is traced with venality – they are in it for the money, fiddling their expenses while Rome burns. We contend that British politics is many things – baffling, sometimes demoralising, occasionally dull – but it is not institutionally and irredeemably corrupt. If you want proper, ocean-going corruption, just try living in Naples instead of Nottingham. This is not because all British politicians are saints, although we suspect that most of them do go into it for honourable reasons. (Full disclosure: some of our best friends are politicians; one of us even married one. But then you could say this puts us in a reasonable position to judge, since we see them when the cameras are off. Also, first thing in the morning.) The lack of corruption is for one boring and obvious reason: politics is not where the money is. The men and women who go into parliament have the exact same qualifications that the big corporate raiders look for: if they really were so greedy and corrupt, they would go and join some dodgy offshore multinational and get to screw the world without guilt.

The pernicious idea has twined around the public mind like bindweed: all this politics is disconnected from the daily concerns of the fabled 'ordinary person'. Sage commentators talk of The Westminster Village, just as in Washington they refer to Inside the Beltway, as if what goes on in the seat of power has absolutely no relevance to an individual living in Carlisle or Poughkeepsie. Politicians do not help themselves, with their on-message and their bizarre management-speak (going forward, year on year, measuring the outcomes). No wonder politics can sometimes seem little better than a parlour game: who is John Humphrys going to trash this morning on the *Today* programme? We know one women who is so demoralised by the whole shooting match that she refuses to listen to the news at all, because it's so damn depressing that even the pills don't work.

But just because your politicians might not be the towering figures that you subconsciously want them to be – better and cleverer, without a stain on their moral character or a blot on their private lives, and yet, of course, just exactly like you, understanding all your needs and desires – does not mean that politics itself is something to be written off as of no importance. Politics affects everything, from the wages you earn to the bus you take to work to the very air you breathe.

If you don't believe that last one, consider the Great Smog of 1952. There is a tendency to think of the famous London Particulars and pea-soupers as some quaint, even charming, chapter of the national story, to be looked at with nostalgia, as part of the Good Old Days. The smog of 1952 was not so very comical or charming for the 4,000 people who died in it. Cattle at Smithfield were asphyxiated where they stood. The fog in the Isle of Dogs was so impenetrable that people could not see their own feet. On each of the five days of fog, 800 tonnes of sulphuric acid was belched into the atmosphere. Just consider that for a moment: 800 tonnes of sulphuric acid insinuating itself through the streets of the city, invisible and deadly. Oh, those Good Old Days.

It is politics that has made such a disaster a distant memory. The City of London Act of 1954 and the Clean Air Acts of 1956 and 1968 banned emissions of black smoke and ordered conversion to smokeless fuels. Pea-soupers were also consigned to history by a combination of slum clearance and urban renewal, both political acts.

None of these pieces of legislation has the swagger or glamour of gunboat diplomacy or tearing down the Berlin Wall; most people today could not even tell you that there was a Clean Air Act, let alone when it was passed, or by whom. (It was guided through the House by Duncan Sandys, an Eton and Oxford Tory who served in Norway during the war and was Minister of Housing under Anthony Eden. As well as fighting for clean air, he invented the green belt.)

So, the next time you take a deep breath in a city street, you might reflect that it was those despised politicians who enabled you to do so. Politics is not perfect, or always fascinating or edifying, but it absolutely does matter.

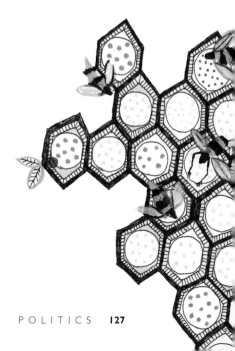

RIGHT WING, LEFT WING, NO WING AT ALL.

Long ago, the Right had a moment of nobility. In the nineteenth century, the entirely charisma-free but strictly principled Robert Peel split the Tory party over his quixotic opposition to the Corn Laws, over the howls of vested interests. Hated by the rich landowners, he became a hero of the working classes. In the twentieth century, something very strange happened, and the Right Wing became emblematic of a nasty type of ruthless social Darwinism, all survival of the fittest and pulling yourself up by your bootstraps. It appeared to hate and fear single mothers, homosexuals and almost anyone in the arts. Now it has become modern and kind, and talks a great deal about global warming and social engagement, and is not really awfully right wing at all. The hanging's too good for them rump has slunk off and joined splinter groups, where it can mutter darkly about all those migrants coming in to take the jobs and steal the women.

Meanwhile, the true Left has become vanishingly rare. It used to have revolutions to fight, and proper causes to champion; modern Leftists remember with tearful nostalgia the moment when everyone could go off and join the plucky Republicans during the Spanish Civil War. It had the enduring underdog glamour of always being out of power. Then there was the Blairite revolution, and the Labour party went from stalwart of the People to Public Private Partnerships. It was all middle ground, all the time, with a few inexplicable foreign adventures thrown in for seasoning. The old Left, with nowhere to go, was reduced to fighting amongst itself, mostly in the pages of weekly periodicals.

You might think that this massive shift to the centre would mean that at last it was the glorious moment in the sun for the modern lower-case liberal. The true liberal has little to do with party, tends not to be obsessively tribal, and will actually vote on the issues. Surely, the new political consensus would usher in the liberal century.

Not a bit of it. As if the old adherents of right and left were so furious about being pushed out of the argument, and having to trim to meet the demands of an increasingly centrist public, everyone started picking on the poor liberals. They are routinely derided as smug and self-satisfied. They are called chatterati, liberati, Islington do-gooders. They are branded as a sinister elite that secretly runs the BBC and looks down its nose at the opinions of the good ordinary people. They are accused of being devotees of the nanny state and political correctness, which has usually gone clinically insane.

In fact, far from sitting about in a haze of self-congratulation, drinking their green tea and wearing Fairtrade shirts, liberals have a perfectly horrible time. This is because they strain to see every side of an argument, attempt to hold several opposing ideas at once, and have a fatal tendency to feel personally responsible for past evils, such as slavery and the more egregious acts of empire-building. They are so determined never to have a common thought or mean, especially towards any beleaguered minority, that they can spend half the day tied up in ethical knots.

In the post September 11 world, they have to deal with all kinds of thorny debates about civil liberties, religious freedom, and cultural stereotyping. They are particularly sensitive to the status of Muslims as a newly demonised constituency, but are revolted by honour killings and the muzzling of the press in the wake of the Danish cartoon row. They know that they must defend to the death the right of anyone to say the things they themselves find abhorrent, although extreme expression sometimes makes them want to shout. But they must not shout: they are liberals.

By the time the liberal has hacked through the thickets of the moral arguments that haunt her daily, she is so exhausted that she has to go and

lie down. This is before she has even started to think about her general belief in the state versus her dislike of its manifest inefficiencies and wasteful spending. Don't even get her started on the difficulties of the hijab or the intricacies of positive discrimination or the complications of multiculturalism. Sometimes the only therapy for this is a box set of 24. Many hardcore liberals secretly adore Jack Bauer. They love that he breaks the rules, prizes loyalty above all, and holds iron certainties about who the bad guys are (there is an element of envy in this: such muscular sureness is a state of which liberals can only dream). They cheer as he defies the stupidity and bureaucracy and occasional villainy of those in power. But afterwards, they feel a little sick, as if they have eaten too much fast food, because they know that in the real world you really can't go around breaking people's arms just because you suspect they might have smuggled a bit of plutonium.

At least things here are not so bad as in America, where liberal is a dirty word on a par with axe-murderer and Quisling. Websites are set up proclaiming Death to Liberals, and Liberals are Idiots, which features a photoshopped picture of Hillary Clinton *hugging* Osama Bin Laden – both are smiling broadly. And, of course, our personal favourite, Liberalscum.com, where you can find enchanting slogans like 'I want YOU to take your traitorous liberal ass back to Canada' and, cleverly, 'YOU shut the fuck up, WE'LL protect America, Keep out of our fucking way liberal pussies'.

In the face of the tectonic shift in modern political life, where tribal loyalties no longer pull at the heart and old certainties are hard to find, it is no wonder that many people are choosing no wing at all. Commentators tend to decry this: they see it as part of the mythical apathy that makes them fret so. But the rise of the pressure group and the internet campaign suggests that it is quite the opposite of apathy. Mad chauvinist partisanship can be tiring and self-defeating, and not at all helpful in social situations. Instead of identifying as Tory or Labour or Lib Dem, you can find your cause and get all the guns blazing. There is something wonderfully liberating about this. You are not just a cog in the party machine, but your very own advocate. It is politics in its purest form. And you may even find that you actually make a difference.

MORAL RELATIVISM.

Moral relativism is a distant cousin of liberalism. Because of the family resemblance, they quite often get confused. This is a mistake.

In its purest form, moral relativism says that all belief systems, ethical positions and cultural mores are equally valid. There are no moral absolutes. On paper, it is an alluring notion; in theory it might mean that people would stop bombing and killing and going to war to defend their various beliefs; it would put all those shouting talking heads on Fox News out of business at a stroke; it is almost utopian.

In practice, it doesn't work like that. Contemporary moral relativism goes along the tired old lines of: who are we to judge other cultures by our own Western mores? In this way, it is oddly self-hating, since generations have fought and died for the Western canons of democracy, free speech, and women's rights. But the moral relativist will insist that genital mutilation and forcing women to cover their entire bodies, and banning homosexuality, are perfectly acceptable practices, because that is what *they* do over *there*, and the West should not be so superior, considering its own human rights record.

This same reasoning is what drove the traditional moral relativist support for Fidel Castro (also an incoherent rage towards America, but that's a whole other story). Many ostentatiously right-thinking people will claim that Castro was perfectly marvellous, with his comedy beard and his indefatigability and his amusing habit of making seven-hour speeches. There is the famed healthcare system, and the glittering rate of literacy. Of course literacy isn't much good if all you can read in the papers is propaganda, but you know, let's not quibble.

Actually, let's. We don't care what the relativists say: it is patently *not* all right to lock up gay men and journalists and librarians and ageing university professors with dodgy kidneys. To say that dictatorship is fine for Cuba is to say that the poor Cubans are simply not up to democracy, which is cultural snobbism of the most horrid kind.

In the same way that the moral relativists might applaud pornography as liberty of expression but die of shock should their daughters run off to join the Teen Dirty Sluts, broadcasting proudly from downtown Los Angeles, so they would leave the country should Fidel and his thuggish cohort come marching up Whitehall, sack parliament, nationalise all industry, lock up Matthew Parris and Dame Mary Warnock and Julian Clary and convert the BBC to a censored mouthpiece of the state. (At least this would put an end to the limping arguments over whether poor old Auntie is institutionally biased to the left: it would be official.)

What is most tragic about the moral relativists is that the deference they offer to disparate cultures is not returned in kind. The men who decree that no woman should show an inch of flesh do not look at pretty girls in summer dresses in Hyde Park and think: ah, well, it's just their funny old Western way of life. They think (like a bad Monty Python impersonation, except without the laughs): stone her.

Even odder, the relativists seem selective in their defence of alien practices. There is not much sympathy with the military junta in Burma, for instance: not much talk of, 'well, they do so love those crazy uniforms and placing elected women under house arrest'. We have not, so far, heard moral relativism brought to the service of the tribesmen of Papua New Guinea, who have taken to burying children alive from a fear of AIDS.

For women, the fight against moral relativism is of acute importance. If you concede that those who refuse to let women go out in public, become bishops, drive cars, marry whom they want, or even have jobs, might have a point, you might as well give it all up and chain yourself to the kitchen sink. This is not some distant problem in a faraway Third-World country. There is muttering in twenty-first century Britain of allowing Sharia Law; in America, the Republican Right would like to appoint strict constructionist judges to repeal Roe versus Wade, so that women would have to return to back-alley abortions, coat hangers and gin.

As Simon Blackburn, the majestic professor of philosophy (and we must admit, one of our very own personal heroes) has pointed out: the main flaw in moral relativism is that it is not at all useful. So you think that gay marriage is an abomination leading to certain hellfire, and I think it is two happy men with a list at Harvey Nichols, and we agree to disagree – and then what? Tolerance and understanding and liberty, which we believe to be Universal Goods, have always had to be fought for. It is the clash of ideas that has led to progress. It seems peculiar to have spent so much blood and treasure to fight fascism, a struggle that is still within living memory, only to decide that all ideas are, in fact, equal. We are having none of it. We are with Kant, and his idea of universal absolutes.

With reservations, of course. We're not crazy.

HOW TO DEPLOY COUNTER-MEASURES WHEN PEOPLE TRY TO USE KANT AGAINST YOU.

The Categorical Imperative is a lovely moral tool, still as shining and useful as when it was first thought of, 200 years ago. It says: 'Act only according to that maxim whereby you can at the same time will that it should become a universal law.' So you can easily prove that lying is wrong, because if you imagine a world where everybody lied, you see at once that there would be no society, no trust, no security, even no certainty. Sadly, some bigoted people will try and use this philosophical gem to prove their own prejudice. Ah, they say, a triumphant gleam coming into their eye: What about homosexuality? What about homosexuality?, you will say, innocently. Well, they say, would you want everyone to be gay or lesbian? No, they say, before you can answer; ergo, it must be wrong.

Take a deep breath. Remember that these people almost certainly suffered some terrible trauma in childhood. Point out, politely, that this is a false question. First of all, it would never happen, in the same way that all humans could not wake up one morning and decide that they had the ability to fly. Second of all, it is not a moral choice. It just is. Throughout history, regardless of social mores and cultural dictates, homosexuality in the general population has hovered steadily around the 3–5 per cent mark. The idea that an overbearing mother or any other random stereotype can make someone gay is the fattest and reddest of herrings. The corresponding idea, still terrifyingly popular among religious fundamentalists, that you can cure homosexuality is more than a herring: it is outrageously wrong. (It was this horror that drove Alan Turing to suicide: a shy, brilliant man, who through his work on the Enigma machine did as much to defeat the Nazis as Churchill himself.) No one, in the 1950s, was going to wake up one morning and think: I know, I'll go gay: that way I can get called names in the street, and risk arrest, and have to go to clandestine clubs in Soho where everyone calls each other Mary.

So, you might like to observe, the correct Kantian question is: would you like everyone to be prejudiced against homosexuality, hating and defining a person on the narrow basis of their sexuality? The answer to that must be no.

Sometimes we do secretly like to ponder what an entirely gay world would be like. Much less war, we suspect, and dictatorship right down – when was the last time you saw a homosexual tyrant? Saturday nights in city centres would certainly be quieter – for some reason, it is always the heterosexuals who so love to pick fights after coming out of the pub (Are you looking at me?). And, obviously, the arts would thrive. Well, we like to dream.

FEMINISM, AND FRIGHTENING THE HORSES.

In the early part of the twentieth century, British women asked for the vote. Mostly they asked nicely. Occasionally, when they were feeling very frustrated, they attached themselves to railings. At this point they were arrested, force-fed, and subjected to the entirely unlovely Cat and Mouse Act.

Then they all became flappers, and everyone breathed a sigh of relief.

Then there was the war, and they joined the WAAFs and looked very fetching in their uniforms, and some of them did astonishingly brave things for the Special Operations Executive behind enemy lines.

Then there was the 1950s, and everyone became a Stepford wife and wore New Look dresses and took a lot of tranquillisers.

Then there was the 1960s, and the pill, and all the women suddenly wanted to sleep with a Rolling Stone.

And then, oh, *then,* there were the seventies, and the Second Wave of Feminism. This was when women realised that it was not enough to wear a flower in your hair and have free love with rock stars. They burnt their bras, got organised, and began talking about scary things like equal pay for equal work. They remembered the sight of their mothers, whacked out on Valium and housework, and decided that they wanted something better for their daughters. They wrote books and had gatherings. Some of them even declined to wear lipstick.

This was extremely alarming. Some clever person came up with the idea of putting it about that all these women were angry bitter lesbians, or just plain flat-out man-haters. The follies that flourish at the extremities

—

'I MYSELF HAVE NEVER BEEN ABLE TO FIND OUT PRECISELY WHAT FEMINISM IS: I ONLY KNOW THAT PEOPLE CALL ME A FEMINIST WHENEVER I EXPRESS SENTIMENTS THAT DIFFERENTIATE ME FROM A DOORMAT OR A PROSTITUTE.'

Rebecca West

of any protest movement were highlighted: they wanted to call history herstory, they said all sex was rape. The press started referring gleefully to the 'Wimmin'.

The women, startled that their plan for a brave new world was being seen as some kind of hormonal hissy fit, dolefully slunk off and formed communes (mostly in Wales, for some reason) where it was said that they knitted their own yoghurt. Some of them just stayed at home with the blinds drawn, reading Sylvia Plath. Yet others put on sharp suits with shoulder pads, marched into the eighties, made a fortune in the City, and kept very quiet about anything to do with bras and conflagration.

The Second Wave took such a battering that it was a long time before the feminists dared put their heads above the parapet again. When they did, they were wearing artfully applied lipstick and calling themselves post-feminists. They had lots of great hair, carefully arranged to hide the bruises from bumping their heads on the glass ceiling. Some of them were occasionally heard to mutter that Andrea Dworkin had been misquoted.

The cracking of thin ice was heard throughout the land. People started getting shifty again. These new feminists looked like normal people; they did not wear dungarees or Dr Marten boots, they did not say that cosmetics were the work of Satan. Many of them were married with children. But could it be that, deep down, they were just like those terrifying Second Wave lesbo 'wimmin' of myth and fable, only this time dressed up in hot clothes?

The pundits got all revved up and started blaming these new feminists for everything from the decline of the family to the lack of council houses (all those cunning single mothers going to the top of the queue). One American evangelist even accused feminists of being responsible for the terrorist attacks of September 11th. Admittedly, he did say that abortionists and homosexuals were equally culpable, but even so.

Most baffling of all, much of the backlash actually came from other women, which made the post-feminists feel very sad. They started considering the lure of communal living in the valleys all over again.

There is an honourable history here, so when people trot out the creaking line about feminism being irrelevant, we are prone to get on our high horse and start galloping. The implication is that feminism is a passing fad, a crazed irrational whim. With a bit of luck, the ladies will have got it out of their systems soon, and then they can go back to doing what they do best. Which is, obviously, baking cakes.

And anyway, feminism, what is it good for? The Western woman can do whatever she wants, so surely she should brush that chip off her shoulder and calm down. The modern feminist might calmly reply that it is not all about her: she might mention honour killings and genital mutilation; the girls of Iraq who dare not go to school for fear of kidnapping or rape; the burka making a comeback in Afghanistan; the girls of Yemen who are married off when they are as young as twelve.

We say that, just as the gay men rehabilitated the word queer, women should dust off the word feminism and make it acceptable in normal usage. It is salutary to remember that all those brave women who came before us fought for was freedom; they manned the barricades with just as much élan as Che Guevara, so why should he get all the great posters? Thanks to them, we have the liberty to work, and enjoy sex, and wear trousers, and be prime minister, if we want to. Thanks to them, most men now realise that the clitoris is not in fact a character in a Greek tragedy.

But changing 2000 years of accepted culture is a delicate business. You may find you have to tread carefully. Victim status does not automatically confer moral superiority. Resist lectures and statistics – this only induces a state of catatonic boredom in the listener, and makes otherwise perfectly charming men start to yearn for the days when lipstick was a woman's main concern. Also, however tempting it may be, do not fall into the trap of blaming men for all the world's ills. Men tend to get defensive and monosyllabic if you do this, and will refuse to do the washing up in protest.

At the same time, it is good to remember the old maxim: never explain, never apologise. There is no need to recount meekly why you believe in the sisterhood. Be proud. If you feel downcast at the lack of progress, remind yourself that women in France only got full emancipation sixty years ago, and by 2007 Ségolène Royale was running for president. Admittedly, they did end up electing a short man who married a supermodel, but even so. If you feel really depressed, you could consider relocating to Sweden, which triumphantly tops the league for gender equality year after year. (All this and Abba too.)

Embrace the complexities of your female heritage: you can be a feminist and still wear scarlet satin and fishnets. (We are personally very fond of the haute courtesan look.) You are not betraying the movement with your love for kitten heels, although it might be worth reminding people that the old trope that all women live for shoes is a devilish reductive *lie*.

And finally, most importantly of all: never, ever, forget your sense of humour.

THE CRAZINESS.

There are days when it does seem as if the mid-market tabloids might be right, and the world, has, in fact, gone mad. You take in – almost by osmosis through the newspapers, the television, the internet – the wars, the earthquakes, the stubborn dictatorships; the car bombs, the suicide bombs, the roadside bombs; the churchmen who forbid the use of condoms in AIDS-ravaged regions of Africa, the rigged elections, the child labour. As if that were not enough, there is the domestic front, where your husband is so overworked that he can barely remember your name, your own salary hardly covers the cost of childcare, your children fail to get a place at the school you have set your heart on, the dog swallows a bee and must go for emergency veterinary treatment. Oh, and there's the credit crunch and the liquidity squeeze, which sound like a breakfast cereal and a type of washing-up liquid but are much less benign, and if you should forget to recycle one week then the poles will melt and the people of the South Seas shall have to live on barges. It's just one damn thing after another, and if you hear one more minister coming on the news and pretending that it's all under control, just a little local difficulty, then you shall do something foolish.

There is no real solution to this. You are right: it's a crazy crazy world, my masters, and even those people with a benevolent god to pray to, secure in the knowledge that He has a plan, must get a twinge of uncertainty from time to time. R.D. Laing famously said that madness was a sane reaction to an insane world, and there are days when we think he was right.

Faced with this, you can lapse into despair and lock yourself in a darkened room and listen to a great deal of Edith Piaf at her most mournful (and what an insane world *she* lived in), or you can take a categorical decision to catch the beauty as it flies by, literally and metaphorically. There is the beauty: the love, the principle, the marvellous free aesthetics of a cathedral or a night sky. There is the good politician, the determined philanthropist, the dauntless crusader; there is the programme that works, the policy that makes sense, the peace that finally comes after a seemingly intractable war. You just have to look for it as hard as you can, squinting into the glare.

THE NEW ORTHODOXY.

The old orthodoxy was a straightforward thing: patrician, male, white and aristocratic, it came out of the mouths of the Establishment with convinced simplicity. Britannia ruled the waves, Johnny Foreigner was definitely suspect, children should be seen and not heard, and women must know their place (at the stove, or in the missionary position). Now, with the explosion of democracy, human rights, the internet and the modern refusal of the ladies to sit at home with their tatting, the old orthodoxy has shattered, and a hundred new ones have rushed in to fill the breach.

Some have ancient origins – the orthodoxy that we are all doomed has centuries of form, as does the idea that the Young People of Today have no health in them. (Personally, we adore the young people of today, and think that the rumour that all they are capable of is texting is not only wrong, but cruel and unusual. If you look at the roll of fallen soldiers from Afghanistan you will find that they are very young people indeed, and most of them died while protecting their fellow soldiers from harm.)

Some are brand spanking new. The orthodoxy of the natural is very recent – in an odd spasm against the technology that gave the modern world clean water and inoculations and electricity and neurosurgery, suddenly everything chemical or artificial has become the Enemy. Homeopaths are found offering cures for malaria; organic has become a synonym for ethical. This new orthodoxy has taken such a grip on the popular imagination that people had to start writing entire books to counter it.

The orthodoxy of political correctness and how insane it has gone is about ten years old, but feels as if it has been around forever, it is so tired and trite. It is an orthodoxy that seems to belong exclusively to very cross middle-aged men, presumably yearning for the good old days when people could talk about spastics and wops and fags. Personally, we rather like the fact that people no longer routinely refer to women as hormonal bitches, but we are a little old-fashioned like that. As for free speech, it has never been more various or robust. People spin entire careers out of saying the unsayable. If PC's true mission was to fetter the cherished British freedom of expression, then its report card would say: must try harder.

THE ORTHODOXY AND THE WOMEN.

When it comes to women, the orthodoxy is all over the place. The old wisdom that women belonged in the home – the delicate sex, fit only for having babies and hanging curtains – was finally, after some argument, replaced by the orthodoxy of female liberation. The notion of women's equality hardly had time to find its feet before it was being blown over by a new suspicion that in fact all this modern freedom was a trap. Certain elements decided that Western women are being traduced by the beauty myth, enslaved by their own sexuality and bound by capitalist imperatives.

There is the occasional suggestion that it would be so much more liberating to follow the example of their Eastern sisters, and cover themselves from head to toe in black cloth (we personally can't wait for that glorious day). The reactionary Right has come up with its own orthodoxy, which is that all this mad liberty has led women to go against all their biological imperatives and try to turn themselves into men, which has left them so confused and miserable that they would be much happier if they got out of the boardroom and went back to the nursery.

For women of the forty-something generation, the orthodoxy is especially twisted: if you have not found a man and had a baby by the age of forty, you are officially On the Shelf. If you have done both, but carelessly forgotten to pursue a dazzling career, then you are On the Scrapheap. If you have done all three, then you are almost certainly On the Make. You may also be attempting to Have It All, which is clearly just selfish and wrong.

There are other more amorphous, but just as stupid, orthodoxies when it comes to the ladies. If an extra-terrestrial landed and spent a week reading the newspapers and magazines, she would conclude that her earthly sisters were all, every single one, obsessed with: shoes, sex, diets, and George Clooney. (We admit that this last one might have a pinch of truth in it, and what's not to love about a talented actor who goes to the UN to talk about the suffering in Darfur *and* has a sense of humour? But the idea that he is *all* the modern woman dreams of is reductive and stupid.)

These new orthodoxies carry an odd strain of intellectual laziness. The ticking biological clock, the sex and shopping obsession, the agonising over diet and thinness: when it comes to modern women, all the idle clichés come out to play. Most demoralising of all, the zeitgeist is crowded with the implication that this education and career is all very well, but none of it means a thing without a big strong man and an adorable baby. The error lies in turning a cheap cultural conceit into a universal truth. Even people who should know better often seem helplessly incapable of distinguishing between the two. If you want proof of this, look at the actress Renée Zellweger, whose most famous role is that of Bridget Jones. She is beautiful, rich, talented and wildly successful, and yet most articles about her focus entirely on the fact that she can't find a man. It is mournfully noted that she has several houses, but not enough free time to turn any of them into a proper home. Poor pitiful Renée: all that hard work, all those trips to the gym, all that pulchritude and, look, look – she can't even get a boyfriend. The triumphantly inevitable conclusion is that her life is meaningless, and she is a sad, empty, lonely individual.

This is patently nonsense. More likely, Renée has not met a man who makes her laugh, does not trade in stereotypes and can deal with the fact that she almost certainly is more successful than he is. What if – and now we really are drifting onto the wilder plains of possibility – what *if* she has decided that she is quite happy on her own?

THE ORTHODOXY
THAT WOMEN ARE
ALWAYS WRONG.

This is a silent, secret orthodoxy: no one actually says it out loud. Of course not, because all the battles have been won and everyone knows that the ladies will do whatever the hell they damn well please. They can be molecular biologists or astronauts, or sit at home and make cheesecake.

But there is a snaking theme that runs through the culture which is not quite so lovely. The Women, variously, are too fat, or too thin. They are consumed with vanity if they pay attention to their appearance, or, if they choose not to, they are plain and dowdy. They must go out to work and contribute to the economy, but then they risk scarring their children for life by missing the formative years. If they are opinionated and funny, they risk being cast as shrill and alienating; if they are not, then they are dull and submissive. If they are feminists, they are, of course, bitter and angry; if they are not, then they are surrendered wives. If they are ambitious, they are tough and grasping; if they are not, they are mousy and uninteresting.

It is hard to think of any woman currently in the public eye who has not been torn down for something. The only amnesty comes when the females pass a certain age, and then, mysteriously, in an instant Pass Go moment, they morph into national treasures. Helen Mirren's acting chops used to be obscured under press hysteria that she had once taken her clothes off on stage; now, she is as beloved as Our Own Dear Queen, mostly for playing Our Own Dear Queen. Germaine Greer has gone from terrifying Antipodean gorgon (one *look* from those burning feminist eyes and you would surely turn to stone) to a beloved part of British life.

All this is true, and the modern female should be aware of it, and remain on her guard. But here is the thing: it's not actually that bad. It's irritating, and stupid; it's the death throes of an ancient patriarchal imperative which is fabulously spooked by any kind of change. The women have not quite got there yet, but in the West, they have come a bloody long way, baby. The orthodoxy is the last twitches of an outdated argument. No one is knocking down the door at three in the morning, literally or metaphorically. It's just that the incredible strides that women have taken leave some people disconcerted and uncomfortable, and the new reality needs a little time to settle.

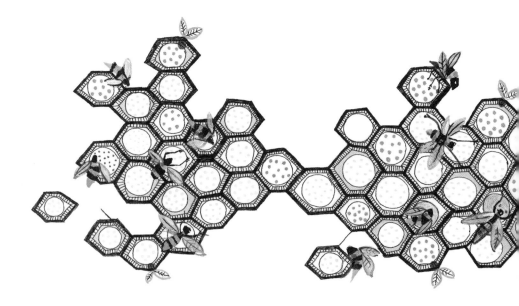

THE ORTHODOXY THAT WOMEN MAY SAY ANYTHING ABOUT MEN, HOWEVER RUDE, WHILE THE MEN MUST SIT QUIETLY AND POLITELY IN THE CORNER AND SUCK IT UP.

This is an interesting one, because it does not easily divide along political lines, but appears randomly from commentators of all stripes. It is even sometimes propagated by women themselves. It is closely related to the idea that the women have Gone Too Far, and has echoes of the pulling memory that people of a certain age will hold, of a time when ladies were Ladies, and everyone knew where they stood.

Oddly, its proof most often comes from advertising. Look, say the sages, who have clearly stayed up all night watching ITV – every single ad now features a wonderfully capable woman, while the men are portrayed as hopeless or rude or wimpish. From this they extrapolate that being offensive about men is the new national sport, while anyone who says anything even mildly questionable about women is arrested by the PC brigade and frogmarched off to Belmarsh, to be held indefinitely without trial. The ineffable conclusion is that all women, everywhere, insist that men are emotionally illiterate idiots. And so, a new orthodoxy is born.

The reason that this received wisdom gained traction is partly because most women are too busy doing jobs and bringing up children and managing their marriages to have time to rush into the breach every time a new and idiotic falsity about them is invented. They simply do not have time to fight every fight; they know to keep their powder dry for the important battles. And partly it is because this orthodoxy does have a minute fraction of truth in it.

We freely admit that when women gather together and have a couple of martinis they may, at some stage, dwell on the utter impossibility of the male. They may complain about how the men want them to have the babies, but then are absolutely of no practical help; they might gripe about how he feels his job is somehow more important than hers; they may take a few cheap shots about inability to talk about emotions or, actually, you know, grow up. They might bitch a little about the state of the bathroom once he has finished with it, or the socks that never end up in the laundry basket, or the snoring. They have a tendency to kvetch about the lack of flowers on Valentine's Day and discuss whether that story about a husband giving his wife a dust-buster for her birthday is true or just an urban myth. Oh, the poor beleaguered men, how do they stand up under such a relentless barrage?

But just let us consider for a moment what the women could really complain about but almost never do: gang rape, sexual slavery, hardcore porn, prostitution. Murder. Violent crime. Wife bashing. Dictatorship. Forced marriage. Oh, and yes, why not, while we're at it, just for fun: female circumcision. And don't let the misogynists come back at you with Queen Isabella of Spain or Tzu Hsi, because everyone knows that the history of tyranny is the history of men.

All right. We are better now. We don't normally let that list go out in public – no woman does. Considering what women have suffered at the hands of men, we think that *not* going on about this stuff is in itself a remarkable feat of self-control. (Also, we know well that it would turn us into hideous bores and we would never be asked out again.) A few jokes about commitment-phobia is surely a small price to pay for thousands of years of male dominance. The emasculation orthodoxy is not funny or clever, or even true. If men really want to develop a plausible victim theory then they're going to need some better statistics.

THE RAY OF HOPE.

All orthodoxies, eventually, burn themselves out. Someone comes along and has a better idea, like those lovely brave women in the early twentieth century who decided that the female brain was in fact capable of voting and getting educated and, in fact, thinking. Old ideas leave shadows behind them, like faint cultural ghosts, so, even now, there is still the idea that women can't drive cars because they are too busy putting their lipstick on. But the lovely thing is that all orthodoxy is open to challenge from the open mind. You can do this in two ways. You can arm yourself with scientific fact and irrefutable statistics (car insurance companies offer lower prices to women because they actually crash *less* often than men) and argue your head off whenever faced with cheap points or tired assumptions. Or, you can just refuse to fall for it. It doesn't have to be a fight. You can look into your own heart and understand that none of these reductive, trotted-out ideas applies to you. You can be a one-woman rolling radical show, and mount a revolution in the barricades of your very own mind.

WOMEN AND INVENTION.

An old notion which never really got updated is the idea that women have never invented anything. Should you need any ammunition to counter this one, here is a short, but not exhaustive list.

Susan Mather invented the submarine telescope in 1845.

In 1871, Martha J. Coston perfected and patented the pyrotechnic flare, which was taken up by the American navy, and formed the basis of a system of communication that helped to win battles and save lives.

Margaret Knight, born in 1838, was a soaring child prodigy, who at the age of twelve, when other girls were playing with rag dolls, had the idea of a stop-motion device to be used in textile mills to shut down machinery and thus protect workers from injury. She eventually had some 26 patents to her name, including a machine for making paper bags, which is still used today.

Hedy Lamarr is famous for being described as the most beautiful woman in Europe and notoriously running naked through the woods in the film *Ecstasy* in 1933. (*Naked*. In the *woods*. In *1933*. Just ponder that for a moment.) Astoundingly, she also invented a system for guiding torpedoes using a technique called frequency hopping. She was desperate to help the war effort, but the US military ignored her miraculous invention and suggested that she would be better employed entertaining the troops and selling kisses at $50,000 a pop for war bonds. What is even more extraordinary is that when her frequency hopping idea was dusted down in the fifties, it went on to form the basis of spread spectrum technology, which is now what makes mobile telephones and the internet possible. So it is worth remembering that every time you send a text message or receive an email, you owe it in part to a naked girl who once ran through a forest in 1933.

Hypatia of Alexandria, born 370, invented the pane astrolabe, which measured the position of the sun and the stars. Also the hydroscope, the first laboratory instrument to measure the specific gravity of liquids. As a reward for these remarkable achievements, she was branded a heretic by furious Christians, and, on refusing staunchly to recant her scientific thinking, was dragged from her chariot to a church, where she was stripped naked, and, as Socrates Scholasticus described it: 'they raze the skin and rend the flesh of her body with sharp shells, until the breath is departed out of her body; they quarter her body, then bring her quarters unto a place called Cinaron, and burn them to ashes.' How perfectly charming and godly of them.

Lady Ada Lovelace, the daughter of Lord Byron, was a mathematician and scientist, called by Charles Babbage, whose work she helped and improved, 'the Enchantress of numbers'. She invented the binary system of numbers to be used by Babbage's analytical machine in the 1840s, which led to her being known by later generations as the very first computer programmer.

In 1966 Stephanie Kwolek invented Kevlar, now used in bullet-proof vests.

In 1893, Josephine Cochran unveiled the world's first practical washing-up machine at the World's Fair, having exclaimed (one imagines in purely female exasperation) 'If nobody else is going to invent a dishwashing machine, I'll do it myself.'

In 1959, Rosalyn Yalow invented radioimmunoassay of human blood and tissue, still one of the most significant methods of chemical analysis used in medicine. In 1977, she won the Nobel Prize.

Also invented by women: the brassiere, the jockstrap, cotton sewing thread, the beehive, Tippex, the Barbie doll, the circular saw, non-reflective glass, coffee filters, the space helmet, chocolate chip cookies and, of course, windscreen wipers.

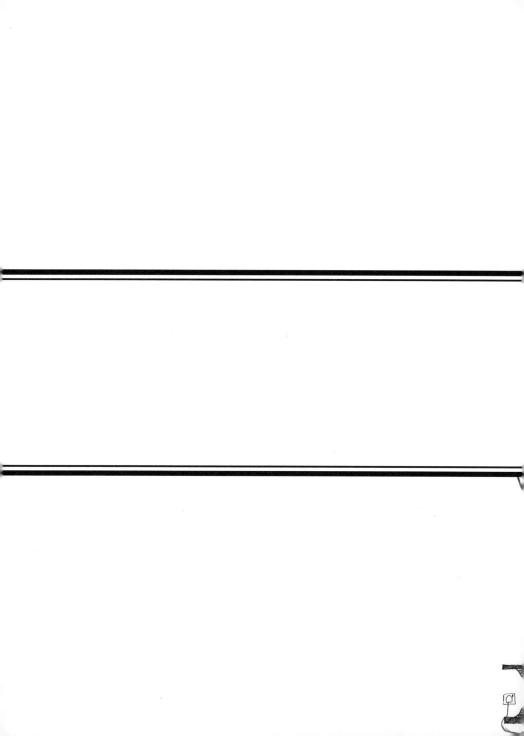

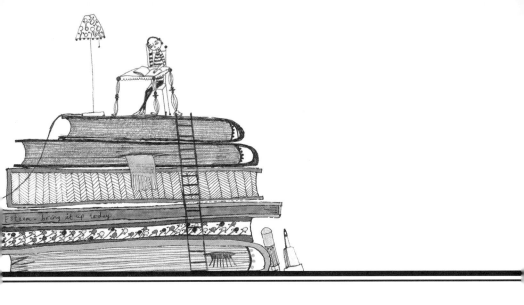

PHILOSOPHY OF LIFE, SELF-ESTEEM, AND THE WHOLE DAMN THING

—

CHAPTER SEVEN

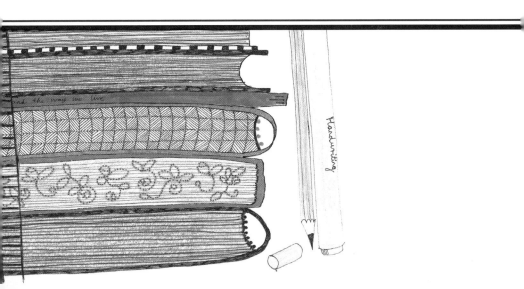

DEVELOPING A WORKING PHILOSOPHY OF LIFE – JUST IN CASE YOU HAVEN'T ALREADY.

Here is the biggest, hoariest, most ancient nut of a question asked by anyone, man or woman, when they get to a certain age: Is This It?

It's like some great cosmic joke: when you are young and arrogant and know all the answers, you don't have much time for asking the questions. You are far too busy falling in love with the wrong people and shooting for the moon. You have no fear. You think you know everything, even though you know nothing; when you get to the age of knowing something, you realise that you do, in fact, know nothing. The Chinese say that the wise man is the one who *admits* he knows nothing, and Socrates had a nice little riff on the same theme, but we find this of absolutely no consolation. The world is very big, and life is very short, and none of it makes much sense.

By this age, you have certainly loved and lost. You have been through a couple of career crashes and worked your way through bad hair and financial crises, and the realisation that all your childish dreams will not come to fruition. You have discarded youthful ideologies and toyed with

'MY FORMULA FOR LIVING IS QUITE SIMPLE. I GET UP IN THE MORNING AND I GO TO BED AT NIGHT. IN BETWEEN, I OCCUPY MYSELF AS BEST I CAN.'

Cary Grant

cynicism. You may, if you are one of the rare and lucky few, have come to a lovely equilibrium. In which case, you should not be reading this book, because you know everything already. Go out and pick yourself some flowers and bask in the glow of your own brilliance.

For the rest of us, there is still the drawing board; by which we mean that any philosophy of life is, by definition, a work in progress: shifting, ephemeral, and prone to abrupt swerves in direction.

In times of particular confusion, the Buddhist notion of the moment can be oddly helpful. It's so simple in theory, yet so hard in practice, but the idea of mindfulness, of noting each moment as it passes, can bring a troubled mind back to some kind of calm. Or you can look at Jung, who said that if we look at what a person fears, we can see where she will develop next. You can even ponder Plato's huge idea that everything is just a shadow of one perfect template. There are the physicists and their eleven possible dimensions and their contention of parallel universes, although personally we can feel our brains stretching and boiling at the mere contemplation. Sometimes we just want to go back to the perfect pop song: when the Rolling Stones told us that you can't always get what you want, but sometimes, if you try, you get what you need, we heard the perfect note of a universal truth.

But the truth is that you can read all the books, you can think all the thoughts, you can make your own mistakes and even, if you are very clever, learn from those of others; you can lie on a couch for years, you can study the newspapers, you can pay *attention*, and you still may not know what the hell it is all about. And strangely, that is sort of all right.

Here is what we believe to be true:

Frailty and confusion are the human condition. It is perfectly all right to admit to them. People will not run away screaming, but sigh with recognition and relief, and quite probably want to talk about it for the rest of the night.

It's not a competition, although it feels like it quite a lot of the time. In some obscure, hard-wired way, you are programmed to think of life as a competition, and that is part of what gets you out of the house. But actually, literally, we are all in it together.

Some platitudes are true: the ones about doing your best, and the comfort of strangers, and in fact it *not* being the end of the world, are pretty much on the money. A stitch in time does, quite often, save nine. And, you know, you do only get one shot at it, because life is not actually a dress rehearsal.

Mostly, whatever you do, you aren't going to change anyone's mind. We ourselves have shouted and cried and raged at people who hold ideas that we find abhorrent and horrifying. It makes little difference. There really are people who believe that someone is worth less because of their skin colour or gender or sexual orientation, and what is confusing is that they do not wear black hats or have horns; they quite often are perfectly polite in every other way. Personally, we think a good woman should always stand her ground. Believe, with every fibre of your being, in your own idiosyncratic ethos, but don't expect to make mass conversions over the dinner table on a Saturday night.

It is important not to dismiss the little things. You might not be destined to win a Nobel Prize or conjure World Peace or go to a Third-World country and offer succour to the afflicted, but you might be able to make your oldest friend laugh when she has just been made redundant. Not every one of us is cut out to save the children of Africa, but you can pick up the telephone when someone you love is in despair. You can *listen.* This is not nothing.

E.M. Forster once wrote: 'Kindness, kindness and yet more kindness.' We think he was right.

BEING FABULOUS.

Fabulousness is essentially an American concept – it's a little too extravagant and shameless for the more prosaic British. It was most frankly expressed in *Sex and the City*, where a devotion to fabulousness was seen as the cure to all ills: from having a man leave you to being diagnosed with breast cancer. It's a 'put on a glorious frock, have a martini and watch me go' defiance.

On a more subtle level, it's a canny use of the superficial (dresses, cocktails, make-up) to counterbalance the profound (existential despair, illness, events beyond your control). We think the very word superficial gets a bad rap. It first appeared in around 1420 (from the Latin *superficies,* meaning surface), and originally meant what was apparent on the outside. It took about a hundred years for it to reach the meaning of not deep or thorough, when applied to thoughts or perceptions. It then carried on its unsteady way to reach its most common application as we know it now, with all its implications of not serious, shallow, vacuous. It has also, oddly, come to have its most damning meaning when applied to women. It is in the fabled female obsession with baubles and lipstick and shoes that superficial rises to its cruellest. After all, it is the frippery *women* who dye their hair and paint their faces while the men go about the serious business of life.

We say: don't let the superficial be dismissed so easily; what is on the surface does, in fact, matter. A judicious dose of fabulousness will not solve the Arab–Israeli conflict, but it can shine a ray of light in a sometimes dim world. A bright scarlet lipstick is not just a confection of wax and pigment but a statement of intent: look at me, facing down the odds. A little rouge, a lilac eye shadow, an inky black mascara mean nothing when broken down into their constituent parts, but have a disproportionate psychological effect. They can arm you for the world, and bring back the cosmetic approximation of the bloom of youth when you are feeling old and worn: it is no coincidence that make-up is often called war paint. Applying make-up is a subliminal sign that you have not Given Up, even though sometimes you feel like giving up altogether. Used carefully, it can be theatrical, amusing, diverting, a tiny but potent addition to the general aesthetic.

The ancient Egyptians would not leave home without applying a reddish purple plant dye called *fucus* to their lips (and the Egyptians were all about the fabulous, just look at the tomb of Queen Hatshepsut). In seventeenth-century England, an English pastor called Thomas Hall called the painting of the face the Devil's work, and a hundred years later parliament actually passed a law against the use of lipstick, stating that women who seduced men by cosmetic means could be tried for witchcraft. (This law also, entirely bizarrely, condemned the use of Spanish wool, high-heeled shoes and iron stays.) Yet during the Second World War, officially Our Finest Hour, it was regarded as a patriotic duty to 'put your face on'; the application of powder and paint expressing some collective defiance in the face of potential destruction.

Of course, make-up and other outward manifestations are only a part of fabulousness, which is essentially a state of mind. It's posture, girls, posture, literally and metaphorically: standing up straight and marching out to meet your destiny. It's good jokes and what the hell. It's allowing the eccentric and celebrating the implausible. It's understanding that not everything must be about the practical and the mundane and the quotidian. It's sometimes pretending that you are in your very own movie.

TO SHRINK OR NOT TO SHRINK.

Even in this pop psychology age, the stiff-upper-lip British have some very strong ideas about shrinkage. We know one man who once marched up to a highly respected psychologist loaded with PhDs and said: 'Are you that charlatan who ruined X's life?' (The charlatan, to his credit, roared with laughter. X, when told of this, said, edgily: 'But I thought I was doing rather well.')

Even the collocations around psychotherapy are loaded: are you getting *help*? They are couched in frightened euphemism: have you thought about *seeing* someone? It is still, even in this age of letting it all hang out, a secret, subversive activity.

Unless you have been brought up by the Waltons, it is conceivable that there may be times in your life when you need a little assistance. Doing everything by yourself is not a badge of honour. No climber would attempt Everest without Sherpas and some excellent boots. The counsel of a heavenly bearded gent with a thorough understanding of the human mind can be a balm of the highest order. It does not mean there is anything wrong with you. (There are shrinks who say that the ones who

really have something wrong are the ones who never go, but that's another story.)

Here is what a good psychologist will do: she will tell you that you are normal. One of the greatest of the skewed constructions that gets developed and lovingly nurtured in the darker parts of the cerebellum is that your problems and frailties and crazy thoughts are somehow unique, and that everyone else is running around being operatically normal and sensible. The wonderful thing about a good shrink is that he has seen it all before; nothing shocks or startles or fazes him. Also, you cannot bore him, since the human condition is his enduring fascination. So if you want to go somewhere where you can rant and be unreasonable and repetitive and not be judged, a good, comfortable couch is where you will find it. (Avoid the grand Chesterfields of Harley Street; the professionals there wear off-putting suits and ring a bell at the end of forty-five minutes, even if you are sobbing at the memory of your mother's hopeless Valium addiction.)

The misconception about therapy is that it always involves regression and agony and unearthing all those scarring memories that you have taken so much trouble to sweep under the rug. You can absolutely do that if you want, but you can also go for a specific problem and a finite number of sessions. The really good therapist will tell you firmly when your training wheels are off, and send you back to the world, once she has checked your levels of separation anxiety. The best and most useful school is Jungian–Adlerian, in our experience, because when you say 'Why do I do that?', the answer will not be: 'Why do *you* think you do it?' The Jungian–Adlerians will actually give you practical advice, and even helpful mental exercises that you can do in times of stress. They will also encourage you to explore fascinating intellectual concepts like the shadow side, the collective unconscious, and the balance between the animus and the anima.

A season with a great shrink stops you driving your friends demented; it offers the perspective of someone who really knows, and at the end you get a lovely ontological lollipop which is: we are all of us a little nuts, in our own nutty way, and that is not a matter for shame or regret.

THE MADNESS OF
SELF-HELP.

We hold the slightly controversial view that most self-help books are written by idiots. Admittedly, many of them are extremely successful and vastly rich idiots, but idiots nonetheless they are. The reason they are so rich is that even you, with all your cleverness and success, sometimes feel at such a loss you develop a dangerous idea that if only there was a great book out there, which revealed all the secrets of life between hard covers, it would all be all right. So you slink, shameful and foolish, into the Loser section of the bookshop and get something with a title suggesting that if only you could feel the fear, or let go of the struggle, or gather the secret and dance with life, everything would miraculously be all right — and hope that the assistant thinks you are buying it for your sad sister.

It's not only that most of these books are written in execrable prose, or that they offer manifestly stupid and plagiarised ideas, or that they have a fatal tendency to instruct you to stand still and wait for the Abundance, whatever that might be. It's not just that they are sometimes actively egregious (many state authoritatively that every single human being is filled with the same golden potential, which is a bit of a problem when it comes to Joe Stalin and other assorted villains and tyrants), it's that they do not actually *work*.

The reason that self-help writers are so rich is that their books are the mental equivalent of diet books. There is no one perfect diet book, because the only diet that works is to eat a little less and move a little more, and you can't spin that into three hundred pages. So it's the F-plan, and then Rosemary Thing with her hips and thighs, the Miami Beach farrago followed by the GI con-trick. In the exact same way, one self-help manual follows another, because, like diet books, they are too reductive and, paradoxically, too complicated to achieve any lasting utility. (We are huge for utility, we don't mind admitting.) It starts off all shining and lovely. It feels as if some great revelation has arrived and you see the world in a slightly different way, and you too can share the Abundance. You say your affirmations in the morning, and remember to let your thoughts flow by and not Define your Reality.

But then the prescriptive regime becomes a little tired, and actually you are really not sure if everything really *does* happen for a reason, and even though you are remembering to do your three kind things each day, you still find that there are elements of life and love and the whole damn thing that confuse the hell out of you. So you get a little disillusioned, and you go and buy another book, even though you really know better, and the entire mad tango starts all over again.

The problem is compounded because the great promise of pretty much all self-help books is that you have the power to be whatever you want, if only you will follow the precepts of whichever cut-price guru you have chosen. If only you truly believe, and open your heart to the universe, whatever you need will be presented to you. This is NOT TRUE. Horrible things happen to good people, and we defy you to make much sense of that. And no matter how much Abundance you welcome into your lives, you may not have the talent to write a sonata or build a cathedral or discover a new planet, however much you wish it. If your daughter has run off with a junkie guitarist and become a crack-whore, it will be of no consolation to discover that it is only your *thinking* about this that represents the reality of the situation.

So, in thrall to the spurious authority of these books, you end up believing that it is somehow your fault that you are not waltzing with life. You are not affirming quite enough, you are not good enough at following the maxims and dictats. It follows that it must be you who is the failure. And you end up feeling worse than you did before.

THE TRULY MAGNIFICENT DOROTHY ROWE.

Occasionally, for reasons we do not understand, the toweringly brilliant Dorothy Rowe gets lumped into the self-help section. We think she should have an entire shelf to herself with a huge sign saying 'Wisdom and Delight and All Good Things Here'.

The reason that Rowe is not self-help, although she writes about depression and the pursuit of happiness and other great life problems, is that she offers no pat solutions, no delusional five-step plan, no easy write-on-the-back-of-a-napkin homilies. Instead, she explains how it is that we came to this, she corrects many common delusions, she charts, with enormous empathy and compassion, the travails of the human spirit, and we love her for it. And she does it all in lucid, elegant prose.

If you read any of her books, you will not come to the end with a blueprint for living, but you will be enlightened and soothed, and you will know that you are not an aberration, because there is someone out there who absolutely understands and sympathises and can explain pretty much how it was that you got this way.

We recommend her with whole-hearted admiration, and hope that she lives forever.

THE OBLIGATORY HOW-TO SECTION.

At the risk of inviting derisive laughter and rolling eyes, we now dare to offer a few of the things that we have learnt in our combined eighty-two years. In the light of what we have said about self-help, this might seem a crass act of hypocrisy, but we write these not as a cure-all to everything that ails you, nor as a didactic programme for living; we present them in a spirit of absolute humility. This is all we know.

We are certain you will know quite a lot of these things already. What we hope is that you will see them as confirmation that we really are all in it together, and that you are not alone. If even one of them raises a tuning fork reverberation of recognition, we have done our job. If not, well, sue us.

HOW TO CALL IN THE PERSPECTIVE POLICE.

The traffic won't move, the rain has just ruined your new velvet coat, you pressed the delete button by mistake and lost a day's work; you burnt the dinner, developed a hideous head-cold the day before a big date, smashed your favourite piece of china. All these are daily irritants, even occasions for sorrow, but they are categorically not worth much expenditure of emotion.

The key, when the stock miseries and frustrations come, is to call in the perspective police. You may have just had a fight with your husband, but you are not living in a war zone. Your brother might have forgotten your birthday, but your home has not been repossessed. You may have discovered a new indelible wrinkle on your forehead, but you have all your arms and legs.

The perspective police will break down the door with a battering ram and remind you of your blessings. They also know all about waiting until you see the whites of people's eyes. What they mean by this is that you have reached the age where you will inevitably have to face some deep griefs. They mean: don't use up all your emotional capital on the small things that are not the end of the world.

The only caveat about the perspective police is not to let them become trigger-happy, otherwise you may develop a full-blown case of First-World guilt which means that you never allow yourself to feel sad about anything, and go on to develop an ulcer.

HOW TO STILL THE VOICES IN YOUR HEAD.

Even the women who do not stalk the city streets with sandwich boards proclaiming the end of the world suffer from the voices in their heads. Shrinks like to give the voices fancy schmancy names, like Mother Introject. In layman's terms, the voices are essentially a cocktail party of Critics from Hell.

They set up shop in your cranium, down a couple of stiff gins, and start barking about how you are not good enough, and your hair is a mess, and why did you ever think you could become a useful member of society when you can't even get your tax return in on time. They are the voices you have internalised from your family, your school, newspapers, random pundits on the radio, the culture itself.

The first thing to do is to identify the voices. Women are so accustomed to them that they often don't even know they are there; it's a static so constant that they think it usual. So just stop, occasionally, and listen. It's the end of a long day, and you are tired, and the kitchen is a bit of a muddle, and you forgot your dentist's appointment, and there it is – the voice that says: 'Call yourself a grown-up?' It is the voice that lashes you for every small lapse in the insane drive to scale the pinnacles of achievement.

You are a nice, decent human being. We are assuming that you do not run around breaking up marriages and laughing at people selling the *Big Issue*. You quite possibly give money to the Red Cross and worry about global warming and think that Amnesty International is a Good Thing. You are certainly kind to children and animals. You would never, ever, in a million years, talk to your worst enemy in the way that you sometimes talk to yourself.

You do not have to do the whole Warm Worthwhile Human Being affirmation gig – this can feel silly, and even fraudulent – but you can tell the voices to bugger off out of it and have their nasty little party somewhere else. The voices become discouraged and grumpy if they are not invited in and given canapés. Eventually they will give up.

HOW TO STOP BEING A PERFECTIONIST.

Perfection is boring. Oh my God, it's the dullest thing in the world. Stop trying to achieve it, now. Step *away* from the impossible demands.

Think of the people you love and why you love them. It is not for their brilliant careers and immaculate houses and infallible way with a soufflé; it is for all their flaky little habits and endearing flaws and entirely human failings. This is also why they love you.

If you did, by any bizarre miracle, become perfect, you would have no friends and no one to talk to and you would have to go and live in a small shed somewhere up a mountain and only communicate with the Dalai Lama – and there is no guarantee that even he would return your calls.

THINGS THAT YOU SHOULD NEVER TAKE FOR GRANTED.

OPPOSABLE THUMBS.

No, really; think about it. It's not just that you are lucky to have them, because it means that you can do up buttons and type. The opposable thumb is a crucial component of almost every human invention. And it's vital for the judicious use of a screwdriver.

THE SUN.

Not just when it's shining and you can go out and bask in it and get brown and sexy. The wonder is the mere fact that it's there at all, at the exact distance that is required for life on earth. If for some reason the sun decided that it was bored and sailed away to another galaxy, we would all be for the dark – both literally and metaphorically.

THE ENGLISH LANGUAGE.

You multi-culturalists out there can stop panicking. We're not saying it's the *best*. We know perfectly well there is beauty and grandeur in Pashto and Serbo-Croat and Urdu. All we're saying is that English is a vast repository of complexity and style and subtlety. It gave us Shakespeare and T.S. Eliot and Robert Frost. It is a fantastic mongrel of a language, shamelessly stealing anything it can get its hands on, from entrepreneur to kedgeree to chukka.

And while we're on it, sometimes we like thinking of the mysteries of language in general. We want to know: who was it who first looked at the sky and decided it was going to be called blue?

THE WEATHER.

It gives us the National Conversation. Even the cleverest meteorologists don't know what it is going to do next. It surprises us and reassures us, in equal measure. In this country, we are insanely lucky to get a temperate climate, with rain to keep the island green and sun to bring the flowers out. We are on the same parallel as Moscow and yet the Gulf Stream guards us from the berserk swings in temperature that the Muscovites must endure. We get warmth without hordes of mosquitoes and cold without ice storms. We get those crazy mackerel skies, which make even the most desolate heart soar.

THE FEMINIST REVOLUTION.

It's not perfect, for the women. We would never say that. Double standards, glass ceiling, objectification; all are still going strong. But you can be pretty sure that, barring disaster, your daughter will be able to do whatever she wants, and that is thanks to all those women who came before and made a noise and tied themselves to railings and got sneered at and called unnatural. Every time you get in a car and drive down the road, think of the women of Saudi Arabia, who can't do that because they didn't get their revolution yet.

LAUGHTER.

The human being is the only mammal who laughs, with the possible exception of the hyena, which really does not count, for reasons that we cannot be bothered to go into. Laughter is a thing of wonder: it defuses tension, cements friendships, drives away demons, restores sanity. It gives the diaphragm a fine workout – there are ladies in India who stand in public squares laughing at nothing at all, for an hour each morning, instead of going to the gym, and we salute every one of them.

EGGS.

We are serious. It was only sixty years ago that the powdered egg was the accepted staple. Just think of life without proper eggs – no omelettes, no cakes, no mayonnaise.

THE NIGHT SKY AND THE MORAL SENSE.

We can't put it any better than Kant, who said: 'Two things fill the mind with ever new and increasing admiration and awe, the oftener and more steadily we reflect on them: the starry heavens above and the moral law within.'

ELECTRICITY.

One of us had a power cut the other day. It was snowing, and the lines came down. For half a day, she could not cook, boil a kettle, work at her computer, keep warm, turn a light on. Electricity, she thought, it's a bloody *miracle*.

RUNNING WATER.

All right, we really are going to stop now. You get the point. But there is a daily wonder in clean, clear, cold water, instantly available, instead of walking ten miles each morning with a bucket on your head, because you don't have a tap, and it's always the women who do that, for some unknown reason. No, no, we are stopping.

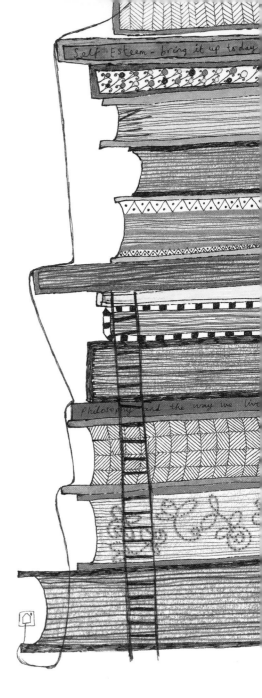

Self Esteem - bring it up to date

Philosophy and the way we live

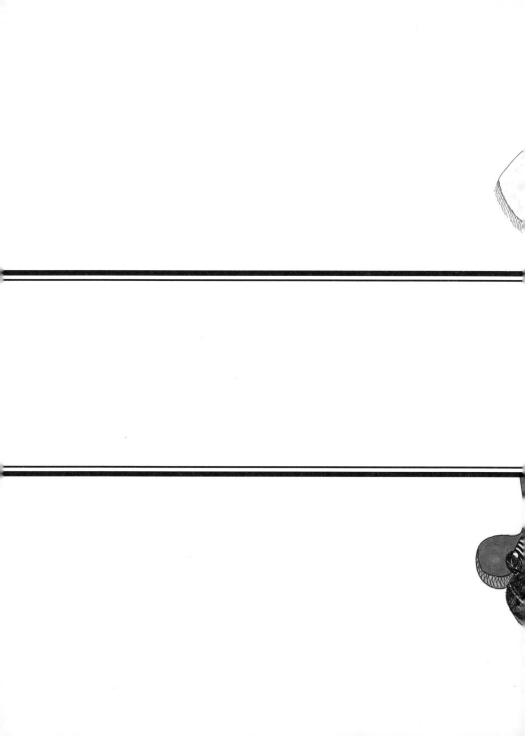

DRESSING AND SHOPPING

—

CHAPTER EIGHT

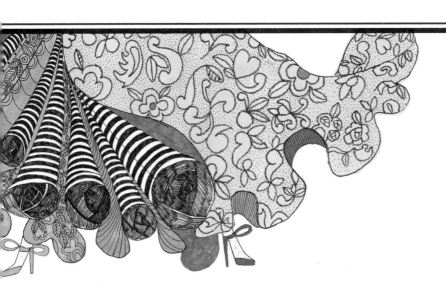

'I BASE MY FASHION SENSE ON WHAT DOESN'T ITCH.'

Gilda Radner

HOW TO READ A FASHION MAGAZINE WITHOUT WANTING TO CUT YOUR HEAD OFF WITH A PENKNIFE.

There can come a time, in your middle to late thirties, when you cast aside the fashion magazines you loved in your youth. You realise that you do not have the time, money or flair to ape Jacqueline Kennedy; you may even feel a twist of disgust at the shallow desire to transform yourself into a fashion plate. You fall back with relief into a standard uniform of black trousers and think that all the stick idiots with their absurd outfits can take a running jump because they have nothing to do with the way that real women live, and anyway, here are your eyes, and here is the wool, and there will be no pulling, not today.

Fashion, which has always been slightly bonkers, seems lately to have grown even madder. It has started using jargon as bizarre as anything that middle managers employ: *must-have, on trend, fashion forward.* It has also developed an alarming tendency to try and flog you incredibly ugly objects for hundreds of your precious pounds. The peculiar trend for enormous baggy leather handbags, decked out with hideous tassels and buckles, and costing thousands, which the fashion editors tell you that you are absolutely mad not to buy, mostly because Sienna Miller has one (which she almost certainly got sent free by a grateful manufacturer) is a case in point. The clinically insane phenomenon of waiting lists, where women are not only told that they must have one of these nasty items, but that they also must put their name down for it and wait three months, in a humiliating state of style penitence, is something which even the most brilliant sociologist would be stretched to explain. The fashion mavens have clearly never read Bertrand Russell, who said that to be without some of the things you want is an indispensable part of happiness.

Fashions, which used to last for a season, even a year, now come and go within four weeks, as if the people who are trying to sell you things are so hysterical that they cannot wait for one trend to settle before throwing another one at you. Magazines run by perfectly intelligent women insist, with great conviction and seriousness, that you really *must* be wearing cobalt blue or mustard yellow this spring. If there is one thing we know, without doubt or equivocation, it is that there is no woman in the world who looks her best in cobalt or mustard. It's a law of nature.

These same emancipated working women also tell you that you certainly should be running about town in shoes with four-inch heels. Clippety-clip, girls, totter totter totter. We sometimes wonder why they just don't tell you to bind your feet and be done with it. Mrs Pankhurst did not chain herself to the railings so that the women who came after her should be forced into footwear in which they can hardly walk.

And yet, for all its bogusness and bonkersness, fashion can be amusing, if you learn to read it right. It can be peacock display, dressing as high theatre, a potent dose of eccentricity and even beauty in a sometimes

'CLOTHES MAKE THE MAN. NAKED PEOPLE HAVE LITTLE OR NO INFLUENCE ON SOCIETY.'

Mark Twain

drab world. Occasionally, taking the time and trouble to put together a really sharp outfit can lift the spirits in some arcane way, and send you out into the streets with your head held higher.

The psychological impact of clothes is undeniable: you can use them as armour, as flirtation, as an expression of self. When the New Look came into vogue in the fifties, the critics scoffed at the madness of wide swirling skirts requiring yards of fabric when there was still cloth rationing. But for many women, exhausted and scarred from the long dark years of the war, the New Look was like a beacon, a shaft of frivolity and femininity after the constraints of Dig for Victory and utility suits. Perfectly ordinary women, who would never drink martinis at the Ritz and had never even heard of the Faubourg St Honoré, sat down with their sewing machines and ran themselves up imitation Dior models in their own front rooms.

So, there is a balance to be struck. The lovely thing about getting older is that you begin to know yourself. You understand that you look like hell in orange (along with everyone in the world except for Burmese monks, who carry it beautifully and bravely); you know that you do not suit high necks or shift dresses; you begin to develop your own style. You have the confidence to understand the utter meaninglessness of the Must-have: there will be no *Must* about it. You also know the world better, and can see the fashion business for what it is, which is a vast commercial enterprise so obsessed with novelty that it must compulsively hurl differing and contradictory styles at you like a teenager with a raging case of OCD. Once you approach it in this spirit, it is safe again to open a copy of *Vogue*.

Reading fashion magazines is like shopping in Argos: you have to rummage through an awful lot of rubbish to find the good stuff. This is not entirely their fault: sometimes it seems as if designers go through stages of producing clothes whose only purpose is to make a woman look as ugly as possible. But there is beauty there, if you look hard enough. The secret is to regard a magazine not as some didactic bible, handing down sartorial diktats on tablets of stone, but as a Cecil Beaton confection of frippery and absurdity, with the occasional pure dose of aesthetic pleasure. Just as long as you understand that you absolutely don't *have* to wear any of those clothes, whatever anyone says, then you can see the whole enterprise as adding to the gaiety of nations, and there is something to be said for that, in these crazy post-millennial days.

SHOPPING FOR THE SOUL.

The single greatest shopping expedition in literature is Nicole Diver's eclectic spree in *Tender is the Night*. Admittedly, it is helped by Fitzgerald's ravishing prose, and it is a list — something he was particularly good at (the sublime litany of guests who came to Gatsby's parties is one of the most perfect passages in any book, ever) — but it is also shopping as it should be. There is something magical as well as comical about buying honey and lovebirds on the same trip.

Nicole bought from a great list that ran two pages, and bought the things in the windows besides. Everything she liked that she couldn't possibly use herself, she bought as a present for a friend. She bought coloured beads, folding beach cushions, artificial flowers, honey, a guest bed, bags, scarfs, love birds, miniatures for a doll's house and three yards of some new cloth the

Coco Chanel said that the great rule for dressing was to look in the glass before you go out, and take one item off. There is always one necklace, belt, scarf, too many. This is wise advice for the stylish, but it should also be remembered that Chanel ended up going out with a succession of not very nice men and collaborated with the Germans during the war. Which might be a little parable of its very own that says: just wear whatever the hell you want.

colour of prawns. She bought a dozen bathing suits, a rubber alligator, a travelling chess set of gold and ivory, big linen handkerchiefs for Abe, two chamois leather jackets of kingfisher blue and burning bush from Hermès.

Admittedly, not everyone can afford to buy a 'burning bush from Hermès', whatever that might be (we have never quite worked it out ourselves), or even a dozen bathing suits in one shot, but it is this kind of shopping which is an art rather than a random surrender to a messy capitalist imperative. Puritanical pundits love to sneer at the consumer society, and there is no doubt that excessive and compulsive buying of pointless and useless objects, which amuse for a moment and then are consigned to a dusty cupboard, leaves the same nasty taste in the mouth as junk food or too much cheap wine. But shopping, when done well, can act as pure pleasure, and we don't think that there is anything immoral or tawdry about that.

There is high style in Nicole Diver's list, and Fitzgerald, for all his drunken melancholy, was all about style, in life and prose. You have worked hard for your money, and there is a difference between squandering it on trifles, which can be profoundly satisfying, and throwing it away on gimcrack, which is not. It is the difference between buying an absurdly expensive bottle of Aqua di Parma cologne, with its beautiful yellow box and its lovely simple bottle, as favoured by Cary Grant and Audrey Hepburn, smelling subtly of summer and the Riviera, and splashing out on some horrid synthetic modern scent endorsed by whichever contemporary celebrity wants to cash in on their name.

We personally hate shopping for clothes, and dispute the myth that all women love to go off in a gaggle and buy many frocks. In a world where most things are cut to fit boyish twelve-year-olds, clothes shopping is a fraught affair, and we think it should be done in absolute private, possibly after taking half a Xanax. But shopping for alluring objects has none of the emotional freight of being the currently prescribed size or shape, and, if done well, is all about aesthetic pleasures.

Our own fantasy version of Nicole's list would include: a botanical print, a second hand copy of *Don't Tell Alfred* with its pretty Cecil Beaton cover, a candle smelling of figs, the complete Mahler symphonies, a bag of rich Guatemalan coffee, a silver paper knife, a pair of suede gloves, a verdigris box, a bunch of anemones, a Lee Miller photograph, a Cross pen, and, obviously, a jewel.

Such a list is extravagant, sybaritic, and entirely indulgent. It is unremittingly frivolous. Yet we think that those adjectives, which all carry negative connotations, have a case for rehabilitation. Sometimes a little indulgence is just what your harried mind needs. You are not raping the land or depriving old ladies of their pensions. A judicious dose of the ephemeral can be marvellously restorative.

There is an idea abroad that you cannot be the kind of woman who shops for fig candles *and* is ethically responsible. If you happen to love cashmere you cannot possibly care about the situation in Burma. It's absolute unmitigated baloney, and yet somehow it sticks. So when you sneak out to a store filled with fripperies, you have to barge through an invisible curtain of low-level guilt to get through the door. And yet it is perfectly possible to buy yourself a delightfully impractical hat and send money to the Red Cross every month. There will be no hair shirts in this book – they are too last season.

Indiscriminate spending is no fun – you end up waking at three in morning in a muck sweat about how you will ever pay off your credit cards – but judicious shopping in the elegant Fitzgerald manner is a simple joy, and you can always comfort yourself with the idea that you are not only keeping entire industries ticking over, but you are also obeying the law of William Morris and taking home nothing with you that is not beautiful or useful.

All this is of course wonderfully rational – see how we have made a massive and logical justification for a little touch of extravagance in the night. The rational is important, because although we do not share the simplistic sneering at the consumer society that is so fashionable just now, we do acknowledge that sometimes it seems as if women are under constant bombardment from people trying to sell them something, usually with spurious promises: if only you buy this you will magically become younger *and* sexier *and* more successful *and* the envy of your friends. So you do need to take your power back, as the shrinks love to say, and the rational is a vital part of that. But, just occasionally, there is nothing wrong with the entirely irrational. One of us, we are not going to admit which, once went out for a cup of coffee and came back with a Picasso lithograph. It was not necessary (it had to be paid off painfully on the never-never), but it sits now, propped up on the mantelpiece, a magical square of blue, from the hand of one of the great geniuses of the twentieth century, and even though there is absolutely no justifying it in any rational frame, it gives undilute pleasure every single day. In the same vein, we know a playwright who, when young and penurious, won a cash prize for his work and spent the entire sum on a Henry Moore sketch, even though he could not afford his rent at the time: forty years on, he can pay the rent, and he still has the picture, and has never regretted it for a moment. There is something magnificent in that.

So sometimes, even you, with your responsibilities and your good sensible mind, can do something in the spirit of sheer folly. Just as long as it is not one of those nasty, over-priced, saggy handbags.

THE PERFECTING OF THE SIGNATURE STYLE.

There is absolutely no need to develop a signature style. But there are advantages. You save money, because you have established, with glorious finality, that cap sleeves make your arms look like sausages and that the colour grey gives you a mildly diseased tinge. You save time, because you know exactly what you will put on in the morning. It also means that never again will you stare dolefully at your wardrobe and decide that you have absolutely nothing to wear, which is a profoundly demoralising feeling.

There are two discrete secrets to formulating a style all your own. The first is to be ruthlessly realistic about your body. This can be alarming, but there is also a great relief in it. Once you accept that your neck is short and you do not have a perfect jawline, you will never again have to buy any kind of polo neck and wonder why it just doesn't look quite right. Coming to terms with your magnificent embonpoint means that you understand that you need nipped-in tailoring – shirts with darts to follow the curve of your body, dresses that go in at the waist, low necks to show off the full munificence of your cleavage – because any straight shape will just hang down from your bosom and make the rest of you look like a box. If you have a rounded stomach, as all sane women do, a flirty silk camisole will skim over the bulge without making you feel as if you are wearing a sack of shame. You will develop the strong certainty that the low-rise trouser is a devilish invention designed only to reveal too much bottom in the ghastly manner of the builder's crack, which is not a look anyone wants to embrace, unless they are, in fact, a builder.

This makes the entire shopping and dressing process much more pleasurable and straightforward, because you are not trying to cram yourself into clothes that actively work against you, and then peering tremulously in the mirror with that sick tearful feeling, which even you, with all your qualifications and your hard-won wisdom and your place in the world, are prone to when the sartorial thing goes horribly wrong.

The second secret when looking for your own style is not to go to the fashion magazines. Because fashion is so febrile and unpredictable, and in certain seasons actively antithetical to any discernible sense of well-being, it is no help in developing a style for life. Part of fashion's job is to keep women in an eternal cycle of sartorial dissatisfaction – that way they are far more likely to be in thrall to its whims.

Instead, be guided by your pocket, your life and your personality. There is little point in developing a signature style based around two-ply cashmere twinsets if all you can afford is boiled wool. (We rather love boiled wool; it makes us think of the thirties, when all the women slept with poets.) Having a signature style does not mean that you cannot, when the mood swings through you, trip out of character. You may decide on one finely honed look and stick to it, where you know you look and feel best in a uniform – so you might discover the perfect white shirt and chic tailored trousers, heaving a low sigh of relief that you no longer have to mess around with flirty little skirts and heels that make your poor feet sore. But you may prefer the idea of dressing as theatre, as telling a story, and vary it according to your mood. Do you want to channel Diane Keaton in *Annie Hall*, or Grace Kelly in *To Catch a Thief*, or Julie Delpy in *Before Sunset*? You can broaden this out to embrace wider characterisations. So today you are a bookish intellectual, while tomorrow you may be a hippy chick. You can be Diana Vreeland one day, and the Bloomsbury set the next. You can do existential Left Bank (if you have the neck for the black polo necks) or funky Lower East Side. You can travel through time: 1955 on Monday, 1972 on Tuesday.

The only caveat is not to allow yourself too many radically different stories, otherwise the whole thing collapses into confusion, and you end up with the same muddle that you started off with.

SHOPPING LOCALLY, AND THE LOST ART OF COMMUNITY.

The local shop, once the very heart of any community, where gossip was exchanged and information gathered and even problems solved, died a slow lingering death some time in the dark days of the seventies. By the eighties, it was not even called the local shop any more; some idiotic desecrator of the language decided that convenience store was a more charming collocation. The problem was that while you could buy a pint of milk and a packet of Jaffa cakes at ten at night, some devilish central intelligence decreed that these shops should be stocked with a random selection of dispiriting foods – whether you were in Sunderland or Southampton, there was the identical display of packet soups, tinned vegetables, and nasty processed cheeses. Meanwhile, the vast shining supermarkets took over the barren land, and the idea of having a butcher, baker and candlestick-maker seemed as quaint and dated as a character in a Restoration tragedy.

For the busy working woman the supermarket does offer a remarkable service; everything the family might ever need, right there under one roof, with a free car park. It seems churlish to cavil; to turn one's back on the supermarket would seem as pointless and Luddite as replacing your washing machine with a mangle in a frenzy of misplaced nostalgia. And yet there is something so entirely soulless about the weekly supermarket visit; navigating your wayward trolley down sanitised aisles filled with unsmiling strangers. On occasion, we have been so overwhelmed by the crowds and the queues and the cascade of *stuff* that we have abandoned our trolley halfway through and run for the exit. Supermarkets are finely honed marketing tools; faced with such abundance, people always buy more than they actually need, and end up throwing away a vast amount of rotting food at the end of the week. Unless you have dogs *and* pigs *and* a compost heap, that's an awful lot of comestibles going for landfill.

As the mood of the nation changes, the local shop is starting to seem like something to be cherished. Unless you live in Ludlow, which, for no known reason, is the foodie capital of Britain, you are unlikely to find yams and lemongrass and smoked oysters in your village shop, but you will find something more precious than exotic ingredients flown in from farther shores – you will, if you are lucky, find a sense of belonging. The great psychologist Alfred Adler said that a human being needs three things in life – love, satisfaction in work, and a sense of community. (In *Tales of the City*, Armistead Maupin brilliantly bastardised this into: great lover, great job, great apartment.) In the supermarket, you are no more than a number on a credit card, a series of electronic beeps as your chosen items pass through an impartial infra-red bar-code reader. In the local shop, you are the bundle of quirks and likes and dislikes that you know yourself to be. The local shopkeeper will remember that you hate red onions, ask about your sick dog, sympathise when your work is going badly; if you are really lucky, she will laugh at your jokes.

Sometimes, when she is feeling particularly deracinated, one of us will do a little tour of our local shops – by the time she has gossiped to Kay at the grocer, and Diane in the newsagent, and Kathleen at the post office, she feels restored to sanity. She admits that she happens to be particularly lucky in her local shops. There are some out there which are run by furious misanthropes who can talk of nothing but being imperial martyrs, and there is nothing romantic about that. But generally we think the point holds: a friendly local shop will soothe your troubled soul in a way that an impersonal hypermarket can never dream of.

THE DULL PRACTICAL NOTE.

Oh, you are crying, it's all very well, waxing on about the adorable local shopkeepers with their charming ways, but what about the necessity of the jumbo pack of kitchen roll and packets of washing powder as heavy as bricks, which have to be lugged home?

Because we love our local shops, but realise that they cannot quite meet all our needs, we do the boring stuff on the internet. Once a month, we order vast amounts of Andrex, floor cleaner, j-cloths, washing-up liquid, lightbulbs, dustbin bags, and all the other uninteresting but necessary stuff, and a helpful man with a van brings it to our door. For the rest of it, we really do go to our fishmonger, butcher, and grocer, where we get a nice chat and a slightly holy feeling of supporting local businesses.

It doesn't work for everyone. But it's something to consider.

DEBT.

Everyone knows what you should do – incomings must be higher than outgoings, write everything down in a little book, go to the comparison websites, blah blah blah.

If you have serious debt on several credit cards and seem entirely powerless to stop shopping for things you clearly do not need, and wake up shouting at 5am because you have no idea how you are going to dig your way out of the deep black hole, there is a real danger that you are using shopping as an analgesic, and you might want to stop and work out what ancient pain it is you are trying to buy your way out of.

On the other hand, you may be a demonic filler-in of spreadsheets and have your budget fixed and pristine and immutable, in which case we absolutely salute you, through faintly gritted teeth.

If you are, like us, somewhere in the middle, your finances are a bit of a muddle, but not fatal, then we think you should stop beating yourself up for not being perfect. Too much debt is horrible, exhausting and debilitating. It eats up your mental energy like almost nothing else. Living on tick and damning the consequences is not glamorous and carefree. but eventually disabling. On the other hand, sometimes it is wildly exciting to buy something gorgeous that you can't quite afford.

In the realm of ordinary objects which eat up money, there are some very easy ways to resist unnecessary spending without feeling that all joy in life is gone. You can take your own delicious sandwich to work instead of buying a plastic confection at inflated prices, carry your special blend of coffee in a Thermos rather than buying soupy cappuccino in a bucket, walk everywhere, join one of the swap websites which are springing up like dandelions. Everyone has their favourite parsimony. Personally, we are huge fans of the public library system, a sad neglected Cinderella of a service, whose budget is chipped away every year by unimaginative political operatives. Librarians are a miracle, in our eyes: not only do they encourage children to read and work with schools and do all kinds of wonderful things, but they will find you the most obscure out-of-print books, even if they have to get them delivered from the other end of the country. We adore books, and have entire rooms lined with them, but since we have joined the local library we find that we no longer spend pointless money on books we will only ever read once, or give up on halfway through, or just find dull, but only actually pay for the books that we know we will go back to again and again, and want to see on our bookshelves like old friends.

We have also stumbled on a little trick which works when we are suddenly overcome with the fierce acquisitive desire for random shopping. We go to our favourite sites on the internet – Amazon, or John Lewis (not glamorous but full of good stuff), or The White Company, or Plumo – and we buy like crazy, choosing anything we want without caution. But then, like wily *foxes*, we save our shopping basket without completing the credit card details. The shopping urge is mysteriously sated, even though we have not paid for anything. Then we go back 24 hours later and look at what we wanted so pressingly the day before. Almost always, we realise that we do not need any of those things at all, and feel vastly smug that we have just saved ourselves a hundred unnecessary pounds.

And if the worst comes to the worst, and you find yourself riddled with shopping guilt, gazing hopelessly at all the pointless objects cluttering up your shelves, you can always sell the entire contents of your house on eBay.

SHOPPING STYLES.

The way you shop, and what you like to shop for, are part of your self-definition. No one likes to admit this, because it sounds so frippery and lacking in moral depth, but unless you have run off to live in a commune, it is true.

There is a theory that the sexes divide on this according to ancient imperatives; evolutionary psychologists have floated the idea that the hunter-gatherer past explains why it is that when you send a man to the supermarket, he is likely to come back with everything except what was actually on your careful list: it is the equivalent of getting distracted by a wild boar, which he absolutely *must* chase. We are in the swampy ground of the massive generalisation now, but it does seem that men take much greater delight in going out and shopping for a single big item: a car, a humming stereo system, a state-of-the-art computer. This is their modern version of slaying the wildebeest and dragging it home. Women, whose job in those old cave days was to search and sift for herbs and vegetable matter, are much more likely to browse, to read the label, to discern between many similar products. This is why you see men getting impatient in shops, as the women touch and consider and ponder.

It is worth taking a moment to work out your own shopping nature, so that you can go with the grain instead of against it. You may adore practical shopping: we know some women who are never happier than when in a hardware store, with its shiny array of nails and hooks and hammers, or who actually take pleasure in visiting Costco for crates of washing powder and cut-price china. You may regard shopping as a solitary activity, where you can make your own decisions quickly and without any helpful suggestions. On the other hand, it might be your dream day out with your closest friends. Perhaps you are a planner, a maker of lists, or you prefer to buy more whimsically. You may have secret shopping loves: we, for instance, are never happier than when in a stationer's, and have an odd attraction to museum shops.

Once you know your own shopping preferences, you will never again say yes to an expedition that you know you will hate. You can proudly admit that you find no joy at all in spending an hour looking at shoes with four other people, and go quietly to search for Moleskine notebooks on your own. You also know, when the sky is dark and the news is unremittingly horrible and you have a pulling feeling of gloom, exactly where to go for a tiny fillip of comfort. We personally believe that nothing terribly bad can happen to us once we are in the bright walls of the shop at the National Portrait Gallery; three postcards of Rupert Brook are not going to solve all our problems, but carrying them away in a little paper bag gives us an odd sense of comfort.

Of course, *of course,* you are much, much more than the sum of what you shop for, but what and how you buy are a telling part of your character, and the more you know yourself, the more you will be freed from the stretched tentacles of ruthless advertisers, and the less money and time you will waste. Because of your ability to say no, you will be able to devote more of your good mind to, finally, getting round to reading the *Comédie Humaine.*

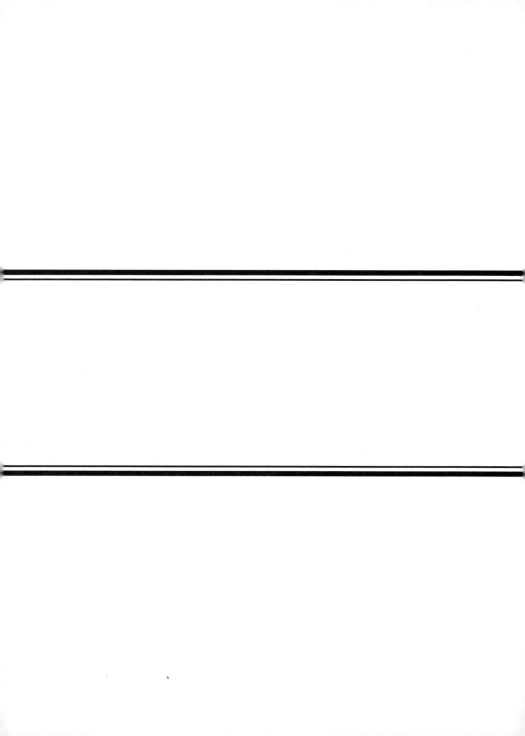

MOTHERHOOD AND FAMILY

—

CHAPTER NINE

Being a mother is quite possibly one of the most complex undertakings you will ever embark on. If you thought the Myth of Romantic Love was exhausting, wait until you encounter the Myth of Motherhood: even more demanding, only with less sex.

Modern motherhood is riddled with contradictions, confusion and, above all, clichés: the have-it-all generation, the too-posh-to-push, the ticking biological clock, the work-life balance. Women who have children can never just be *mothers*; there must always be a qualifier. Stay-at-home mothers, working mothers, full-time mothers (show us a mother who is part time, and we'll show you a pig with actual wings); earth mothers, alpha mothers, pushy mothers, single mothers, teenage mothers, geriatric mothers and, of course, the dread yummy mummies. (Whoever thought up that phrase should be taken out and shot.) Society sees all these women going about the business of raising children and, instead of delighting in the continuation of the human

race and expressing profound gratitude for this new generation of tax-payers, it goes out of its way to judge them. Mostly, they are found wanting.

THE THIN BLUE LINE: THE ANXIETY BEGINS.

According to the press release, pregnancy is one of the most special times in a woman's life, dreamy months of wafting around in empire-line tops and gazing doe-eyed at sleepsuits in Mothercare. In reality, technology and society have conspired to turn pregnancy into an exhausting and sometimes frightening period of scrutiny. Modern pregnancy, with all its guidelines and scans and statistics, is eked out in a succession of physical examinations – and, by implication, a series of potential failures.

With so much new-fangled machinery around, the medical profession finds it hard to resist the temptation to scan, monitor and generally poke and prod the foetus at every stage of its development. And yet, surely there is such a thing as too much information.

In our mothers' day, if you thought you might be pregnant you went to the doctor. A test was done. If positive, you then received a short lecture on the importance of not lifting heavy items before being instructed to go home and return in nine months' time. Barring obvious complications, pregnant women were mostly left alone to let nature take its course. Nowadays expectant mothers are treated as though they were suffering from a potentially fatal disease. This is understandable, since pregnancy tends to culminate in birth, one of nature's more perverse practical jokes and undoubtedly a risky undertaking. Nevertheless, things do seem to have got a little out of control. Blood tests, urine samples, physical examinations (internal and external), endless weighing and measuring and, of course, numerous scans now define the experience of pregnancy. Most babies can expect to be importuned at least four or five times during gestation, more if their mothers have engaged an expensive private obstetrician. Women are repeatedly warned during their first trimesters not to tell anyone the news, 'just in case'.

If there is a problem, it will most definitely not be the fault of medicine (we did all the tests, see) but almost entirely down to the fact of the mother not having eaten enough oily fish, or having eaten too *much* oily fish, or drinking the wrong kind of water, or dancing to the wrong kind of music, or whichever other fashionable theory happens to be doing the rounds. There is really only one thing a pregnant woman can be certain of: whatever she's doing, it's probably wrong, and sooner or later someone will publish a study to prove it.

There is much to thank science for, and we are by no means ungrateful; nor would we advocate a return to the nineteenth century, when maternal deaths totalled between 500 and 600 in every 100,000. But it is worth pointing out that, while the introduction of antibiotics in the 1930s slashed these grim statistics, earlier improvements were brought about principally by midwives, whose specialist expertise made them far better suited to the task of extracting babies from ladies than their more stuffy medical cousins, the doctors. The foremost expert on the subject, Irvine Loudon, a family doctor and distinguished medical historian whose 1992 book *Death in Childbirth* is considered a seminal work on the subject, writes, 'During the 1920s and early 1930s, the lowest rates [of maternal deaths] occurred in Scandinavia and the Netherlands, where well-trained midwives undertook the majority of deliveries. The highest rates occurred in the United States where midwives were despised, and most deliveries were undertaken by doctors.'

The scans are the most unnerving aspect of all this obstetric surveillance. All mothers feel a close connection with their baby in the womb, but the real bond is formed after it emerges. Now, women form relationships with babies when they are at the tadpole stage. They study their profiles ('Who does he look like, darling, me or you?'), they choose names ('Ooh, Charlie is kicking a lot today') and count their weird, alien-like, fingers and toes. If something does go wrong, you are not just losing a hypothetical, you are losing an actual tiny human, one whose ultrasound picture you may already be carrying around in your purse.

Surprisingly few of these tests can materially alter or improve the path of foetal development. Some of them seem more like an exercise in statistics-gathering than anything else. One little baby we know, who arrived very politely and punctually on her due date (most uncharacteristic, as it turned out), was pounced upon just hours after emerging from her mother's womb by medical professionals wanting her to have an MRI scan. She didn't need an MRI scan – there was nothing wrong with her; but the teaching hospital where she was born wanted to collect data on the brain activity of newborns delivered on their due date. Her mother, who had frankly had a bit of a time of it, acquiesced to this procedure through a fug of morphine and exhaustion, and so it was that just hours later she was standing in her slippers, watching her baby slide into the tunnel of an MRI scanner. A few years later, when the little creature was running around in a positive bloom of health, the mother underwent an MRI scan herself. She was absolutely horrified to discover that being inside that metal tube was not only fiercely claustrophobic but incredibly loud, full of frightening thudding noises. Had she known, she would never have submitted her baby to such an ordeal. Even now, she

wonders to what degree the horrid process might have scarred her daughter's tiny subconscious mind, all so that some hospital statisticians could collect new data.

We know women whose babies passed all their uterine tests with soaring colours only to be born with severe, unexplained disabilities, and women who lay awake at night fretting because their babies' legs were too short whose children are now the tallest in the class. At twenty weeks the doctors can tell you that your child might have Down's Syndrome, but it's not as if they can offer a cure. The most they can give you is a potentially fatal amniocentesis – and if that confirms their suspicions, the offer of a termination.

Of course, there are plenty of women who find all the technology reassuring; but there is no doubt that it contributes to the oppressive, even obsessive culture that defines Western childhood. From that first foetal viability scan (such a cold, inhuman piece of terminology) to a newborn's Apgar scores, to the age at which baby takes those first steps or utters that first word, your children's lives are measured out, test by test, and along the way so too is your ability as mothers. It shouldn't be a competition; but sometimes it feels like it.

THE GREAT CONSPIRACY OF SILENCE.

The unwritten rule of parenthood is that you never let on to non-parents what it's really like. This is particularly acute in the early stages, pregnancy and the pre-school years. This was once described by one sleep-deprived father as the great parental conspiracy of silence. It goes like this:

Your friend announces she is pregnant. You are, of course, delighted. You meet, for coffee (yours is a double espresso, since the children have been up all night), to talk about it. She wants to know everything, or so she says.

HERE'S WHAT YOU TELL HER:

1. It doesn't matter if she gets fat, the weight will drop off afterwards, especially if she breastfeeds.
2. The birth itself isn't that bad, and anyway your body is biologically programmed to forget the pain.
3. Breastfeeding can be a little tricky to start with, but in the end she'll get the hang of it.
4. You get used to not having as much sleep as you used to.
5. The experience of looking after a newborn can really bring two people together.

HERE'S WHAT YOU ACTUALLY *MEAN*:

1. Her stomach will never be the same again, not even if she goes to the gym every day (which she won't be able to because she won't have the time), breastfeeds until her child goes to university and observes a strict vegan diet.
2. The birth is quite terrifying, gas and air doesn't work like they say it does, having stitches is horrible, midwives don't always get it right, there will be more blood and bodily fluids than an episode of *CSI Miami*, and having half the world staring at your most intimate parts while you make noises like a demented pig is not, in any sense of the word, empowering.
3. Breastfeeding can be very hard indeed, you feel like a useless failure if you can't do it, you will almost certainly get mastitis (which is like the worst toothache you can imagine, only in your breast), old ladies will give

you horrid stares if you try to do it in public, breastfed babies do get colic, you may have curious and uncomfortable anxieties about being a prize heifer, you will leak in public, your nipples will feel like they've been sandpapered and your breasts, like your stomach, will never really recover.

4. You will go insane with sleep deprivation. You really will. Even the hardiest of military men were reduced to wrecks after three days of no sleep in Japanese prisoner of war camps, and you were not trained for this. There will be days when the very act of putting clothes on your shattered body will feel like a major achievement.

5. Once the initial euphoria has subsided, you and your partner will effectively become shift workers: when he's awake you will be dropping off to sleep, and vice versa. You will become resentful of his ability to leave the house in the morning, bound for the comparatively stressless world of work. In the back of your mind will be the sneaking suspicion that he is spending longer and longer in the office because he would almost rather be anywhere than at home sterilising bottles and dealing with a frazzled you and a wailing babe. Sex will be implausible, not so much because of the physical changes wrought by giving birth, but because you will both be spectacularly exhausted, and no one feels like having much sex when they're tired. And smelling slightly of sick.

That is one side of the story: the disruption and chaos. The other, often equally unexpected development is the degree to which you adore your baby. For many women, the love they feel for their child far and away surpasses anything they have ever experienced before. At first you don't really notice it – sure, this small pink bundle is adorable and absorbing, but you are still getting used to each other. And then somewhere around week three, quite possibly when you are dozing off at 4am, with this little milky person asleep by your side and the soothing sounds of the BBC

World Service drifting from the radio, it suddenly hits you, with the force of an oncoming train: you love this thing more than life itself.

This love is a new kind of love. It is, in the true sense of the word, unconditional. The media, society, other mothers with something to prove, like to hymn this great novel love as a tremendous nirvana, the deepest truth of the female heart. But paradoxically, it can be extremely frightening, not just for the mother, whose happiness now depends on this highly unstable bundle of new human flesh and blood, whose very sanity can feel as if it hinges on one tiny human continuing to *breathe*, but also for her partner. Adjusting from being the centre of a person's universe to being a distant satellite is never easy, especially if the ego involved is male.

All this is why you can't really tell your pregnant friend the truth. She doesn't yet understand the peculiar feeling of being hopelessly trapped and unspeakably elated at the same time – nor will she, until she's given birth. You have to let her experience it for herself, in her own way. Far better – and easier – to toe the party line. Which is: my child is an angel/genius/source of endless joy, I am deliriously happy being a mother, my partner and I have as much – if not possibly more – sex than before and no, of course we do not miss the lie-ins/foreign holidays/expensive consumer durables/actual freedom.

ADVICE, EXPERT OPINION AND WHY THEY'LL THROW THE WHOLE DAMN LIBRARY AT YOU IF YOU LET THEM.

Dr Spock, that lovable guru of childcare, was right: as a mother, you know more than you think you do. Oddly, there are plenty who would disagree. These are the individuals and organisations whose prescriptive and inflexible views on childcare have given rise to a culture where those who can do it by the book are loved and lauded; and where those who don't, or can't, are vilified and made to feel like rank failures. Both sides of the baby debate are guilty of this. On one side are the breastfeeding zealots, who advocate that any other form of nutrition is tantamount to feeding your baby Chinese takeaway. Ranged up against them are the disciplinarians who essentially treat newborns as an invading army to be subdued through the use of complex regimes and implausible scheduling. The battle is aided and abetted by the media, which sometimes seems to love nothing more than fanning the flames of parental paranoia.

We have only one thing to say on the subject: ignore them all and do the best you can. Children are not machines and motherhood is an inexact science. Trust your instincts and don't be too hard on yourself. Above all, do not make a habit of putting your child's needs ahead of your own: being too exhausted to speak – or even eat – is not going to help anyone. And besides, no one likes a martyr.

The only real duty you have is to stay as sane and as healthy as possible so that you can be there, with a clear head and a calm(ish) disposition, when your baby needs you. And if that means giving up breastfeeding, or having the baby in the bed with you, or using disposable nappies instead of the eco-friendly washable ones, then so be it. Whatever gets you through. After all, your job is to equip your offspring for life in the real world. And the real world, as everyone knows, is an imperfect place.

IT'S NOT ABOUT YOU, DEAR.

This is a difficult one. The modern generation of mature females has developed a strong belief in an individual sense of self. It's what our mothers were not allowed; it's what the liberated women of the 1970s fought so hard for, and you do not like to let them down. Many contemporary forty-somethings are ferociously independent, emotionally, sexually and financially go-getting; it's a matter of principle to decline to be backwards about coming forwards. Then along comes Baby. Motherhood is about many things, but it is not about the exploration of self. It can be hard when, at the age of thirty-five and after a lifetime spent essentially pleasing yourself, you are suddenly not the centre of anyone's attention any more, least of all your own. Those days of spending entire Sunday afternoons in a scented bath, or re-reading *The Sun Also Rises*, or making crucial adjustments to your hair are over. Suddenly, you find yourself packing into fifty seconds what used to take you at least half an hour to achieve. You learn, because you have to, to get dressed while at the same time making breakfast, helping a small person with their homework, doing the washing up and filling in a tax return.

THINGS YOU WOULD NEVER HAVE DREAMT OF DOING BEFORE YOU HAVE CHILDREN BUT WHICH NOW SEEM AS NATURAL AS BREATHING.

- Going to theme parks.
- Spending £7.50 (£7.50!) on a flashing Thomas the Tank Engine light stick.
- Sharing a lavatory cubicle with one, sometimes even two, other people.
- Holding someone's willy for them when they go for a pee.
- Eating cold fish fingers.
- Pretending to be a horse.
- Going to the beach in the rain. (It's raining. You're on holiday. What the hell else are you supposed to do?)
- Reading the same book over and over again every single night of the week.
- Saying any or all of the following: 'Eat up, there are starving children in Africa', 'Keep quiet in the back there, please', and 'If you don't stop doing that right now I'm telling your father.'
- Going to bed at 9.30pm. Alone. And sleeping in it.
- Calling your partner 'Daddy'. (And we don't mean in the Daddyo sense of the word.)
- Being insanely elated when someone gives you a small piece of kitchen roll with three stickers and a wonky felt-tip drawing on it for your birthday.

This is one of the reasons why, contrary to popular myth, mothers actually make fantastic, exemplary employees: they are focused, they respect a schedule (if you have to pick your child up from school at five, you damn well learn to have everything done by four), and they are demon multi-taskers. They become fiercely practical: lofty ideology gives way to a kind of raw pragmatism: a mother whose child is faint with hunger doesn't care whether the food has been genetically engineered by ICI or hand-grown by virgin nuns; they just want to get something into that little empty stomach.

This cultural adjustment can also create seismic shifts in your social life. Once you have children, friendships change and evolve. Some even get lost altogether. People you once loved and adored fall by the wayside. Childless friends without whom you could never have imagined a fruitful Saturday night's entertainment suddenly exhaust you. In turn, they may mourn the loss of their old mucker: *why* don't you want to go clubbing until 3am any more? Why can't you blow £500 on a wild weekend in Barcelona? You, meanwhile, are frustrated by their benign failure to comprehend what it means to rise at six after only three hours' sleep, or not to be able to afford so much as a new pair of sensible shoes. Gradually you stop seeing each other; then you stop calling each other. Before you know it communication is limited to the occasional email, Christmas card and guilt-ridden birthday wishes.

You should bear the above carefully in mind when selecting godparents and guardians. Choosing someone whom you either know won't (or can't) have children as a godparent for your child is an excellent idea from a number of perspectives (good disposable income, rigorous attention to the latest fashions, a high likelihood of tickets to the ballet), but you may have to make an effort to stay connected with them. Childless friends may be perfectly delighted to buy cashmere pants for your newborn, but it is unlikely that they will greet chapter and verse on little Molly's love of green beans or your struggle to get her into a good school with quite the same enthusiasm and empathy that a fellow mother might. Chances are they have refrained from having children of their own in the first place precisely because they wish to avoid such topics.

Don't be put off by your differences. Persist. These are some of the best friendships you will ever have. Having an active non-mummy friend is every actual mother's key to sanity. A resolute refusnik is a breath of fresh air when you are feeling irretrievably bogged down in nappies and homework and teenage tantrums. The fact that you still know someone who can at any given moment drop everything and open a bar on a beach in Mexico makes you feel young and free again in a way that a warm glass of wine at a PTA meeting just doesn't. It reintroduces keenly missed opportunities, and gives rise to vicarious fantasies which, while invariably a long way from the truth, provide some vital escapism. Having someone who doesn't connect you entirely with your offspring reminds you that you were once, and may yet be again, an individual – and not just someone's boring old mum.

TO WORK OR
NOT TO WORK.

For many women, work is not a choice, it is a necessity. It is not just the fact that few families these days can afford to exist on a single income, it is also that many women enjoy work, and do not view having children as an end to their professional existence.

Whatever the case, when it comes to mothers in paid employment, society is madly schizophrenic. Women are a vital part of the workforce, fully expected to pull their weight financially. Culturally and educationally, they are trained for full-scale equality – even if the pay gap between the sexes still hovers around the 25 per cent mark. On the other hand, mothers who go back to work are often felt to be neglecting their biological duty. It all adds up to a lot of confusion and misunderstanding.

Elect to give up work altogether, or even just take some time out, and there may well be a sharp intake of breath from friends and colleagues. From the feminist point of view, you are letting the side down. From the employer's point of view you have proved yourself a bad investment, something that, as a woman of child-bearing age, they always secretly suspected you might be. The perception, wrongly, is that you are somehow opting out.

In fact, mothers who make the transition from the office to the home are simply changing the location of their work. Bringing up the next generation is every bit as vital as working in the mainstream economy, and no less hard. Looking after a baby or a small child is like working for the most demanding, unreasonable and exhausting of bosses. As a mother, it is not just your job to keep them watered, fed, and out of harm's way, you are also expected to act as mentor, guide, educator, nurse, teacher and shrink. It requires almost infinite patience, guile and resourcefulness.

All that, and you don't even get paid. In fact, you are roundly penalised: if a woman is not making National Insurance contributions she is not filling her pension pot. In Britain alone, many women miss out on a full state pension because they have taken time out to raise their children, leading to frankly scandalous figures relating to women's poverty in old age, and a situation where the average female pension is half that of men.

If, once the children are at school, a woman decides to return to work, she will invariably have to do so at a far lower level, both in terms of status and pay, than her male peers, or those women who have not taken time away. It is hardly surprising that many choose to press on, taking minimum amounts of maternity leave and either paying through the nose for childcare, or relying on relatives for support.

This presents its own set of problems. On a purely practical level, the world of work isn't equipped for mothers. Very few workplaces provide crèches. Despite the internet, emails and instant messaging, and all the other technological paraphernalia, working hours remain stubbornly inflexible. And while legislation is in place to protect new mothers from losing their jobs, employers still find it possible to sideline women, either during pregnancy or while on maternity leave. True, the latter has been extended to enable women to take up to a year of absence after having a baby, but most of that leave will be on little or no pay. You now have the right to stay at home with your baby for longer; quite how you're expected to pay for the roof over your heads remains unclear.

On the subject of childcare, things are even madder. A working mother who employs full-time childcare is not only responsible for her child-carer's tax, National Insurance and an extra employer's tax, she also has to pay all this out of her net salary. Childcare – despite being a necessity for working mothers – is not tax deductible. Unlike, for example, company chauffeurs, which are considered a legitimate business expense. We have come a long way in the battle for equality, but while society thinks it is perfectly fine to have tax relief on *chauffeurs* but not on childminders, there is still a way to go.

Because of the impossible financial burden placed on working women, many simply pass that burden on, usually to other working women. Child-care providers are often paid cash-in-hand simply because their employers cannot afford to do otherwise, with the result that these already low-paid women are the ones most at risk of a pensionless old age.

All that, and we haven't even touched on the psychological and emotional pressures. Working mothers have been implicated in almost all of society's ills, from childhood obesity to antisocial behaviour. Ours has been cruelly branded the 'have it all generation', implying unprecedented levels of greed and selfishness. For the record, we would like to say that having it all is not what it's cracked up to be.

WHY THERE IS NO SUCH THING AS A GUILT-FREE WORKING MOTHER.

The guilt and incipient paranoia of the working mother is Wagnerian in scale. It stems, principally, from having to leave your child with someone else. This is especially bad if that someone else is on the payroll: it increases the guilt by roughly a factor of ten. Leaving a child with an unpaid minder, such as a grandmother or kindly aunt, feels so much more wholesome than leaving them with a childminder or in a crèche. This is clearly irrational, since a qualified carer is much less likely to a) indulge your child on a diet of sponge cake and Hula Hoops, b) indoctrinate it with all the prejudices it took years of therapy for you to expunge, or c) have its hair cut into an unattractive pudding-bowl shape without your permission. No matter: in your head, the very fact of your baby being cared for by a blood relative means that they are more likely to give your child love and affection that is genuine, and not bought and paid for.

Leaving your child with a virtual stranger is a very peculiar experience indeed. It doesn't matter how many references you check, or how glowing the qualifications, in the back of your mind will always be the sneaking suspicion that the shy twenty-six-year-old you have just taken on will turn out to be a lunatic, baby-shaking, sadist sociopath.

Newspaper stories about nightmare nannies and television programmes in which undercover journalists film tiny children being horribly treated don't help. You visualise your precious little one being locked in a playpen all day, while the person you are handing over half your salary to files her nails and gossips to her friends on the telephone. You worry that your strict nutritional instructions are being disregarded, and that your baby is being weaned on a diet of tinned hot-dogs and Fruit Shoots. When you get home at night, you scan the house for signs of abuse. Even the fact that your baby is clearly extremely happy and very well looked after doesn't reassure you: there has to be something wrong, you know it in your water.

As the children get older, learn to speak, and start to express their affection for their carer, a new type of paranoia creeps into your bones. Do they love her (or him) more than me? Do they have more fun with her? Why, when sleepy at the end of a rigorous day's play, do they accidentally call you by her name? Are you losing them? Has it all been a terrible mistake? Will they be scarred for life when she hands in her resignation to go travelling with friends, or return to Australia, or get married, as all minders invariably do? It's a strange relationship, this one of mother to carer, and one that very few women are equipped for. It is only relatively recently that the concept of a nanny has ceased to be confined to the upper classes, and extended to the expanding middle class, where working mothers now provide substantial percentages of the family income. For many women, their inability to get to grips with the work/nanny conundrum can be instrumental in their decision to stop work altogether: they can feel a strong need to reassert their authority as mothers.

In fact, children are perfectly capable of telling the difference between their parents and their carers. Competition and jealousy between the two is not constructive or desirable. Open rivalry can be disastrous, akin to the uncertainties caused by divorce. If your child loves his or her carer, be happy for them. Unless you are a Cruella de Vil of a mother, there will be plenty of affection left over for you.

It's not just their children that working mothers feel guilty about; there is also such a thing as employee guilt. It goes like this: where once you would have happily dropped everything to fly to Vancouver for a conference, now you break out into a cold sweat at the very thought. It's not that you don't want to go – a couple of nights in a four-star hotel could be just what the doctor ordered. It's that you can't, see, because you need to spend the weekend making costumes for the school play, or fashioning a three-dimensional object out of clay, or baking cakes for the summer fête. You simply cannot give your employer the attention and dedication he or she is used to, and this is a worry. It worries you because if you won't do it, someone else will, someone who has no obligations or constraints, and that someone is going to get your promotion; and it worries you because it reminds you of the universal and unerring truth about working motherhood. Which is: no matter how hard you try, how many lists you make, how early you get up in the mornings, you can never please everyone all of the time. And you can never, ever, get to the bottom of your to-do list.

WORKING MOTHERS VERSUS NON-WORKING MOTHERS.

Call us paranoid, but we sometimes get the distinct impression that the biggest unresolved conflict in the world is not between Palestine and Israel but between working mothers and non-working mothers – or, as the latter often prefer to style themselves, 'full-time' mothers. This conflict is ludicrous: there is no such thing as a full-time mother, since the idea of a part-time mother is ludicrous. The idea that simply having enough money to be able to bring up a family without having to work somehow makes you superior to all those who don't is infuriating and vacuous. As is the idea that if you engineer yourself into a position where the work that you do is both financially and intellectually rewarding, you are somehow acting selfishly and not in the interests of your child.

The trickiest genus of stay-at-home mother is the highly educated and career orientated. She has given up a successful job, and doesn't she want you to know it. She is now dedicating herself 'full time' to her children because she believes that they deserve the best start in life (implication: yours are being neglected). The combination of a competitive spirit coupled with too much time on her hands and a strong need to validate her position makes her a force to be feared, especially in the school arena. While the working mother's children turn up at school dishevelled and with a lunchbox full of hastily prepared Marmite sandwiches, the child of the non-working mother is impeccably turned out and looking forward to tucking into her nutritionally balanced organic chicken and avocado wrap. The stay-at-home mum's child is never left sitting alone in the school office because her mother has got stuck in a meeting, or on a train. And when it comes to competitive thank-you notes, or best costume prizes, the working mum's child doesn't stand a chance. How can a hastily assembled loo-roll rocket compete with an exact-scale representation (in painted gesso) of St Paul's Cathedral?

The conflict is exacerbated by the fact that, secretly, mothers who work do feel their inadequacies keenly. Combining full-time jobs with children is not only stressful and exhausting, it also means less time spent on or with your babies. These are uncomfortable truths and impossible compromises. None of this would matter a whit were each side not so keen to prove their inherent superiority to the other. We've been on the websites, we've read the books and newspaper articles: we know what it's like out there. The amount of vitriol and resentment between the factions is quite astonishing. Where is the support, the love, the understanding that women are supposed to be famous for? Either some women are very good at hiding their true natures, or there are an awful lot of right-wing preachers from Texas out there posing as mums.

CHILDREN, AND YOUR RELATIONSHIP WITH YOUR PARTNER.

If your relationship is on rocky ground and you're looking for methods of shoring things up, do not, whatever you do, have a baby. It is not that having children together cannot be a wonderful and exciting adventure, it's that if there are problems, the birth of a child will only exacerbate them. Sort your differences out first, and only then, when you are absolutely certain of your commitment to each other, should you think about children.

The old-fashioned idea that you can somehow fix a crumbling marriage by having a child only works if by 'fix' you mean retreating into separate worlds, with only a joint mortgage to keep you under the same roof. Having children will test you in ways that you cannot begin to imagine. If you find the way your partner slurps the milk in his Rice Krispies slightly annoying, wait until you've been up all night with a colicky baby. A little innocuous milk-slurping can suddenly seem like reasonable grounds for homicide. Many separated couples say they can trace the real start of their troubles back to the birth of their second child. The parental/child ratio of two to one is much easier to cope with than the apparent parity of two versus two. Three versus two, especially if they happen to be under the age of five, and you've got a situation where the children unquestionably have the upper hand. Four restores parity, but not necessarily sanity. Five, and you are either so deranged you no longer care – or else you are attempting some kind of record, in which case we wish you the best of British luck.

The children themselves are unlikely to be the direct cause of difficulty – it's the domestic climate they engender. Extreme tiredness, financial difficulties, emotional pressures and the fact that being a parent is a 24-hours-a-day, seven-days-a-week, 365-days-a-year job can conspire to create tensions in even the most stable of couples. If one parent stays at home while the other goes out to work, a situation can arise where you begin to live parallel lives. Technically, you are both travelling in the same direction, but your cultural paths cross less and less. This can come as a cruel shock if you have always based your relationships on intellectual and sexual equality. A woman who has been brought up to get married, get pregnant and dedicate the rest of her life to her husband and children will have a far easier time adjusting to parenthood than someone whose entire emotional and cultural education has been geared to independence and self-expression. And since females conforming to the old stereotype are rarer than a taxi in a rainstorm, difficulties are bound to arise. Intellectually, we may all be post-feminists now, but as far as evolution is concerned we are still animals. And in the animal kingdom, it is the female that cares for the young (apart from seahorses, or something) while the male struts around doing the occasional bit of fighting and quite a lot of showing off. We are generalising, obviously, but you know what we mean.

Even in couples where both partners could effectively be described as alpha-types, this retrograde shake-down is very hard to resist. Except in rare or self-consciously forced cases, it is invariably the woman who takes on the bulk of the childcare. Sure, you will see plenty of men at the school gates, but the person organising the babysitter, dealing with the childminder, arranging play-dates and generally taking care of all the mundane yet vital aspects of parenthood is often, still, the mother.

In fairness, this is not because men are unwilling to do all this stuff. It is to do with the lioness that lurks within all mothers. Men love their children deeply, but they don't get it in quite the same feral, visceral way as women do. Mothers can be irrationally territorial, even within the home. The man is in danger of feeling sidelined and inadequate. If, every time he does the shopping, or gets the children dressed, or brushes your daughter's hair, he is judged to have done it wrong, in some small, imperceptible way that is only noticeable to you, he's going to do it less and less. And if when, on a Saturday afternoon, he proposes that he take the children while you have lunch with a friend you chastise him upon your return because the house is a mess and the cat hasn't been fed, you can hardly blame him for giving up and going to the cinema instead.

The thing to remember about men and babies is that both parties very much desire your love and attention. Inevitably, it's the man who got there first, which is why it is perfectly understandable that he feels a bit

miffed when suddenly all you care about is this little usurper who not only has the manners of a hog but is also infinitely more demanding than he would ever dare. Managing that situation, not just in the early years but as your family's needs and demands grow, is vitally important. And it is the key to keeping it all together.

NOT MOTHERS BUT FIGHTERS.

There are certain mysterious creatures who, despite coming fully equipped with fallopian tubes, decline to enter motherhood. (*Entering motherhood*: such a strange expression, when you get to thinking about it, as if Motherhood were a model village, twinned with Cagnes Sur Mer, winner of the Britain in Bloom competition three years in a row.) The newspapers are oddly fascinated with them, and periodically hunt them down and interview them about their controversial decision. The media never, *ever* asks a mother of four for the rationale behind *her* decision, because it is considered so natural, so expected, so much in the order of things, to need no explanation. In an even odder twist, the chosen subjects are always selected in a subliminal confirming bias: they are not the ones who have really sat down and examined their motives, the ones who have given it considered and serious thought. They are the ones who just didn't fancy it much, or didn't dwell on it, and then it was suddenly too late and now they must justify their barren state.

In a criminal disservice to autonomous women everywhere, the papers and magazines haul out these happenstance non-mothers, who say, listlessly, that it's awfully nice that they can still afford to go on holiday and wear smart clothes and do, you know, jobs without worrying about maternity leave. It is all madly unconvincing, and gives the same papers excuses to run terrifying statistics about monomaniacal career women who refuse to listen to their biological clocks until it is too late, punctuated by screaming headlines about *epidemics* of childlessness. And so the prejudice chugs on: the childless are selfish and unnatural and unfulfilled. How monstrously self-centred they are to prefer trips to the Isle of Capri to giving birth. But why is the act of procreation regarded as the ultimate act of self*lessness*? Surely it is all about the self, the propagation of *your* genes, *your* family tree; the production of a little mini-me: just *look* what I made. Surely the only truly selfless (if we are to see that very word as a measure of moral worth, which is in itself questionable) way to make a family is to go to China and rescue the little girl babies that they don't want there.

There is another kind of woman who decides not to breed, who has contemplated her choice from so many angles, and examined her grounds so comprehensively that she has practically drawn graphs. You rarely hear from her in the press, but this is what she thinks:

She believes that producing and loving an entire human being is arguably the most important, complex and demanding thing a woman can ever do. Of course companies must be run and government policy invented and black holes explained, but to have responsibility for a fragile human heart – ah, that, *that* is off the chart.

She does not decide not to have children because she does not love them, as people carelessly and idly assume; it is the precise opposite. It is exactly *because* she loves them that she knows that having them is not a thing to be taken lightly, just because of some random arrangement of biology, or a momentary longing in the belly. She respects small people. She is moved by their questing natures and their unsullied dreams and their unconstrained laughter. She finds them fascinating and contradictory and individual. She likes that they are so wholly themselves, lacking the self-consciousness that comes with adulthood. She is fascinated by their robust childish passions, their wild loves and hates, their imperious demands and their sudden, shocking vulnerability. She remembers keenly what it was to be a child herself, and knows how easily all those crazy enthusiasms and hopes of youth can get scarred and mashed by one crushing adult remark.

She accepts, because she has thought about it, the limits of her own nature. She knows that she does not have the patience for the endless repetitions of child-rearing; she has no interest in finger-painting or singing along. She may be essentially solitary, unable to tolerate too much noise and mess. She may fear herself too slapdash and impetuous to be confined by the routines of children. Conversely, she may love order and the expected too much to adapt to the mild and constant chaos of the early childhood years.

She may have darker, more secret fears. She has read *The Blank Slate*, she knows that it is not all nurture, but that nature too must have its say. What if she had a dull child? What if she produced a pedant or a bigot? Is she so confident in her own impartiality that she knows she will love it still? She imagines having to live with someone for twenty years who has *no sense of humour* and is not sure that she could fake it. She knows perfectly well that these thoughts are not worthy, and dares not say them in public, but she has seen those families where one child is clearly favoured over another, is loved more simply because it *is* more lovable, even though not one of the breeders will ever admit it. She has watched the older generation carefully cover up its dismay that it produced an estate agent when it wanted a poet. She has observed the pathos of a child who knows that it is a dark disappointment to its parents, or will never live up to its adored brother or sister. She might very well carry the ancient hurts of her own neglected or damaged or fucked-up childhood, and decide that she damn well is *not* going to do that to another human being.

For all of these reasons, she knows that if having a baby required a job application, she would fail at the first interview. She believes that being a mother is not a biological fact but a talent, and she does not have it. She refuses to do it just because convention requires it, because if she does not she will be branded aberrant and bolshie and definitively odd.

For all this careful thought, she is rewarded with remarks like: 'Well, you have a womb, you must use it.' What she wants to say, but mostly does not, because she is really quite polite is: 'I have a sodding *brain*, am I allowed to use that too?' She smiles courteously when she is told that she cannot really know the meaning of unconditional love until she has had a child. She generally does not say that she gets a little puzzled by the whole unconditional love jive. All mothers have it, apparently, and yet some of them seem to be bored or frustrated by their children, not really that interested in them; they smack them and make them wear stupid clothes and send them out on walks in the rain when the tiny little things would much rather be reading a book in a nice warm room. She would like to ask about this curious paradox, but she does not, because she does not wish to appear rude. What does she know, anyway? She is just the selfish freak who refuses to obey her biological imperative.

Actually, she *does* know something. She knows that motherhood is hard, demanding, unremitting work, with no salary or awards ceremonies or public acknowledgement. All women are assumed to be natural mothers simply because they have the physical equipment, as if all humans could one day wake up and decide to be astrophysicists merely because they have a frontal cortex. Because of this, the ones who do it well get no

praise, while the ones who do it badly get damned. She knows that a happy child is reward in itself, but she still thinks that the good mothers should get prizes.

She also knows that the whole working mother argument is the reddest of red herrings, and wishes that people would just stop. A person who should not keep a dog, let alone have a baby, is not that way because she does a job; the rotten mother who stays at home just has that much more time and opportunity to screw up her children completely. She knows too that the current good mother construct is an idiot artifice, some confused fantasy of devotion and domesticity and utter subsuming of self, and she thinks that it should stop being used as a club to smash perfectly nice women over the head with. Her theory is that the good (enough) mother is one who listens and appreciates and is not trying to prove anything; who does not lay out templates of perfection or run guilt trips or do parenting by prescription; who can laugh and apologise for her own, inevitable mistakes; who is confident and clever enough to let the children be free. When she sees one like that (in fact, she knows quite a lot just like that), she watches in admiration and wonder. She thinks, privately, with relief, that she herself made the exact right decision, whatever the biological determinists have to say about it. Sometimes, if she has had a little red wine, she becomes tearily grateful that the ones who do have the talent for it are out there, having the babies, so that she does not have to, and she thinks she really ought to send them a present.

THE ALTERNATIVE FAMILY.

If you do take the radical decision not to get married and have children, you will have some explaining to do. You can decide not to climb Annapurna because you do not like heights, you may choose not to learn the piano because you have clumsy fingers, you can decide not to become a particle physicist because you are absolutely no good with particles, and everyone nods their heads and talks knowingly of courses and horses. But, oh, decide not to make a family, and you are Freak Girl and that's an end to it.

People will give you strange looks and mutter behind their hands; the newspapers will write articles about how you are undermining the very Fabric of Society. You will quite often be told that you do not know your own mind, even though you have a degree from a fine university and several deep thoughts about the human condition: oh, people will say, breezily, you'll change your tune when you meet the right man. Change your own bloody tune is what we would really like to say, but of course we do not, because our mothers brought us up to have good manners.

If you are one of those who has chosen the path less travelled, we say: Welcome to the Freak Show. It can be a whole lot of fun. You can even revel a little in your own freakishness and celebrate the fact that you did not bow to convention and become just like everyone else. You may decide to regard your decision not to breed as a moral one: it's all very well all those people having the babies at the drop of a garter, but the little tykes are going to grow up and want cars and fridges and cheap aeroplane flights, and how about *those* carbon footprints? You can choose to see your refusal to mate as glamorous rather than sad. There is sadness in every life, however many children you have: because you have decided to stay alone does not mean that you will get more of it than those who move in a pack. We have said it before and we will say it again: just really fuck 'em if they can't take a joke. It's your life, and how you live it is no one's business but your very own.

And the lovely thing is that there is more than one way to make a family. You can make your very own fabulous unit with no more than: a great woman friend who understands your every emotion, a gay man who knows better than anyone what it is not to bow to societal expectation, a male friend you have never slept with and who loves you with no underlying sexual motive, a niece or nephew who can tell you all the things they dare not say to their parents, a couple of godchildren who do the same, a dog who will adore you with every atom of its doggy being, and a rare breed pig who unexpectedly has eleven piglets one summer morning. Admittedly that last one is slightly specific, and is not suitable for someone living in a third-floor flat in Bolton, but if you have a nice field and the time and a good supply of pig nuts, oh, the joy, the profound delight that piglets bring with their snuffly little noses and their delicate feet and their sudden babyish wrestling matches. You really can make a family with a little imagination, some care and attention, and a bit of Mum's sticky-back plastic. Just think of it as a *Blue Peter* of the heart. And the heavenly thing about your very own chosen family is that there will be no divorces, no one running off with the secretary, and no need to call in the lawyers to fight bitterly over access.

PUBLIC NOTIONS OF THE FAMILY.

The Family, as opposed to the family, is a mess of contradiction and warring expectation. It is utterly private: no one can really know what goes on once the doors are closed. At the same time, it is entirely public: politicians and newspaper columnists make statements about The Family almost hourly, as if there is some quota they have to fill. The health of The Family in the life of the nation is monitored closely, agonised and argued over, as if it is a recalcitrant patient with a slightly odd disease.

The Family is also a misty ideal, held up as the very thing that will save us all from perdition. It is as if there is some perfect genetically engineered family out there, and the policy-makers are desperate for it to be emulated up and down the land. On one level the family is just what it is, but in the political sense The Family teems with subtext. When someone from the hard Right talks of The Family, there is the suggestion of distaste for those who do not conform to the Waltons version of Ma and Pa and John-boy, a bat squeak of disapproval for single mothers and feckless dads. It seems mildly strange that the unreconstructed still like to blame single mothers for so many of the cracks in society, when the 1920s saw a huge number of fatherless children because of the First World War, and these were the same children who grew up and gave us our Finest Hour in the Second World War.

The family is also the home of the sweeping generalisation. Statistics on what are horribly termed *outcomes* for the children of broken homes are often trotted out as definitive proof that the nuclear family is the only good start in life. But there is little account taken of all the other factors that go into making a person: poverty, peer pressure, the nature of society itself, the galloping imperatives of a fast capitalist system, individual example. The children of a fraught miserable marriage, where two people are desperately sticking plasters over the cracks in order to keep the family together, will grow up thinking that is what a relationship is: that is their template. They are quite likely, when they are old enough, to go out and find one just like it.

The daughters of a single mother, who is working at three jobs just to buy them shoes, and who loves them madly, may easily grow up to believe that, with enough determination and confidence, a woman can do anything, against all the odds, and go out and live highly successful lives. Yet there is a strange pressing desire to write off everyone who does not fit into the currently accepted version. Any evidence which does not meet the vaunted paradigm is ignored: the family values stalwarts never mention the ten-year study by Professor Richard Lucas of 70,000 Britons, which concluded that those who never married showed the highest levels of happiness. No, no, because it is *The Family* which is the thing.

The family, like all dreamy ideals, can live up to its billing, and be a place of love and jokes and safety. A good one can be a refuge and a delight, but the problem with putting it on a pedestal is that all the ordinary, mildly dysfunctional, messy families feel that they are somehow failing. Quite frankly, with all the contradictory demands and convictions, we are amazed that the family survives at all. Yet it does. For all the alarms and warnings about its imminent breakdown, it is what most people choose. It's just that now they are doing it in slightly different ways than in the past. It might not always be mother and father and two tow-headed angels and a kitten, but somehow, with three wheels and a ball of twine, the family rattles on.

We think that, instead of laying down hard rules about the definitive way to make a family, people should celebrate it in all its forms. It should not be held up as some high ideal, a moral salvation, the very crucible of society. The family values crowd should admit the reality, with all its flaws. The family will not make everything magically all right; that is not its function. But when it is not driving you demented, it can make you feel happy and loved. It can give you the incomparable feeling of *belonging* to something. For good or bad, it is where you are from.

The psychologists, following the precepts of Donald Winnicott, talk about the 'good-enough mother', a lovely idea which gives you permission not to be perfect. We say that there is also the good-enough family, which has nothing to do with the version peddled by all the shouty newspapers and magazines, the stern politicians, the unrealistic misty movie depictions. The family categorically does *not* have to be the pristine building block for a utopian society. Sometimes there will be fights and misunderstandings; it may feel claustrophobic and dislocated. There will be frets about money and never enough time. These are just the daily realities of life, and not a catastrophic failure. As long as there is affection and understanding, a little compromise, some good jokes, and a sense that you are all in it together, then that really is Good Enough.

THE CURSE OF THE PERFECT FAMILY.

You see them everywhere, most especially in upmarket clothing catalogues. There they are, the perfect family, running down a golden beach, dressed in cashmere, with pink cheeks and bright eyes. Everyone has fabulous hair. You just know that those cute little children always eat their broccoli and do their homework on time and go to bed when they are told. The glorious carefree parents are clearly not in a panic about

finding a good local school or worried that they never have sex any more. The puppy (there is *always* a puppy) does not pee on the carpet or eat the chair legs but gambols about being adorable and perfectly trained. Quite frankly, you might as well just give up now, because you will never, ever reach that pitch of perfection.

The famous do not help. Celebrity mothers love to give interviews about how they never understood anything in life until they gave birth. Having a child, making a family, instantly and miraculously resets all their priorities, shows them the true meaning of love, and gives them some transcendental sense of wisdom, as if the mere fact of giving birth turns them into a cross between Saint Theresa of Avila and the Dalai Lama. There is never any mention of colic, or mastitis, or the sheer raw panic that normal mothers feel when a very small new person will simply not stop crying. You hear nothing about painful stitches or forty-hour labours. There is not a whisper about the fact that it does not matter how many books you read, nothing really prepares you for producing an entire human being whom you have never met before. The mere fact that you are a woman is supposed to equip you perfectly for becoming a mother. It's instinct, surely; it's natural; it's what you were programmed for. According to the famous women, it is the moment when your deepest, most wonderful sense of being female is utterly fulfilled.

What is very interesting about the celebrity mothers is that, for all their talk of seeing the world through new eyes and finally understanding what is *really* important, the first thing they do in the months after giving birth is get back into shape, often using extreme methods – cabbage soup diets, bootcamp personal trainers, convoluted machines to wrangle the body back to screen-worthiness – buy some expensive childcare, and go back to work. So much for transcendence.

The only celebrity mother we can think of who did change her priorities was Demi Moore, who gave up her career entirely for several years and disappeared to the backwaters of Idaho to raise her three girls. The fascinating thing about this is that it is not at all what she is famous for. Her reputation is of thrusting ambition: 'Gimme Moore' is what the papers delight in calling her, because she dared to assert herself in her professional life. Articles about her now concentrate almost entirely on her appearance, which *of course* she must have had surgically altered in order to keep her handsome young husband interested. No one seems to care that she put her money where her mouth was and sacrificed worldly success for the sake of her children. They are much more interested in whether she had a knee-lift. Yet the celebrity mothers who play the It Changed my Life card shamelessly, while changing nothing, only have to appear occasionally in public with a small blonde child on their hip for everyone to fall for it. We think this is very peculiar. And also extremely unfair to lovely Demi.

Oh, and just in case you are tempted to fall for the celebrity mother transcendence jive, remember that while they are discovering the deepest truth about the meaning of love, they have *squads* of help. They have expensive cohorts of nannies, housekeepers, assistants, chefs, cleaners, secretaries and personal trainers. No wonder they can retire to a corner and transcend.

The perfect family does occasionally manifest itself in real life. The husband seems happy to help with the housework, the mother manages to run a thriving business while also making drop scones for Saturday tea, the children play the violin and speak Mandarin. The house is a Wonderland of Cath Kidston prints and cashmere throws. The annual holiday is a joyous trip to Cornwall, where the sun always shines and everyone has gleaming buckets and spades and builds perfect sandcastles. Just a single day in their company can make you feel like jumping off a high building.

When assailed by the perfect family, it is very important to keep in mind the example of the swan. It sails serenely across the surface of the river, as if it does not have a care in the world. It seems to know that it is protected by Her Majesty the Queen. But underneath the water, its little ungainly legs are paddling very, very fast.

Even to achieve an appearance of the ideal family takes a huge amount of manic paddling. It may look swan-like from the outside, but it can come from a neurotic perfectionism. It is quite likely that the creators of a picture-book family are suffering from a deep inner sense of inadequacy. What are they trying to prove, after all? It may easily be that they look at more chaotic families, where the puppy does in fact chew the sofa, and the children spend more time making a mess than mastering pure Castilian, and there are sticky handprints on the furniture, with a sense of absolute envy. The perfect families might wish that they had the confidence to let things slide occasionally, but they cannot do this, because then everything will disappear into a mess of chaos.

Of course, they might just, freakishly, *be* perfect, and entirely happy, bizarrely untouched by the travails of lesser mortals. In which case, you are going to have to be very brave about it. But chances are that they might not. So it is just as well not to take any appearance of absolute perfection at face value.

YOUR OWN MOTHER.

We have a theory that for any woman over forty, her relationship with her mother is more complicated than at any other time in recent history. Admittedly, the poor flappers had a hard time of it with their stern Edwardian parents, but we are staunch in our notion.

The parents of modern forty-somethings were born in or just after the war. This was a generation that was raised on duty and sacrifice and societal rules that were mostly unquestioned, except by a few naughty artists who hung around with Augustus John. The teenager had not been invented: women went straight from the schoolroom to the marriage bed. Children were seen and not heard. Homosexuality was illegal. Divorce was rare and utterly stigmatised: divorcées were not allowed into the Royal Enclosure at Ascot, presumably because the Red Badge of Shame would clash with their frocks. Unwed mothers had to go into special homes, and were often forced to give their children up for adoption. The bowler hat was an everyday item of clothing, and respectable ladies did not leave the house without a pair of gloves.

It is hard now to imagine the shocking seismic shift caused by the second wave of feminism, the pill, and the invention of sex (some time around 1963). In some ways, all of these things now seem Whiggishly expected, the simple march of historical inevitability, but at the time it was a Galileo moment: some crazy chicks were actually insisting that the earth revolved around the sun. The debates which now rage around working mothers must seem utterly strange to the 1940s generation. For them, it was very simple. Working-class women went out to work, because they always had, and always would; the middle-class ladies ran the household and did enthusiastic things with the Girl Guides or Women's Institute; the upper-class girls, as usual, did whatever the hell they liked, as long as they eventually married a nice eligible fellow with a smart stately and a stable of corn-fed hunters. Women who went to Oxford were odd rarities known as blue-stockings; there were an eccentric few who became politicians or writers or scientists, but they were such a tiny number that they only emphasised how different from the pack they were.

We ourselves often forget how odd it is that we are the first women in our families to go to university. We have a suspicion that however much our mothers are proud of us, there is also a tiny subliminal element of bafflement lurking in their minds. So much radical social and technological change was packed into the years between the 1940s and 1970s that it is really a miracle that there is any communication or understanding to bridge the gap.

This is why you may carry the lurking assumption that your mother does not understand you. Almost certainly she does not. You take for granted an education that she could not have dreamed of, and may do jobs that in her day were the strict province of lettered gentlemen. You get to earn and manage your own money, and if you should choose to have a husband, you are not dependent on him. You can smoke in the street and fly off to the Rialto on a whim and swear like a navvy, if the inclination takes you. You can set up house without being married and no one will describe it as living in sin. When your children are born, your husband will be right there with you, instead of off somewhere smoking a fat cigar and putting in a quick call to his mistress. You regard orgasms as your inalienable right, whereas your mother was taught to lie back and think of England. She was instructed in the value of discretion and the stiff upper lip, while you can skip off to Hampstead and have a lovely time exploring your psyche with a sage old shrink.

Sometimes you may feel resentful about all the things your mother never told you, but it is important to understand that she could not

possibly prepare you for the strange new world in which you find yourself, because she had absolutely no conception of it. Her mother told her to be lady-like at all times, to defer to her husband on every salient point, not to bother her lovely head with money and politics and business, and to sit up straight. She could not magically transform herself into someone who could advise you on the tiger traps of serial monogamy, or the correct etiquette for condom use, or when to ask your boss for a pay rise. The best she could do was teach you how to make *soupe bonne femme* and always to write your thank-you letters on time. These are not negligible skills, but they are not quite enough. When you get the feeling that you are just making it up as you go along, you are. And this really is not your mother's fault.

Remember too that however much she loves you, there may be a certain wistful envy in her secret heart. You have freedoms that she was never allowed. So when she says the annoying things that mothers will say, about should you really wear so much black, or isn't it time you settled down, whenever she starts a sentence with In My Day, just take a deep breath and remember all the great fortune you have to be living in a time of emancipation, educated up to your eyeballs, and, for all the confusions of the modern world, free.

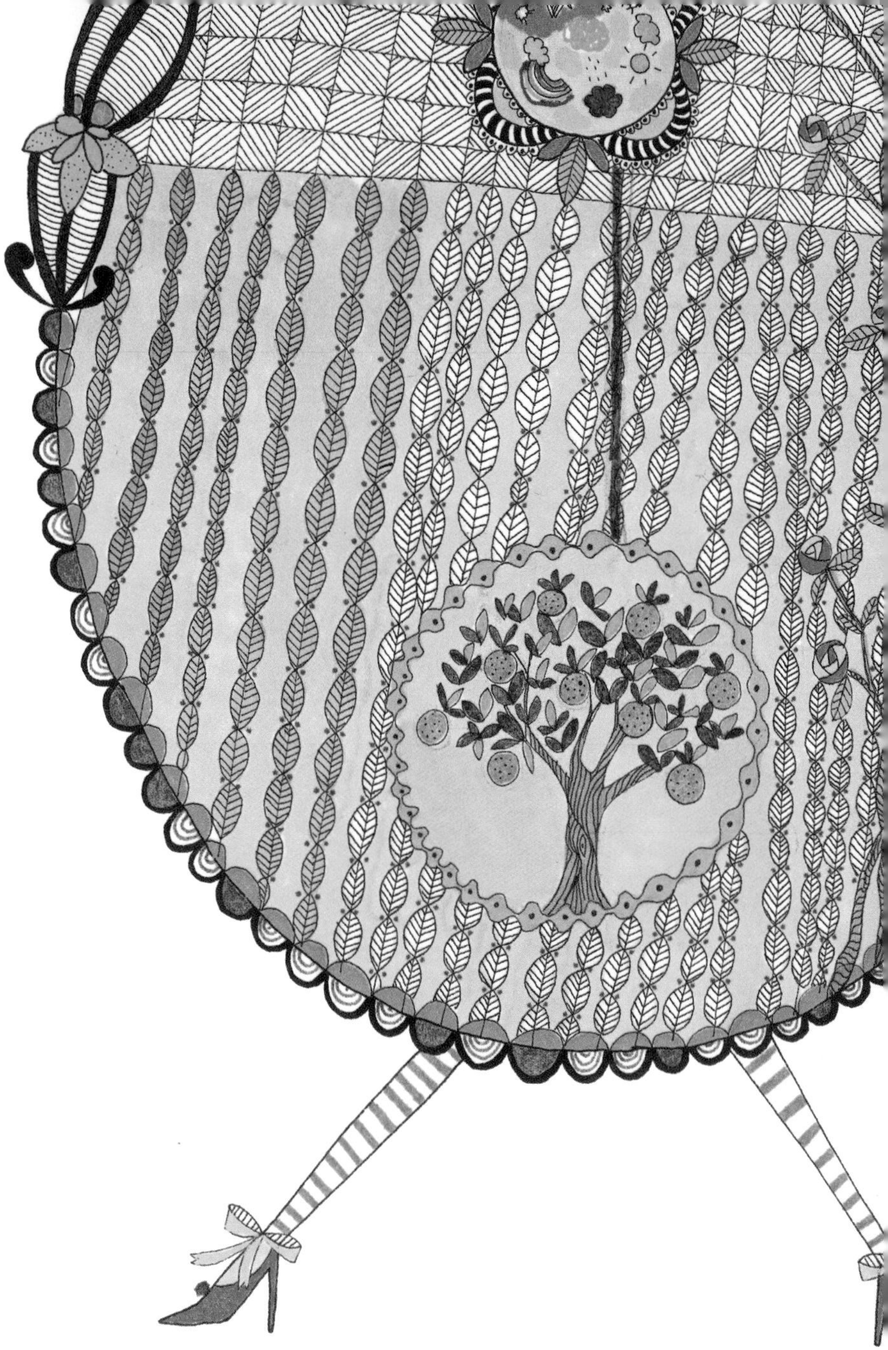

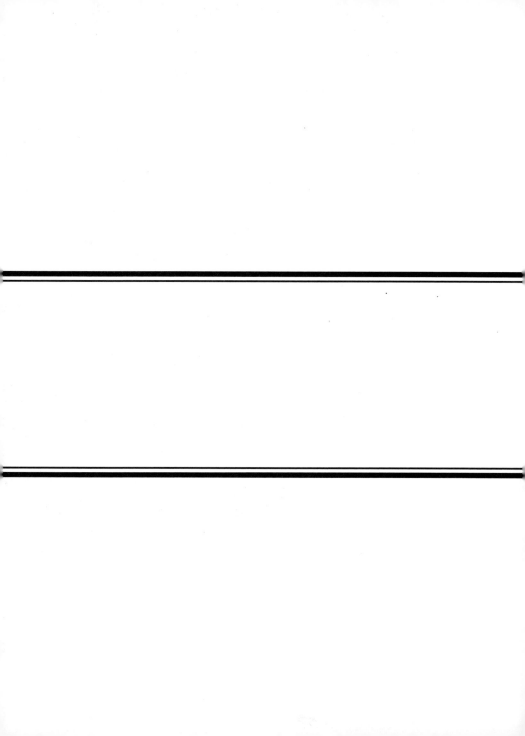

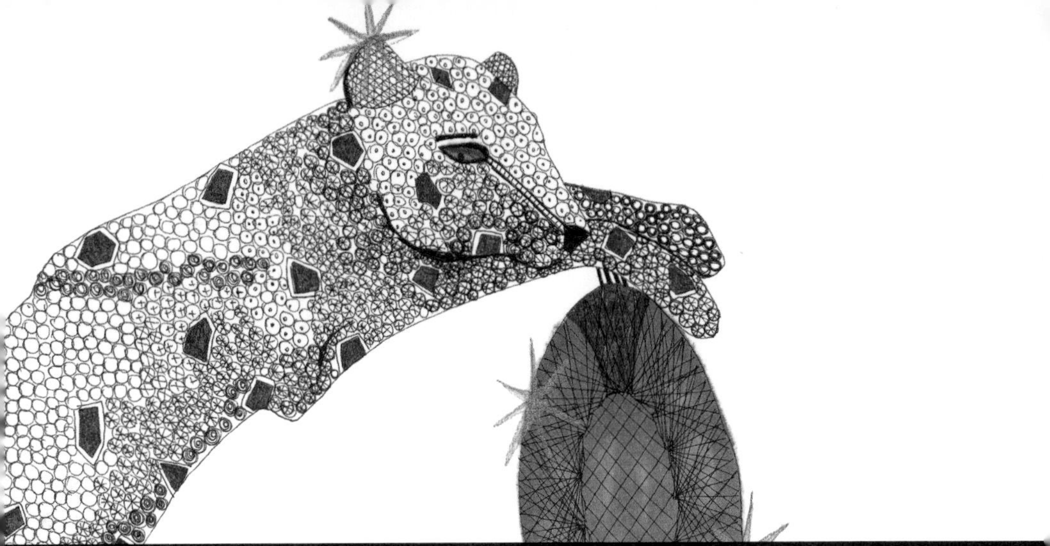

MONEY

–

CHAPTER TEN

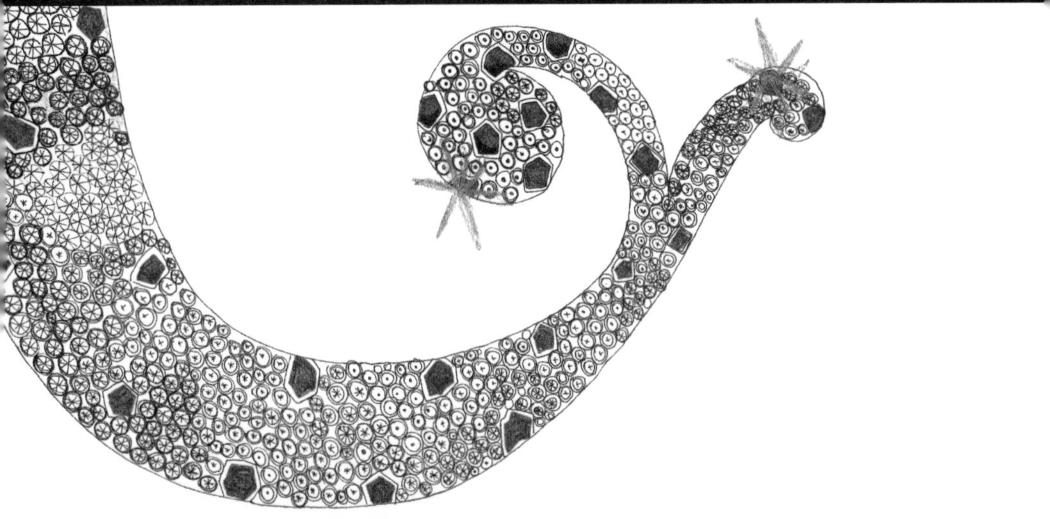

THE IDEA OF MONEY.

Even the *word*. We can feel you yawning; your eyes are skating over the page. You have suddenly remembered a pressing appointment. You are overcome with a powerful urge to do something quite else, perhaps move to Ulan Bator, where barter is still in operation and you can ride over the plains on those enchantingly stocky Mongolian ponies.

But once you really think about it, money is curiously interesting. Not the bare fact of it, the mundane aspects of cheque books and credit cards, pensions and PEPs, but what it represents, the psychological and metaphorical ramifications of it. Of all the subjects we considered for this book, money has turned out to be the most paradoxical of all.

Talking about money is considered inexpressibly vulgar, yet everyone wants it. As a subject, money is regarded as beyond dull, yet one of our finest novelists actually wrote a book called it. The pursuit of money is assumed to be a debased activity, but many people yearn to be rich and famous, two words which go together like carriage and horse. One of the few groups left in society about whom it is permissible to be fabulously rude and prejudiced is the very rich, yet the dream of winning the lottery is enshrined in the national consciousness.

The old rich, with their many green acres and idiosyncratic leisure pursuits, are consigned, disdainfully, to the historical dustbin: toff is virtually a swearword. But the first thing any successful rock icon does is buy a stately and take up riding and shooting; Madonna, the queen of the dance floor, also became chatelaine of a fine country estate and shopped, just like the old landed gentry, in Holland and Holland.

The new rich, commonly categorised as crude and boorish, are considered beneath contempt, with their flash motors, their packs of helicopters, their adoring embrace of bling, and their compulsive habit of buying football clubs. Yet their idiosyncrasies are examined minutely in newspapers and magazines, their shopping sprees followed with fascination, their divorces reported as news stories. They are courted and fawned on by politicians of all parties.

For all its shabby reputation as boring, shallow and corrupting, money is endlessly desired. Books with blatant titles such as 'I can make you rich' race up the bestseller charts like greyhounds. The internet teems with charlatans who promise ways to make thousands of pounds for only five hours' work a week. In the wider arena of geo-politics, the pursuit of money is regarded, in oddly biblical terms, as absolutely the root of all evil. Money is blamed for Western governments' tendency to cosy up to nasty regimes in Uzbekistan (oil and gas), Saudi Arabia (oil), and Equatorial Guinea (oil and gas). Even after all the public outcry and government censure of the hideous Burmese Generals, Total, one of France's biggest companies, maintains massive investment in the Yadana gas project. Money keeps Washington very quiet about Chinese abuses of human rights, quite possibly on account of the fact that China owns a quarter of the American national debt.

But, true to its paradox, money is also regarded as the solution to the ills of the world: raise money to save Africa, donate to rescue tsunami victims, AIDS sufferers, those dying of malaria. Money will provide clean drinking water, inoculations to prevent disease, schools and hospitals where there are none. The minister for International Development is the single post in cabinet that the public has no cynicism towards: this is the department that can send cash across the world to deserving downtrodden peoples.

Even as traces of suspicion around unfettered capitalism persist, and an often well-founded scepticism towards corporate greed runs like a subterranean river through public discourse, there is an idea that it was money that contributed to the defeat of Communism. The benighted people of the Eastern bloc tore the wall down not just because they desperately wanted liberty: it was the bright lights of Western capitalism that caught their eye. They had the high ideal of being free to vote; on the ordinary human level, they also wanted to be free to shop. If you think that is a shallow interpretation, just imagine for a moment having to queue for bread and shoes; picture yourself standing in line for hours in the snow and bitter wind, only to reach an echoing store with empty shelves. Politics and courage pulled down the iron curtain, perhaps even the historical inevitability of an idea whose time has passed, but money played its part.

The other curious thing about money is that it is ubiquitous – everyone has to deal with it, consider it, use it – and yet it is the last taboo in an open society. If you think this is overstating the thing, picture yourself asking someone at dinner how much they earn. It is unthinkable. You can discuss their politics, their sexuality, their last divorce, even their religion, but if you ask about their money you have gone officially beyond the pale and risk never being asked out again.

Yet, contradiction on contradiction, money is bandied about in the media as never before: footballers' salaries, City bonuses, divorce settlements, pay rises, house prices, compensation deals – all are splayed across the headlines without shame. In private discourse, you would not dare demand to know someone's worth, but in the public square the rich lists have become an annual feature of reputable broadsheets, as inevitable and traditional as rain at Wimbledon and the Queen's birthday honours.

The final paradox is that money itself has no actual meaning. It is, literally, pieces of paper. It is an entirely human construct. By some arcane collective fiat, significance has been granted to flimsy pieces of paper with a picture of the Duke of Wellington on them. Intrinsically, money is nothing – sometimes now literally so, as you do not even need the piece of paper, but spend and receive your money through invisible electronic transactions: non-existent figures that you cannot see, flying through an ether you cannot imagine.

But because of the imposition of meaning on the meaningless, money has an extraordinary power to affect the emotions. It can make you feel physically sick, or it can make you feel free as a swift flying south for winter. It can make you ashamed, or proud; it can make you feel strong or weak. If you handle it well, it can make you feel organised and adult; if its management eludes you, it can make you feel childish and stupid. It can bore you or fascinate you. It can disgust you or tempt you. It can make corporeal human beings feel invisible. If you are poor in a society which concentrates on consumption, lack of money can make you appear not to exist: all those glossy ads, all the credit card offers and shiny brochures and tempting mail order catalogues, all the articles in the newspapers about hidden hotels and delicious organic foods and theatrical marvels, all the beauty pages and house and garden features – none of these is aimed

'OVER ALL HISTORY MONEY HAS OPPRESSED NEARLY ALL
PEOPLE IN ONE OF TWO WAYS: EITHER IT HAS BEEN
ABUNDANT AND VERY UNRELIABLE, OR RELIABLE AND
VERY SCARCE.'

J.K. Galbraith

at you. No one even wants to *sell* you anything. You are a ghost in a vast uncaring machine.

Yet money, such a base material, can translate into the transcendental. It was money that built the Sistine Chapel, St Paul's Cathedral, Blenheim Palace. Money commissioned the *Mona Lisa, Whistlejacket, Las Meninas*. It is money that will pay for your doctorate in metaphysics; only if you have enough money can you sit in your study like Montaigne and ponder the sublime. Money allows the physicists to attempt their theory of everything, and the Hubble telescope to look back into the origins of time itself. Yet money, which can turn on a sixpence with more celerity than a London cab, can also trash the sublime. There was something inscrutably demeaning about a Japanese collector paying $82 million for the luminous portrait of Dr Gachet in the gleaming halls of Christies on Park Avenue, before the impressionist bubble burst. It was not just the disparity of the impossible sum and the fact that Van Gogh sold only two paintings in his life and died in degrading poverty; it was as if that uncountable amount of raw cash had almost drained the beauty from the picture itself.

Money keeps the doors of the National Gallery open so that even the indigent can walk in and gaze at the arrayed genius for free, but it also spirits away masterpieces to secret vaults where they will only ever be seen by a single pair of affluent eyes.

Money: we don't understand a word of it.

FEAR OF MONEY.

Although we find money in the abstract fascinating, in all its contradictions and confusions, we must plainly admit that in a practical sense it can scare us witless. What we would really like is enough money so that we would never have to think about it again, but we have absolutely no idea how to achieve this, or even if it is achievable. We also have no idea how much money this mythical 'enough' would be.

Money has a nasty habit of simply disappearing. It does this in small unremarkable ways — a taxi, a visit to the cinema, something to eat, and all that cash you withdrew from the hole in the wall this morning is mysteriously gone. It also does it in a grand newsworthy manner, from the Wall Street crash of 1929 where investors were wiped out overnight and cast themselves in despair from high buildings, to Enron, almost eighty years later, where an entire Fortune 100 corporation, politically connected, restlessly global, simply disappeared as if in a conjurer's puff of smoke, and on to the present day, where the autumn of 2008 saw a succession of black Mondays, as markets tumbled around the world and venerable investment banks vanished overnight.

Money, for all its tough connotations, is curiously fragile. When people lined up in the street to remove their savings from Northern Rock in 2007, it was not so much because they understood that there was anything intrinsically wrong with the company, but more on account of a strange Chinese whisper effect which led people to believe there were nasty things in the woodshed. They literally wanted to take their money home and put it under the bed.

Money behaves in erratic and inexplicable ways. How is it that the actions of a dodgy mortgage broker going door to door in a trailer park in Tallahassee can have a direct effect on the lending rate of a bank in

Cologne? Why did the Asian tiger, roaring in triumph one moment, slink into its lair the next, never to be mentioned again? Does anyone really understand what actually happened on the Black Wednesday of 1992, when Britain famously *crashed* out of the ERM, as the papers liked to phrase it? *The Economist* could surely put it all in words of one syllable, but it does not quite add up to an explanation.

Money is like alchemy, a darkly improbable art. There is an element of the magical in the ways that stock markets suddenly, shockingly, fall – following each other like clicking dominoes from Tokyo through Wall Street to London. A silent voodoo runs through the traders, confidence falters, share prices collapse. It is no coincidence that when they rise again, it is always referred to as a recovery: the initial fall worked exactly like a mysterious disease, one of those viruses that no doctor can diagnose, except possibly lovely Hugh Laurie in *House*.

Powerful governments are not immune from these cryptic alchemical effects. The greatest superpower the world has ever seen has gone, under a Republican party supposed to be in favour of low spending and fiscal prudence, from a national surplus to a debt of *ten trillion dollars*. Ten trillion is on the very edge of comprehension. Like the quark, it is exceptionally hard for the human brain to conceptualise. Does anyone know how this happened? Could the Secretary of the Treasury offer any cogent explanation? Is it just a question of – a billion here, a billion there, pretty soon it adds up to real money?

Money might be less alarming if it was spoken about in ordinary language. But, despite the plucky bulwark of the Plain English Campaign, financial specialists seem determined to hedge it about with fustian and doublespeak, trotting out obscurantist terms that we suspect even they hardly understand. It is as if they have become so proprietary about money and how it works that if they let the laywoman in on the secret all their diabolic powers would mysteriously drain away. At random, here are a few of the most egregious: financial drag, chief rent (which, of course, is not actually rent), liquidity ratio, credit squeeze, trend growth, macroeconomic fundamentals, structured finance, stress scenario, deal flow. So many ugly words in one sentence; it is almost physical pain.

It is impossible for the uninitiated even to guess what 'workout consequences' are: possibly some kind of muscle strain from obsessive visits to the gym? Could 'sovereign investing' mean buying shares in our own dear Queen? One glossary kindly explains: 'Yield to Worst – the yield to maturity if the worst possible bond repayment takes place.' (Yes, yes, it's all perfectly clear now.) If you think we are just gathering together the worst examples of jargon to make our point cheaply, consider this from the august *Financial Times*, where the brightest fiscal minds go to work: 'Rating agencies play a crucial role in the securitisation process. By rating securitisation vehicles, these agencies determine prudential limitations based on data they receive from loan originators.' These journalists are the best of their generation, and *look* what they are doing to the language of Shakespeare and Milton. It is no wonder that even intelligent, well-informed people feel baffled and stupid when it comes to the workings of money.

Money is so capricious, so mercurial, that we have an idea that one day it will get fed up of being abused and misunderstood and will bugger off to somewhere more congenial and everyone will be left with empty bank accounts and have to eat grass. We have no scientific data to back up this theory; we just feel it in our bones.

So if you occasionally feel intimidated and puzzled and slightly panicked by money, and spend much of your time mentally beating yourself up for entertaining such foolish and childish emotions, we think that you might be more rational than you know.

HOW NOT TO BE FRIGHTENED OF MONEY.

Stock up on tinned goods like a Montana survivalist in case the global financial system goes into terminal meltdown. Get used to driving around in a pony and trap so that when peak oil happens you will remain unaffected. Read yourself stern lectures about how it's only numbers on a page and you are a grown-up, and really. Train yourself not to want anything. Learn to add up.

WOMEN AND MONEY.

There is a strangely persistent cultural expectation that somehow men are better at money than women. The obvious jobs to do with money – City trading, chartered accountancy, private equity – are still dominated by men; even the very jobs themselves carry a whiff of maleness, whether swaggering and aggressive, or meticulous and forensic. At the private level of savings and ISAs and pensions, there is a lingering hangover of 'Don't worry your pretty little head about it'. (Oh, our poor fluffy pink little heads, sometimes we think they might just *explode*.) There is some speculation that the reason women tend to have fewer savings than men is that even in this egalitarian age, there is still some subconscious Snow White expectation that a husband with a nice fat wallet will gallop up on a snorting white horse.

Historically, it is easy to see where this pattern comes from. Until relatively recently, married women were not allowed to own property, and any money they had went straight to their husbands, although we prefer to dwell on the fact that in the nineteenth century unmarried women were legally entitled to keep their own cash, and there was a happy band of spinster heiresses running around merrily in furs and jewels.

But mostly it was the men who controlled the cash, no question. And in many parts of the world, it still is: in India, women do two thirds of the work, earn one third of the money – and end up giving it all to their husbands anyway. Still, we don't quite understand where the idea comes from that this automatically means men will be *good* at it. We know many men who are dramatically useless with money, several of them in our own families. If men really were born with an innate financial brilliance, then Barings Bank would never have collapsed, national debt would not exist, hedge funds would not disappear overnight, and there would be no gentlemen going bankrupt. The pensions fiasco was presided over by Gordon Brown; the same man who mysteriously sold off large amounts of Britain's gold stocks when gold was trading at an all-time low. (And we thought it was only impoverished dowager duchesses who ended up having to flog off the family silver.) The scandal of the missing Iraqi billions was overseen by a male colonel in the American army, crates of shrink-wrapped dollar bills which simply disappeared, and for which he unapologetically kept no receipts. The *twelve billion pound* IT system for the NHS was such a massive failure that the man in charge of it, Richard Granger, had to resign in disgrace. The strange thing is that no one extrapolates from this that men are bad with money, although we would say there's some pretty compelling evidence right there.

There is some psychological speculation that money means different things to the sexes, that men are more likely to associate cash with power and status, while women tend to link it to love and care, for themselves as well as other people. In terms of investing, there is research to show that men take bigger risks and go on gut feeling, where women will take time to gather more information before taking a decision. (There is also a lovely American survey which showed that women investment managers beat their male counterparts by almost two whole percentage points in 2006. You go, sisters.)

A nice little cherry on the cash cake is the rumour that men feel emasculated by a woman who earns more than they do. If there is any truth in this, quite frankly we think that they should just butch up and get over it.

It may be true that women see money slightly differently than men do, but attitudes to money have as much to do with the way you were brought up, and your own nature – recklessly spendthrift, carefully precise, incurably generous – as sexual stereotypes and expectation. Your money is your own, and you deserve it, and there is nothing in your biology or evolutionary history that says you cannot deal with it just as well as the big old boys. Don't fall for the rumours. You really do not have to wait for your prince to come; you can buy your own white horse, and charge off into the sunset whenever you damn well feel like it.

WHY EVERY GIRL SHOULD HAVE A PREMIUM BOND.

Premium bonds are possibly the worst investment you can ever make, if you actually look at the possible returns. But they are a throwback to childhood, when a kind godmother would give you one for your birthday, and they are so quintessentially British, stitched into the fabric of national life, that there is something charming and comforting about them. And there is nothing like the thrill of the envelope in the post telling you that you have won fifty pounds. Tax free! They are absurd, but we can't help loving them.

ALTERNATIVE WAYS OF INVESTING.

The rainy day, the old age, the broken leg: everyone knows that they must sensibly and prudently invest some of their earnings for these dread eventualities. If you have the kind of mind that sees the stock market like a racecourse, with the traders as tic-tac men, and the brokers as bookies, investing can be a thrill. If you don't, it can feel like an entirely soulless imperative: putting your cash into companies you don't care much about, because you know you should.

Personally, we like the idea of investing some of your money into actual objects that you can love and cherish. After all, those chatty financial advisers like to talk of nothing more than 'diversifying your portfolio'. Why not diversify into something intrinsically lovely like an art deco brooch, or a Lartigue photograph, or a first edition of *For Whom the Bell Tolls*? You get the arching joy of the thing itself for as long as you can afford to keep it; when the day comes that you must cash it in, you can let it go gently, knowing that you had the privilege of it on your wall or lapel or shelf for a few years, and many people are never that lucky. If a miracle happens and you get a huge promotion or you have a number one hit song or invent a new way of harnessing wave power, you might never have to sell it at all.

And it's so much more fun than flimsy share certificates in multi-national conglomerates who are poisoning the groundwater, or refusing to sell drugs cheaply to developing nations or flogging attack helicopters to the Indonesian government.

WHY YOU SHOULD ONLY MARRY A HEDGE FUND MANAGER IF YOU REALLY, REALLY CANNOT LIVE WITHOUT HIM.

In the eighties, when people behaved inexplicably and did strange things with their hair, we spent a few weeks running around with a pack of futures guys. In those days, the futures market was the newest, shiniest, most out on the edge part of the entire financial system.

The futures guys were absolutely nuts. They dealt with such vast sums of money and took such crazed risks that they ran purely on adrenaline and testosterone. They worked insanely long hours, so that when they had any time off they treated it like a sybaritic version of *24*; packing a week's worth of pleasure into one day. They did not just order themselves a margarita, they ordered a *jug*. Conversation for them meant everyone shouting very fast all at the same time. They drove at high speed from one nightclub to the next, interspersing the manic shouting with sudden boyish practical jokes. They were funny and vulgar and generous and sprayed twenty-pound notes around like confetti, but in the end they were too exhausting for us, and we had to go home and read a book in a very quiet room.

The noughties version of the financial maverick is the hedge fund manager. No one really knows what hedge fund managers actually do, but everyone knows that they make startling amounts of money. They are secretive and very, very serious. One hedge fund guy, interviewed in the *Guardian* in 2006, stated: 'Obviously, one's personal life is very opportunity-driven.' We have absolutely *no* idea what this means, but it doesn't sound a huge amount of fun. He showed the interviewer a huge computer that calculates and performs all his investments for him; he just programs the thing. It is like the massive bank of computing machines that broke the Enigma codes at Bletchley, except solely devoted to making money. When asked what he would like most to buy with the money he makes, the object he most covets in the wide world, he said: 'There are certain military aircraft which are a very nice thing to have. A fighter plane is very nice. Some are not so expensive.'

So, let's get this straight. Here is a man who describes his private life as opportunity-driven, works fourteen-hour days while a computer the size of a room chugs away in the basement, and whose ultimate dream is not a chateau in the Loire or a Rothko or even a sleek Aston Martin V8, but a fighter jet. What the hell do you *do* with a military aeroplane? Fly about over Surrey pretending you are in *Top Gun*? Bring back those nutty futures guys, all is entirely forgiven.

Another hedge fund operative told a journalist from the *Observer* that the reason almost all hedge funds are run by men is that women are 'not logical and not good at making fast decisions'. One American fund manager described the feeling of bucking the market and making a killing: 'You're a genius, you've got a big dick, you're a superstar.' Another admitted: 'My very worth as a human being depended on my continually making money.' There's a poverty of language and imagination here that makes us yearn for a starving poet rather than a big swinging dick with a military aircraft in his garage.

We are certain that there are perfectly lovely hedge fund managers out there, who read Turgenev and dream of planting forests and like dogs. Well, nearly certain. But you might like to tread with care.

BROWN ENVELOPES: A PLAGUE ON ALL OUR HOUSES.

They land implacably on your doormat, pulling a low feeling of dread along with them. They have a vaguely recycled-looking air to them, with their grainy-brown texture, but you know there are rarely good intentions inside this little packet. Often they have a small window, with a tiny plastic window pane. Inside, your name is typed in ominous, official-looking letters on an ominous, official-looking piece of paper. It can only be bad news. A bill; a letter from the council; a notification of planning consent from your neighbour, whose intention it is to build a small tower block in his back yard; or, worst of all, a letter from the Inland Revenue. Either way, you can be sure of one thing: the arrival of a brown envelope means you will almost certainly have to fill in some wretched form, and very likely sign a cheque.

How you deal with this little brown devil is a pretty good measure of your overall approach to money. If you rip it open fearlessly, pausing for just a split second to scan the contents before calmly placing it in your in-tray, or briefcase, you are either an accountant or perhaps even an actual employee of the Inland Revenue. For the rest of us, the options vary from any or all of the following:

Put it straight in the bin. This is bad: the bailiffs are only moments away.

Put it in a pile, along with all the other brown envelopes. We've tried doing this, and all that happens is the buggers breed like rabbits. Before you know it you've got fifty strapping brown envelopes on your desk, and absolutely nowhere to put your nice cup of Fairtrade coffee.

Put it in a drawer. This is worse than the pile because the dark makes them breed even more. And you will definitely forget it's there, which is another shortcut to a visit from Messrs Grabbit and Runn.

Give it to someone else to open. This works surprisingly well, as long as that person is sensible and level-headed, and not someone who will stagger backwards, stare at you in horror before collapsing into rude laughter after revealing, hilariously, that the contents were not in fact a £12,000 tax bill but a circular from the vicar.

Forward it directly to your accountant. This worked very well for a while, until the accountant, baffled by the constant stream of unopened mail for someone else, bundled them all into one massive, hellish brown envelope, and sent the lot back. That was one memorable morning.

One of us, we won't say which, is rather ashamed to admit that she gets her partner to open all brown envelopes that arrive in her name. Yes, yes, we know, years of feminism and all that, but it really is a blessed relief. When they first got together, and they moved house, he uncovered her secret stash of unopened brown envelopes. It was so large that he thought she might have an actual mental illness relating to brown envelopes, a phobia – in the same way that some people have with spiders, or Hoovers. We tried to find out if there was such a thing as an official word for the fear of brown envelopes, and were astonished to discover that there isn't. There are, however, hundreds of perfectly inoffensive things that carry official phobias: fear of otters (Lutraphobia), fear of the colour purple (Porphyrophobia) and fear of flutes (Aulophobia – presumably you get this if you once dropped too much acid at a Jethro Tull concert); there's even something called Hippopotomonstrosesquippedaliophobia, which is a fear of long words, and very useful if you like playing Scrabble. No word for terror of brown envelopes, though. It's a definite oversight.

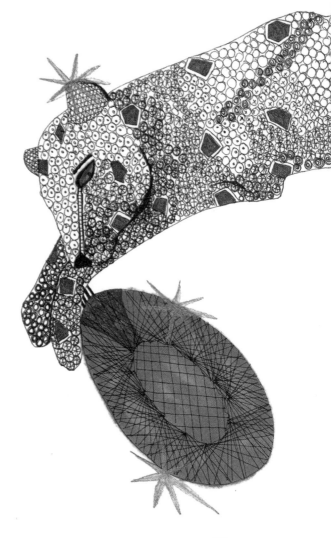

GRIEF

—

CHAPTER ELEVEN

THE TERROR OF GRIEF.

The crucial thing to remember about grief is that people are so
frightened of it – not only their own, but also that of other people.
They are afraid of saying the wrong thing, or just not knowing what to say
at all, because what *is* there to say, when tragedy strikes in its ruthless and
random way? Faced with someone deep in sorrow, a person can feel
entirely inadequate, futile and small. This is why anyone who has ever
suffered the sudden death of a loved one will report that people actually
cross the road to avoid them. This is not callousness, but fear.

There is something peculiarly British in this terror. The British are not
schooled in public mourning; they have no proud national history of
melancholy as the Russians do, or the intellectual fascination with existential
despair that the French embrace. They really do not, unlike some nations,
do ululation. The proliferation of confessional television shows and the
momentary hysteria over the death of the Princess of Wales have led the
media to suspect that the British have embraced a new tendency to Let It

All Hang Out, but in fact the old traditions of stoicism and stiff upper lip still die hard. When someone suffers a great loss and people say 'She's doing so well,' what they really mean is that she is not howling in the street. She is not making a *scene*. Admiration for the bereaved is strongest when she is putting a brave face on it: this admiration comes from both selflessness and selfishness; a gladness that the grief does not seem to be overpowering, but also a sense of relief. It is being dealt with: you do not have to reveal your own fear of being inadequate in the face of it.

The British way is still to shy away from strong emotion. There are no classes at school for grief. When children weep, they are instantly comforted: 'Don't cry,' they are told; 'It's all right. It will be all right.' Adults carry this memory with them, which is why they always say 'I'm fine,' when asked 'How are you?' They tend not to give the honest answer, which might be 'I'm falling apart, actually,' because there is no easy reply to that, and the ancient, ineradicable fear is that to tell the unvarnished truth might be either dull or vulgar, the two great British sins.

The alarm at other people's grief, and feelings of helplessness in the face of it, are compounded by the fears you carry about your own capacity to deal with sorrow. Because it is not spoken of in polite society, the manifestation of any deep grief can come as a terrible shock. Great loss, like great love, can feel like a form of madness. The world may become entirely meaningless, distanced, as if you are seeing it through an unbreakable pane of glass. You might be unable to make sense of the most ordinary things: newsreaders sound as if they are speaking a language you have never learnt, television is reduced to a jumble of meaningless pictures, shops become an assault of pointless objects. Usual daily tasks become as impossible and unknown as climbing a high mountain: you put coffee instead of washing powder in the machine, you literally forget how to clean your teeth, lacing your shoes may seem alien instead of automatic. Some people physically lose their sense of taste, so that food is like ashes in their mouth.

Sorrow affects everyone in different ways: there is no known, familiar template. Some women become obsessively organised, madly polishing and tidying and dusting, as if by asserting control over the home they can fight the feelings of randomness that loss may bring. Others feel that nothing has much meaning any more, and let their house and themselves go to hell: what is the point of doing the washing up or putting on lipstick when the loved one has gone? Some become manically busy, as if to keep the dark thoughts at bay; others may be unable to get out of bed.

Just as there is no common pattern, so there is no accepted timeline, although people like to act as if there is. Time does, miraculously, heal, or at least take the edge off, but it is not a straightforward process. There may be a day when you get out of bed and you can see the sun coming in through your window for the first time in weeks; you think you are coming back to life and the worst is over, and the very next day, you are back in the crushing darkness. This is natural, although it feels cruel and unusual.

It is not a matter of will. You cannot fight it, however strong-minded you are. The only thing to do with grief is to accept its mystery. Sometimes it is so overwhelming that it feels like an actual physical pain, as if someone has bashed you all over with a mallet. At this stage, it can induce feelings of panic: my body is too frail, it will break apart from the agony, it was not built for this. The panic is also to do with the suspicion that it will never end, that this irrefutable sensation has you now, and there is no way out. All we know for certain is that it *will* end. There truly is always a day when the light comes again. You might not be the same as you were before – you will bear the scars – but you can, finally, learn to carry them easily, even proudly, as the sign that you have loved. You can accept them as the marks that you are human.

THE HIERARCHY OF GRIEF.

Because grief is so random and formless, there is a natural human desire to try and codify it. People, whole societies, do this in different ways. There is the idea of the order of the components of grief: shock and denial, followed by anger, depression, and acceptance. This is how it goes: it can be mapped. There is also a desire to put some kind of time on it: you may grieve for a year, and then you must snap back to life. Some people regard grief almost as an illness: there is remedy, there is recovery.

The most obvious ordering attempt is to put grief into a hierarchical category of loss. It is generally considered much worse to lose someone young than an ageing parent, who has, as the ghastly expression goes, had a Good Innings. (So British, that, with its overtones of stoicism and its cricketing reference.) The loss of a child is considered the worst of all, and it probably is; it is almost beyond imagination. Conversely, the death of a grandparent is seen as the natural order and does not garner much sympathy beyond a cursory sorry. Deaths outside the family are considered much less painful than the loss of a brother or sister.

This strange sliding scale has elements of truth in it, and yet it is not necessarily helpful or right. Grief is not relative. If your grandmother was the one person in your family who truly understood you, believed in you, made you laugh, it will not make you feel any better that she slipped away peacefully in her sleep at the age of eighty-five. Her Good Innings is of absolutely no consolation. The very fact that she was around for such a long time means that the hole she leaves behind is that much bigger.

We know one woman whose grandmother was such a pivotal source of sanity that when that remarkable woman died she refused point blank to go to the funeral, on the grounds that if she never saw her buried then she couldn't really be dead. To this day, in her head, the old lady is alive and well and approaching her 100th birthday.

Montaigne was quite undone by the loss of a male friend: not a lover or sister or mother, but a mere friend. He said, of Étienne de La Boétie, that 'He alone had the privilege of my true portrait,' and eighteen years later, still mourned him. 'Since that day when I lost him … I merely drag wearily on.' In contrast, he accepted stoically the death of four of his five daughters in infancy 'without great sorrow'. To modern sensibilities, Montaigne's feelings seem peculiar and disproportionate: surely a daughter is worth more than a friend? This reaction shows how contemporary society judges and grades grief, as if there is some kind of correct assignment of sorrow to each level of bereavement. It sounds shocking when a divorced woman states that she wishes her husband had died, because then at least she would have had some kind of prescribed and accepted mourning. Her loss is way down the hierarchy of grief; no one is going to hold a funeral for her shattered dreams of infinite and enduring love, or bring flowers; people will hardly even make allowances. Yet a divorce can feel like a kind of death, even though the very word *divorce* is so commonplace as to be almost drained of meaning.

Some griefs are so far down the chain that they are considered vaguely comical. The death of a dog is usually greeted with varying degrees of incomprehension and phoney regret. Because, you know, it's only a dog, and you can get another one. Yet for someone who has

—

'GIVE SORROW WORDS; THE GRIEF THAT DOES NOT SPEAK, WHISPERS THE O'ER-FRAUGHT HEART AND BIDS IT BREAK.'

William Shakespeare

experienced the ragingly unconditional love that a dog gives, the faithful patient adoration, the unquestioning loyalty, that death can be like a hammer blow to the heart. But you must put on your brave face and get on with it, because it's just an animal, for God's sake, and they are killing the girl babies in China.

Ultimately, you cannot grade grief. It is mysterious and entirely personal to you. Do not let other people, no matter how well-meaning, tell you how you should be feeling. Loss is loss, and should be honoured.

CONSOLATIONS.

Are there any consolations in grief? There is a fashionable view among the self-help gurus that grief is somehow rewarding, that it opens up new depths in the human psyche, that to go through it forges you in steel and enables your true spirit to flower. The instinctive answer to this, when you are on the floor with a smashed-up heart and your head aches from crying and there is a hole where a person should be, is: you can stick your true spirit up your jacksy.

Philosophically, grief is part of what makes you human. Once you have truly felt it, you may develop greater sympathy and empathy with other people. It shows you that you have loved. It can even bring life into perspective, making you realise what is really important, leading you to seize the day and all those other easily mouthed homilies. The irony is that, although many of the books on bereavement emphasise this positive, even spiritual element of grief, Western society shies away from existential pain like a spooked horse. Doctors dole out pills like Smarties to people who are not clinically depressed but merely a bit down in the mouth, as if they can somehow medicalise sorrow. Why feel the pain when you can take a lovely tablet and all the bad things will go away?

It is easy to judge this: oh, the wimpish moderns, with their terror of anything that actually hurts. But when you are in great psychic pain, it is almost impossible to find any good in it. The pain is unbearable, and the natural human temptation is to make it go away, by any means necessary. People would think you certifiable if you insisted on suffering a chronic headache without recourse to Paracetamol, because the agony is good for you.

Emotional pain, when it is happening, just *is*. It has no point or lesson; it is not a parable. It can make you feel as if you are losing your reason. In its grip, you behave in irrational unfamiliar ways: you may become impatient, rude, restless, when you are usually kind and polite; you may sink into a dark silence where before you were garrulous. The only reason to let it run its course is not a moral one – it will not necessarily make you a better and more profound person – but a realistic one. If pain is dammed or denied, it has a bizarre and inevitable habit of getting you in the end. In subterranean cruel ways, it twists itself up and comes out in ulcers, or rage, or sudden clinical depression, where you cannot speak or eat or sleep. Its imperative is expression, and if thwarted, it will punish you.

The language of grief suggests that it is finite: you get *through* it. Time heals, people tell you, sagely, kindly. You will get better. Actually, you do not get through it: it gets through you, if you let it. If you allow it to roar through you like a river in full flood then one day the rains will stop, and the river will shrink to a slender brook. It will always be there, and in some ways it should be. There is something indecent in expecting great grief to disappear as if it has never been. It is not so much a question of getting better, healing, *recovering*, but more a matter of coming back to a kind of balance, where the shadow of the grief remains, but there is again joy and savour in life. You are no longer overwhelmed by loss and sadness, but can carry the marks of your sorrow on your heart lightly. They are an indelible part of you, the reminder of loves and dreams, but they no longer define every aspect of you. They find, in the end, their place.

Is this consolation? It is a thin gruel. It is only after the worst has passed, and you can look back with some sense of clarity, that you can even see the consolation. Yet you have survived, and that alone is a sort of miracle.

THE GRIEF OF OTHERS.

Seeing those you love in terrible pain can bring on profound feelings of helplessness, fear, even embarrassment. You, with all your knowledge of the world and your years of experience, can be rendered entirely inarticulate in the face of great loss. Grief, like the past, is a foreign country: they do things differently there. The strange thing is that even if you have gone through a similar pain yourself, you may not be able to remember it very clearly – what was it that you wanted or needed during that time? You suddenly cannot recall. Because grief takes the rational brain and pummels it into a primal state, the memories of a time of mourning can be clouded and muddled. And now you are faced with someone you love, in absolute agony, and you don't know what to do. What you want to do, more than anything, is take the hideous suffering away as a surgeon cuts out a tumour, and that, of course, is the one thing that is impossible.

There are books that offer you strict rules for what to do in this situation. In life, rather than on the page, there are no rules. Each occasion calls for a different set of skills and attitudes, because every individual responds to grief in different ways. The only crucial thing to remember is that all judgement must be suspended: there is no correct way to grieve, no right timespan, no empirically proved path to follow. There is no place for the word *should* in a time of profound sorrow.

There are those who are terrified of crying in public, afraid that once they start they will never stop. Some cannot bear to be touched. So in these cases, kind words and let's talk about it sympathy and generous hugs will not work. You have to act like the most advanced radar in the world, trying to sense from moment to moment what is needed. Perhaps it is a lack of nonsense, practical approach: the ones who are desperately trying to keep it together might need you to take over the cooking or clean the house or make telephone calls. If they are unable to talk, possibly the best way to express your sadness and sympathy and love is in a letter, maybe many letters, which they can read alone, where crying feels safe for them. Some people need to talk desperately, and the greatest gift you can give them is your mere presence: a quiet listener is their highest balm. Some will need to be held, like babies, because they are afraid that their very bodies might shake apart from the paroxysms of sorrow. Some need to be allowed to be angry, although anger can feel frightening and even incorrect: not considered the proper reaction. But there is often a raging and irrational fury in grief – at the dead person, for bloody well dying, at the world, at all those people walking the streets, still unheedingly alive, at gods or fate or whatever it is that orders this unfair universe.

Because grief has no ordnance survey map, and those in it can become radically changed, all your resources are called on, every last atom of empathy and courage and emotional wisdom. You will certainly make blunders. No one is perfect in the face of impossible loss. You will say the wrong thing, do too little or too much, misunderstand clouded cues. Try not to beat yourself up for this. The only important thing is that you are present. You can offer all the wisest words and the most practical help, you can recommend intelligent courses of action, draw on all your gathered resources, but really, the only thing that counts is that you are *there*.

REJECTION.

It might sound strange to put such a small daily occurrence as rejection in a chapter that deals with grief. Proper official grieving is reserved for the big things: death and destitution. But we think that there are other, lesser griefs that deserve to be honoured. Rejection strikes right at the core of the human psyche. When you are a child, you are very small and very helpless. As you grow, you develop your sense of self, which involves two basic feelings: a sense of power and a sense of significance. These are fragile and tentative, which is why, years later, the memory of humiliation at the hands of adults can still feel as sharp as that old serpent's tooth. You are trying your best to grow into an actual person, and there are these huge careless adults laughing at you; such easy mockery strikes at the foundation of the edifice you are staunchly building.

As you grow up, you learn to laugh at yourself, which removes much of the sting, as well as making you very good company. But the memory of those early blows remains, like a shadow moving below the surface, and it does not take much for it to be resurrected, and suddenly you feel like you are six years old again, and the grown-ups are laughing and scoffing. This is what is meant when people talk about 'pushing your buttons'. We can't quite decide whether this is a pointless platitude, or a very clever metaphor. Whichever it is, you have buttons, there for the pressing.

—

'BEWARE OF ALLOWING A TACTLESS WORD, A REBUTTAL, A REJECTION TO OBLITERATE THE WHOLE SKY.'

Confucius

There are some lucky individuals who have such a sturdy sense of self that they can take rejection easily, understanding that it is part of life, and that often it is not, in fact, personal — although uniquely personal in the sense that it is happening to them, they see that it springs from something deep in the other person, and so do not take it so much to heart. Optimists particularly deal well with rejection, seeing it as a challenge or a second chance, instead of the end of everything. If their great ground-smashing idea is cast aside, they simply regard it as an opportunity to come up with another, better one. The confident optimist will not make the errors that the rest of us frailer mortals are prone to: if a proposal or book or painting or brilliant new business plan is rejected, they know it simply for what it is — one project that did not fly. They do not regard it as a confirmation that they themselves are no good, and that they will never amount to anything, and what were they *thinking*, ever assuming otherwise? They are the ones who pick themselves up and dust themselves off and start all over again (they quite often sing this, gaily, in the shower in the morning).

For those, like us, who aspire to reach this state of mind, if we ponder hard enough, and scour the philosophers for clues, and remember to breathe, rejection is a less simple proposition. You might be able to rationalise it, intellectually: of course, *of course*, it is just a thing, part of the weft and warp of life's bloody rich tapestry, and there are worse things happening in Chad. But inside, where your irrational demons are having a glorious all-night party, it feels as if you are bleeding.

The ultimate and most famous rejection is the broken heart, the one that the poems and plays and songs are written of. But there are other less theatrical forms of rejection, which can hurt almost as much. Your best friend falls in love with a fabulous neurologist from California and runs off to live in Palo Alto and suddenly does not need you any more.

You try and be happy for her, of course you do, you are not a monster (you are *not* a monster) but there is an insistent childish voice in your head saying: what about me? You remember all the nights that you have sat up with her, drinking the red wine and playing the sad songs and listening to her and holding her hand, and now all that seems to count for nothing, just because she got a flash of some pretty blue eyes. The word *nothing* is used advisedly here. The sense of self is fragile, the search for significance is so fundamental, and even though you know that you should be able to generate it all on your own, occasionally you need your card stamped. You live in the world; human beings are social creatures, they cannot survive alone; the loves you have, the shared histories you build, are an essential part of the map of who you are. So when someone integral to you ceases to see you, it is as if you have disappeared. Of course this is not literally true, and your good mind will eventually understand this; you will retrench and rebuild; but even though there has not been a death in the family, there is still a loss, a gap, something you may allow yourself to mourn.

Professional rejection can also induce this sense of nothingness. Although there is the perennial trope that it is not personal, it's just business, what you do in the world of work carries a freight of self-definition. This is most acute in the area of the arts – a poem, a painting, a song, a novel, is an absolute expression of everything you believe and feel about yourself and the world. A savage review is the direct equivalent of someone walking up to you in the street and telling you that you are stupid and ugly.

But the blow of rejection is just as acute in the less artistic professions. A project involving spreadsheets and powerpoints does not carry the romantic associations of a sonnet; you are not John Donne; you are not pouring out your very soul. Yet think of the language people use when they talk of a big piece of work – 'I really threw myself into that', 'I put everything I had into it.' If it is trashed by a jealous colleague, or ignored by a thoughtless boss, or cast aside because the agenda has changed, it can feel as if a piece of you has been trampled.

This may seem entirely babyish and pathetic. For God's sake, butch up; it's only work. It's the race for the prize, if you have not got the bottle for it, get out and go into something less demanding, like raising sheep. (Although sheep too can break your heart, when your entire flock is wiped out by dropsy.) But in fact it is entirely explicable and to be expected. You are not a machine; you are prey to all the sorrows that flesh is heir to. You will certainly find the capacity to tough yourself up and paint that game face back on; you will put it behind you and begin again. But there is no reason not to allow yourself a small period of sadness for something that has been lost. Quite frankly, we are so sensitive that we sometimes get upset if someone refuses a dish we have lovingly prepared (what do you *mean*, you don't like lentils?).

The problem with the small griefs is that there is no accepted ceremony for them. Human beings are hard-wired to need ritual: this is why you solemnly perform a burial service when your niece's hamster has died. (We say goodbye to Bob, and hope that he has gone to some delightful hamster heaven, where there is plenty to eat and a nice wheel to play on.) All personal and professional rejection involves a crashing of hopes and dreams. A little attention should be paid. Only then can you again show your shining face to the world.

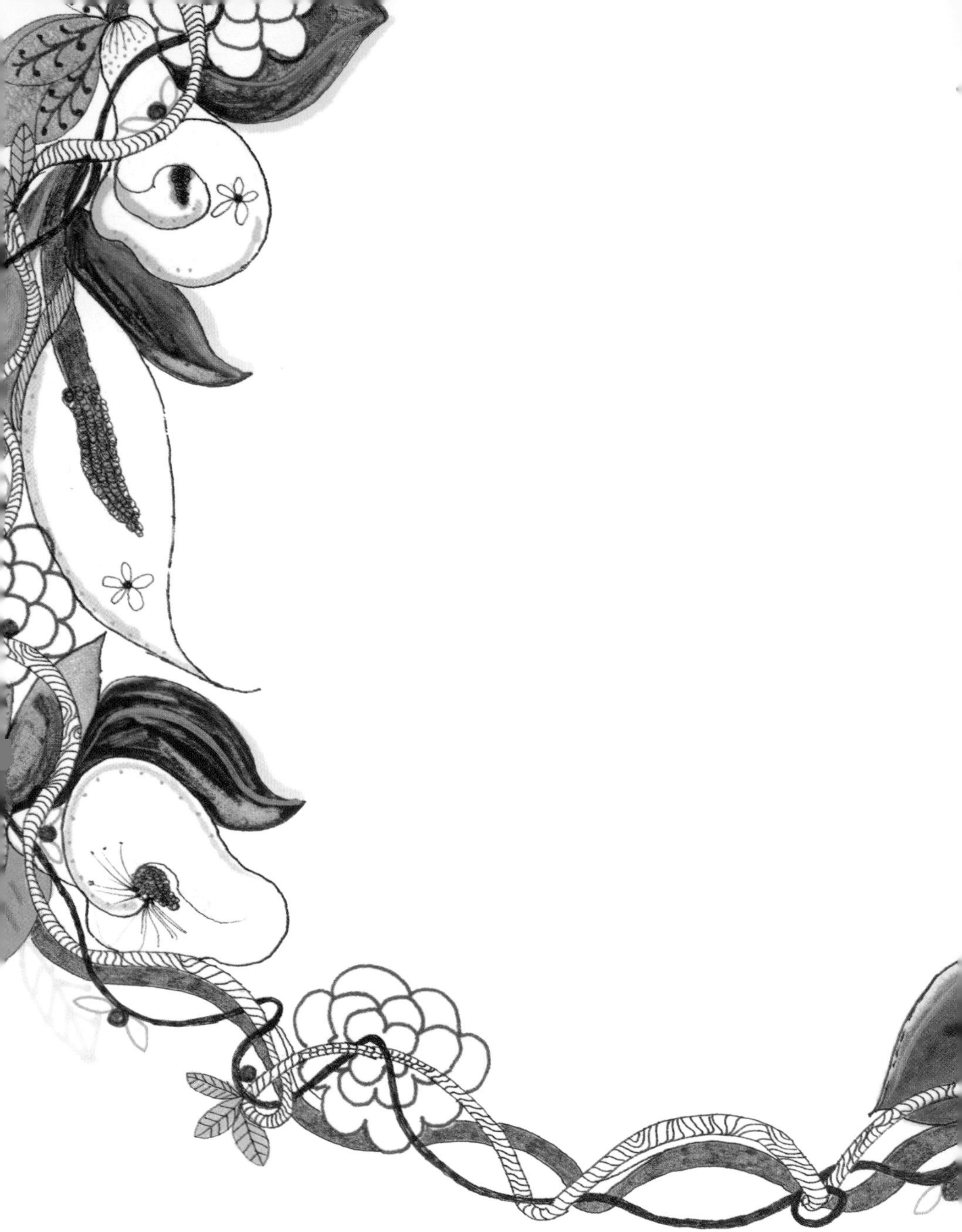

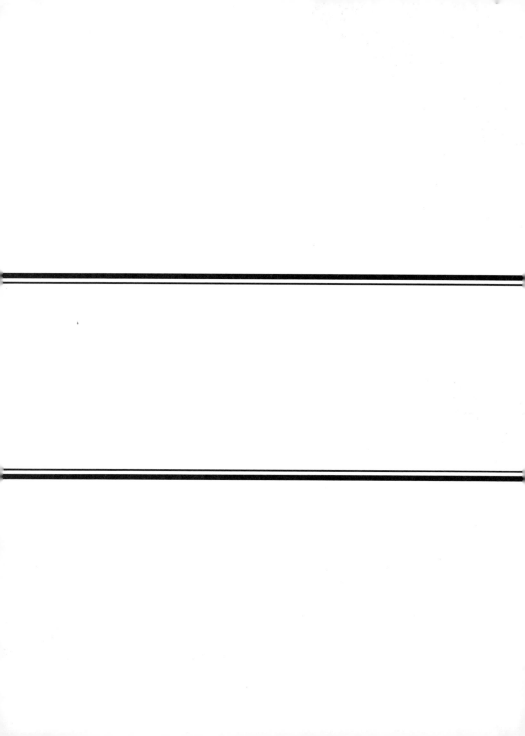

AGE

—

CHAPTER TWELVE

AGE.

The odd thing about age is that it is constantly obsessed over, in private, in public, in the magazines and newspapers, but once you get to thinking about it, it is not intrinsically interesting at all. The only people for whom age rightly fascinates are certain kinds of research scientists who want to find out why the body ages at all (not much biological advantage) and the true role of the free radical in the breakdown of cells. For the rest of us, all that newsprint is not saying much that is especially illuminating, or new.

Here is what happens: you get old. Then you die.

It does not matter how many wheatgrass shots you swig or hormone injections you pay for or facelifts you have, the absolute irrefutable fact of life, the only one that affects everyone the same, whether they believe in gods or the fires of hell or reincarnation or the celestial choir of the tooth fairy chorus, whether they are white or black, rich or poor, cruel or kind, is that they get old and then they die.

We say: get used to it. There are many things in life that are worth

> ## 'HOW PLEASANT IS THE DAY WHEN WE GIVE UP STRIVING TO BE YOUNG – OR SLENDER.'
>
> *William James*

worrying about. You can regulate your carbon footprint, be a better wife or friend or mother, you can make sure that you are in a job where your talents are used to their best and most shining advantage. These are pointful worries. Fretting about age has no point at all.

There are aspects about age that are unlovely. You may find yourself a little creaky in the morning, the good body prey to dull aches and pains; you might grow impatient, because life is flashing past you and time becomes more precious; the grumpy old woman in you wonders why it is that everyone has to be so damn loud and opinionated, especially on radio discussion programmes. If you have made the unforced error of marrying a very shallow man, you could wake up one ordinary Tuesday and discover that he has run off with someone half your age, in which case you should consider yourself well shot of him and go out and find someone who actually has more than an inch of emotional depth.

But there are aspects of getting older which are absolutely marvellous. You will have sifted through an awful lot of garbage and ephemera by now; you will have started to develop a keen sense of what is really important and what is, as a sharp businessman of our acquaintance puts it, just *noise*. You understand that Life is Too Short is more than a truism but a keen truth, and, wonderfully, you discover that it is far too fleeting for bores, bigots and the terminally self-involved. You stop going to impenetrable French films where nothing actually happens, just because you think it makes you look intellectual and continental, and happily

'I'M NOT INTERESTED IN AGE. PEOPLE WHO TELL ME THEIR AGE ARE SILLY. YOU ARE AS OLD AS YOU FEEL.'

Elizabeth Arden

embrace your love of flashy American thrillers. You discover, with a singing sense of relief, that your youthful fantasy of being all things to all people is an absolute waste of time and biologically implausible; you accept that you can only be some things to some people and rejoice in those things.

Most of all, you can stop apologising. You are what you are, and some people will love it, and others won't, and some will not get the point at all, but, wonderfully, that is *their* problem.

THE ABSOLUTELY LOVELY ABILITY THAT AGE BRINGS TO SAY NO.

When you are young, saying no can seem almost impossible. You want everyone to love you, you don't want to miss anything, you still hold the irrational belief that you can do everything and get away with it. Despite the arrogance that youth brings, you do not want to offend.

This is most acute in social situations. Think back to the times you said yes to deathly dull dinners or vapid parties just because someone asked: there was always the vain hope that something fabulous might happen: you could meet the man of your dreams or discover a solid gold networking opportunity or get taken off to Paris on a private jet by a gentleman with a broken accent. By the time you get to forty, you know perfectly well that none of these things ever actually happens, so you really might as well stay at home and watch a box set of *The West Wing*. You know that you hate big dances, would rather chew your own arm off than ever again go to a cocktail party where you will inevitably be trapped in a corner by the most overbearing person in the room, and can't stick dinners for more than six people. Knowing this, you do not have to contort yourself into acrobatic excuses about your sick grandmother or some fictitious deadline, you just, like dotty old Nancy Reagan, say: No.

You can do this at work, in much the same way. You are not going to take on that extra project or sit up going over papers until midnight or cover up for a hopeless colleague as you might have done when you were young and eager and even, possibly, foolish. You understand about priorities; you know that sometimes you must go home and have a rest and you know, see your children and talk to the dog. (One of the most successful men we know sometimes has a little sleep in the afternoon, something he would not have dared do ten years ago.)

You know that all that saying yes when you were younger, because you wanted people to love you and think you were helpful and amenable and generally charming and wonderful, did not necessarily achieve the desired results. Say yes too often and people take you for granted and trample all over you and do not have the faintest idea about all the sacrifices you have made. Sometimes it is the saying no that gets you the love and respect that you crave.

No becomes an easier word in more nebulous areas as well, from the most simple things – do you like green beans, to the most complicated: do you entertain the notion of an afterlife? Suddenly, never explain never apologise actually has meaning. You have had enough time to work out what you really think and believe, and you have the inner assurance to admit it freely in the marketplace and not embroider it with caveats and special pleadings. Do you believe in the Immaculate Conception? No. Do you want to have children? No. Could you ever entirely love a man who owns a Phil Collins album? No.

Do you like oysters? No. Would you like a subscription to *Wallpaper* magazine? No. Do you care what happens to Britney Spears? No.

See how wonderfully easy it is? This is what age does for you. So, you have to pay the price of a few wrinkles and a mild loss of skin tone. Take a step back and survey the wider picture, and suddenly you see that it is a price immensely worth paying.

THINGS YOU CAN DO AS YOU GET OLD.

- Never again have to go to the gym and do physical jerks while an idiot in a leotard shouts things like, 'Yeah, ladies, take it to the max!' or, 'Come on girls, feel where it's coming from!'
- Admit that you actually like going to bed at 9.30pm with a good book and a cup of Lapsang Souchong tea.
- Never have to sit at a bus stop in a very small skirt at 3am waiting for the N70.
- Never have to go to Glastonbury and share a lav with 100,000 stoned people.
- Always have a useful supply of stamps in your purse (older people always have stamps in their purse. It's the Law).
- Stop shopping in Topshop.
- Stop pretending that you like experimental dance.
- Take as long as you damn well need to pull out at junctions.
- Wear socks in bed.
- Stop making excuses.
- Keep the radio tuned permanently to Radio Four.
- Pretend selective deafness.

THE REASSURANCE OF KNOWING YOURSELF.

There is never a precise time when you absolutely and entirely know yourself. You are a work in progress and you and the world are in constant flux; you have the alluring human ability to believe at least seven contradictory things before breakfast. There is not going to be a eureka moment when you can stand back like an exhausted sculptor and gaze at what you have created and say: Yes, see, that's it. Which is just as well, because if you did you might simply collapse out of sheer boredom. But there is a definite sense, as you get older, of knowing more. There are certain things you no longer have to agonise over, because you really have worked them out in your mind.

You will have a greater sense of your own strengths and weaknesses, a growing conviction of autonomy, a fund of experience and memories. You might not know much about art, but you know what you like. Your tastes become more fully formed; your early warning radar becomes finely honed; your desires get sorted into a hierarchy of importance. This does not mean that you have to become didactic or pedantic, or let your beliefs harden into unreflective habits of thought. It does mean that you can save yourself enormous amounts of time and fret, because you are less likely to buy the wrong dress, marry the wrong man, wear shoes that hurt or affect opinions that are not your own in order to impress. Quite frankly, not having to worry about those alone is like a month in the country.

THE INVISIBILITY MYTH.

Here is what people – journalists, voices on the radio, cultural commentators, people in the street – insist is true about women and age: after a certain random number, you become *invisible*. This, like other idiot tropes (all women are on a permanent diet, all females hate their thighs, the XX chromosome induces an irrational yearning for footwear) has become embedded in the national consciousness. It is accompanied by some anecdotal piece of absolute proof, which always, for some inexplicable reason, takes the form of: the builders no longer whistle at me in the street.

Oh, the cruelty of those discerning builders. How can a mature woman carry on when large men in low-slung trousers no longer yell, 'Go on Darlin'', or 'Get 'em out', or the more pithy '*Whooar*'. The days of wine and roses are surely gone forever.

Let us give you an illuminating anecdote of our very own. Not so very long ago or far away, a woman we know celebrated her fortieth birthday in a large and elegant hotel, where a nice gentleman she had never met before took one look at her and proposed a wild night of unspeakable acts, to which she kindly assented. A week later, a twenty-five-year-old Australian screenwriter, who bore a gratifying resemblance to Hugh Dancy, all cheekbones and curling black hair, made her a similar offer, in an illegal basement dive somewhere in Soho. Although she had always had mild dreams of doing a little Mrs Robinson number, she decided that the fifteen-year gap was a little too much, and politely declined. This woman is not a wild beauty. She is a generous size 14, has not much jawline, no ankles to speak of, clouded little eyes, and dyes her hair out of a box in her own bathroom. Builders in fact have never whistled at her, even when she was in her pomp. But interestingly, she did not buy that invisibility myth for a single solitary second, and so, when the witching hour of forty hit, it seemed that she was more visible than ever.

In other words, there is a considerable possibility that this entire fallacy only exists in people's crazed heads. If you decide that age will wither you and stale your infinite variety, then chances are, it will. Men may sometimes seem a little dense, even insensitive; the best and brightest of them occasionally have to have the mysterious traces of the female sensibility spelt out in large clear letters. But what they do have is an acutely accurate internal radar, as finely honed as anything the NSA can muster: they can sense desperation at fifty paces. If you decide that invisibility is your fate, just because you read it in a newspaper, then gentlemen will pick up on that, and confirm your worst suspicions.

In yet other words, this is nothing to do with age itself, but all to do with your own perception of it. The lovely thing about this is it means that how you are perceived as you enter maturity is almost entirely your choice. You will no longer have the thick dewy skin of youth; gravity will take its toll on your body, pulling everything a little further towards the earth; the smiles and frowns of the last twenty years will leave their traces on your face. None of this makes any difference to whether you will be seen. If you hold yourself up proud and tall, and know that inside you are dancing, you can be as visible as you want to be.

The other oddity about the invisibility notion is that it assumes that the mark of a successful woman is that she is still perceived as a sexual object. The idea that as you hit your forties you become some neutered creature that men on scaffolds no longer sexually harass, and that this is a *bad* thing, is almost certainly tied up with some muddled thinking about the menopause. This profound hormonal change in the female body does not generally hit until fifty, but by the time you reach forty, it is not far off; you are moving along the sliding slope to infertility. There is also the comparison to male biology – those old sperm can still do their job, however creaking and crabbed the man; Charlie Chaplin was having children when he was in his seventies.

This has led to confusion: another unchallenged assumption is that men can be old and sexy, simply because they can go on being fecund. If you take a step back and actually compare famous people of similar age, you see how insane this idea is. Meryl Streep and Diane Keaton, deep into their post-menopausal years, are far more aesthetically pleasing than paunchy, balding Jack Nicholson. (We adore Jack, and won't have a word said against him, but he is definitely trading on past glories in the looks department.) Once you cast aside societal assumptions and view the world clearly, uncluttered by prejudice and raddled thinking, you will see that everywhere you look there are glorious, beautiful, sexual older women, revelling in their visibility.

It is easy to get po-faced about this, and make lists of attributes twenty times more important and enduring than sexual attraction. There is nothing wrong with wanting to be old *and* sexy; you just have to work a little harder at it. You can no longer rely on animal attraction and a certain carelessness in your dress. A good haircut and some delicious scent and a pot of wonderful face cream and an alluring lipstick will work wonders when you are past your heedless twenties. But more important still, and the only truly lasting secret of attraction, is the sense of being comfortable in your own skin – what the French call *bien dans sa peau*. Here, age is an actual advantage. Your collagen production might not be what it was, but by the time you are in your forties there is a high chance that you start to know who you are, and what it is you really want, and where your strengths lie: this will give you more radiance than any expensive cream. The growing confidence that comes with age can give you a sheen and a bloom that no cosmetics can approximate.

The builders, no judges of subtlety and nuance, may not be struck by this marvellous inner glow, but that is because they are programmed to whistle at women who look like Barbie. But as long as you believe in your own visibility, you may still be surprised by the occasional indecent offer.

THE PARADOX OF AGEING.

Ageing does bring confidence and a growing sense of self and a certain rash what the hell, but, oddly, at the *exact same time*, you can feel absolutely no different than you did when you were seventeen. You understand, in the good logical part of your mind, that this is not precisely the case. You really do know more than you did twenty-five years ago. You could sit down and make a detailed list of all the things you know now that you did not know then. It is literally so, but there are times when it does not feel so. The powerful irrational part of your brain is urgently telegraphing that all those things you have learnt are somehow irrelevant, or are no more than figments, or count for nothing: the truth is that you are just a crazy teenager masquerading as a grown-up.

It can sometimes seem that the defining feature of human beings is their bizarre ability to hold two opposing ideas at once. This aspect of ageing is a perfect example. You know that you have gained knowledge and wisdom and savvy and all those good things: you have the scars to show for it, because you have learnt the hard way (sometimes we wonder if there is any other way – does anyone ever say I learnt the easy way?). You have a perfect pension fund of emotional and practical experience, ready to be drawn on. Yet there are moments when all this counts for nothing and you find yourself at a loss, convinced that the growing-up police are about to tap you on the shoulder and tell you that you are busted. We wonder whether this is because, somewhere along the line, someone, in a book or a film or even in real life, laid down a template of what an adult should look like: if you do not fulfil this picture in every aspect you feel that you cannot possibly be the real thing. You hope vainly that you can go on perpetuating the illusion; you pray that everyone else is so preoccupied with their own mad simulacrum of adulthood that they will not notice the paper-thin aspect of your own counterfeit.

The only way to get around this paradox is to accept it. Some days you will feel very old indeed, only fit for reading the obituary columns and pondering your pension; on others, you will be filled with youthful folly and want to put glitter on your eyelids and eat iced buns for breakfast. Age is mostly a state of mind, and your mind is a fervid and unpredictable thing. There is no perfect template for being a grown-up, no secret prescription written down somewhere of how you should feel or behave or be. Embrace all your scattered inner selves, and do not bow to any misguided imperative.

HOW LIFE DOES NOT GET ANY EASIER, BUT THE ADVANTAGE OF AGE AND EXPERIENCE IS THAT YOU KNOW YOU WILL SURVIVE IT.

A clever writer once wrote something like: knowing you will survive does not make it any easier to bear. We read this when we were very young, and, fired with a vastly theatrical sense of our own melancholy, thought it was one of the truest sentences we ever encountered. Now we are less inclined to regard ourselves as characters in a film by Ingmar Bergman, we wonder.

There is a low hum of comfort that comes from the knowledge, that only really arrives with age, that you will survive: you did it before and you can do it again. In the wild shores of the young unformed mind there lives the contradictory belief that you are immortal, yet that when the heartbreaks and setbacks come, they will literally kill you. The youthful heart is such an untried organ that when it is assaulted it can feel as if it will shatter beyond repair. By the time it is past thirty-five, it has been through the wars; it is battle-hardened, marked and scarred, and so when it is bashed again you know that it will crack, but not break entirely. This does not make the sorrows of life any less great, but there is a context; there is familiarity – oh, this again, the subliminal mind says, yes, I remember this. The memory of the pain comes back, but also the memory of survival. It can feel exhausting – oh no, says the subliminal mind, not *this* again; it can even feel dull; but the chugging engine of healing will kick in, almost automatically. You know that the worn Nietzschean line about what does not kill you makes you stronger is so readily trotted out that it can make you want to spit, but you also know it is true. You will have to pull on all those inner resources; you will have to concentrate and work at it; you sometimes wonder why life just can't be easier; but you also know you can do this, because you have done it before.

It is not only in grief or loss or heartbreak that age brings advantages. One of the most helpful shafts of enlightenment in getting older is that you start to understand that it is *not* all about you. The young exist in a state of lofty solipsism, which is fabulously tiring; every slight is taken absolutely to heart, every argument turns into not just a scene but a three-act play. The lovely thing about being older is that you know that expressions of anger, moments of irritation, random criticism, sudden misunderstandings, are usually entirely to do with the other person. It is, as the twelve-step groups like to say, *their* stuff. They are angry or insecure or fearful, and these feelings, difficult sometimes to contain, get projected outwards – if you happen to be in the way, you get hit. This knowledge does not mean that you suddenly develop a wonderful thick elephant hide on your fortieth birthday – you may be a sensitive plant and still get hurt or baffled or bashed up a bit – but you have the ability to remember that it is not personal, and make like a duck and watch the water flow off your back. You can, literally and metaphorically, walk away, because if you have learnt one thing it is that you are categorically *not* responsible for other people's feelings. You can allow them to have their rotten day, and decline to brood on it and amplify it and turn it into something it is not. You can shrug it off and go and have a cake and think of something quite else. What you get, as the years pass, is a little objectivity, and that is a gift more precious than emeralds.

THE DANGERS OF AGE.

The most obvious danger of age is that your habits of thought calcify and little rocky outcrops of prejudice appear and you actually start believing what you read in the angrier sections of the newspapers. You risk becoming jaded, or mired in convention, or unquestioning. If you ever hear yourself saying, without irony, that the young people of today do not know they are even born, you might like to take a couple of hours in a quiet room to check your state of mind.

There is absolutely nothing wrong with having a routine, or understanding that there are certain things you will never like or understand; these can save trouble and time. Conversely, there is something faintly worrying about closing yourself off from ideas or experiences simply because you have reached a certain age. Think of the old people that you really admire. The octogenarians you most adore will still have curiosity, enthusiasm and jokes in abundance. They are the ones who surprise you by going off on impetuous trips to the Antarctic, to see the penguins; they astonish you with their understanding of the intricacies of new technology or their knowledge of the latest developments in thrash metal. They might be past it in some departments, but they are still all over Facebook. If you should ever feel your mind creaking shut, remember them, and wedge it wide open again.

The other dark peril in getting older is that, as the fiery energy of youth leaves you, and you understand more of how things work, you despair. You are no longer the romantic revolutionary who was going to change the world; you know that the world will never really change, and that realpolitik is the order of the day, and that there is an acute possibility that the only final destination for the human race is hell, in a handbasket. You start to agree with Schopenhauer, who said that human existence was a kind of error, and that every day it will get worse until the worst of all happens. Your inner Pollyanna, exhausted by events and all evidence to the contrary, has quite given up, and morphed into an inner Eeyore, and the only answer is strong medication or spirit alcohol.

At this point you have two choices. You can just turn into Schopenhauer, which is, of course, your prerogative. Or you can remain calm, and concentrate very very hard on the good news. Looking for good news is like shopping in a thrift store: you have to rummage through an awful lot of rubbish to find the gems, but gems there are, nonetheless. On the day of writing the headlines were all about trouble in Kosovo, fighting in Afghanistan, and the US refusing to meet carbon targets: enough to make the strongest-minded woman abandon hope. But on the website of one of our great national newspapers there was also the first ever film of the long-haired jerboa, an adorable Mongolian rodent from the Gobi desert. Eleven Chinese miners were rescued after seven days trapped underground, surviving by eating paper, a leather belt and some orange peel. £520 million had been put into a programme for disabled Britons. It's not exactly poverty solved and cancer cured, but it's better than nothing. It's the news equivalent of counting your fingers and your toes and being grateful that they have not been removed in an industrial accident.

If you choose to look for it, there is a swamp of empirical evidence that the world is indeed going to hell, but there are also green shoots of hope. The grouches will insist that there was some kind of mythical golden age when everything was rosy, but when *was* that exactly? The thirties, when casual drawing room anti-Semitism was unchallenged and slums snaked through the industrial cities? The fifties, when rationing was still in force and all the ladies were on tranquillisers? Or the sixties, which were fabulous if you were Mick Jagger, but not so great if you were looking for lodgings in Notting Hill and found signs on boarding houses saying No Blacks, No Dogs, No Irish? Or perhaps the great Victorian age, when children were put up chimneys and cholera could wipe out 2000 people in a week?

Sometimes, just to fight against the nasty suspicion that everything has gone to the dogs, it is salutary to remind yourself of all the things you take for granted. At home this means everything from central heating to penicillin, free speech to the vote. Abroad can be harder, when the news only highlights lack of clean drinking water and suppressed democracy and the religious police running mad. But twenty years ago, it was almost unthinkable that the Eastern bloc should ever be free. The young, who are not, contrary to red-top opinion, all Asbo kids, go on marches and demonstrations to make poverty history. Politicians cannot ignore the plight of developing countries, and hold summits about them. It's not perfect, but it's not nothing. You might be getting older, but it does not mean that you have to lose hope. Some days it is easier than others, and unless you are an unreconstructed optimist, it is almost always an act of will. But, like talking yourself down off the ceiling and mastering the art of making a perfect soufflé, it is a skill that can be honed, over time. It is within your grasp.

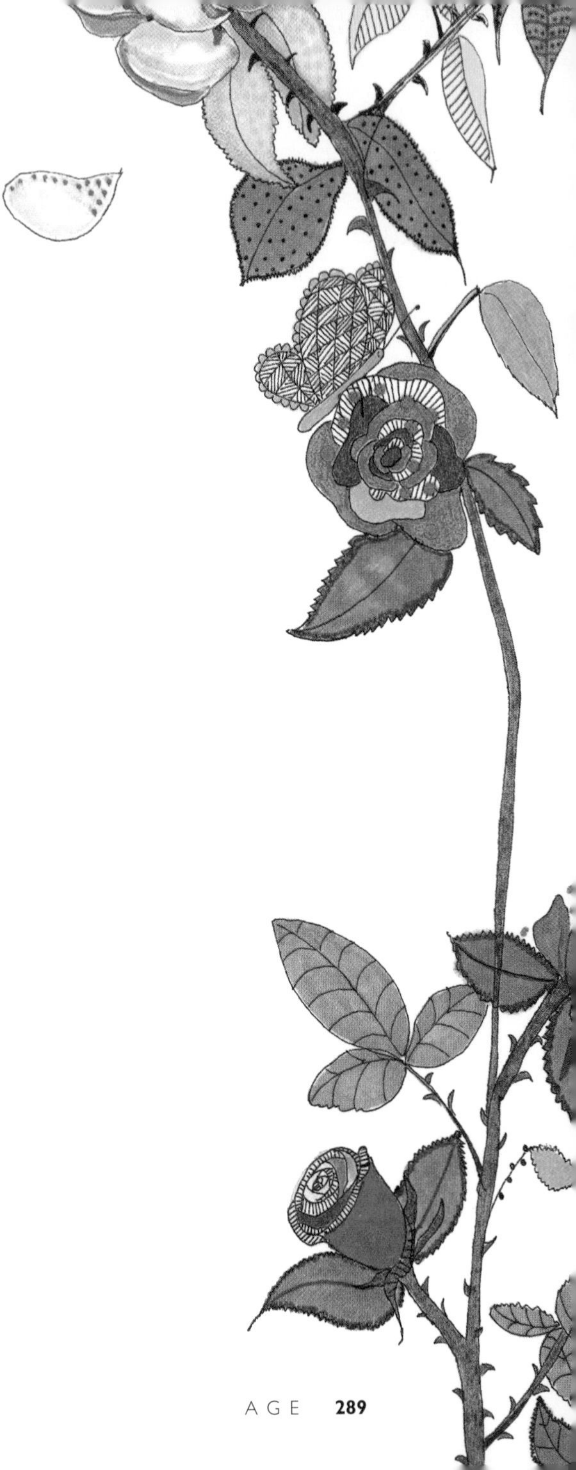

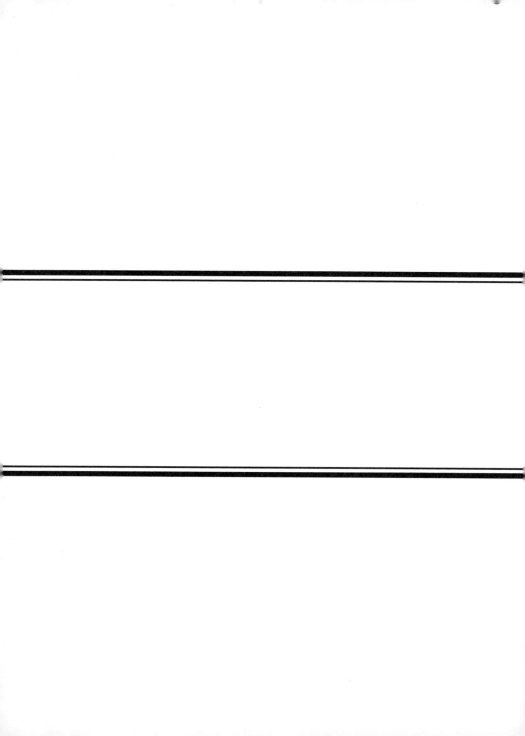

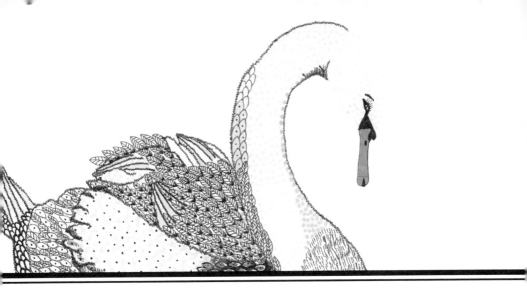

BEAUTY

—

CHAPTER THIRTEEN

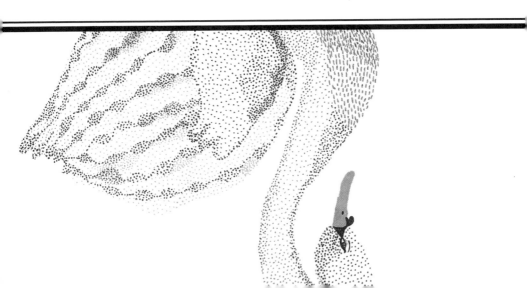

THE MADNESS OF IT ALL.

When one of us was young (sadly, far too young to think of a withering riposte), a member of the opposite sex made the following remark: 'I suppose there's one good thing about being as plain as you: you won't have to worry about losing your looks.' Since it was the eighties, the decade that embraced garish make-up, frizzy perms and unflattering clothes, there may have been mitigating circumstances. Nevertheless, it was a rude and cruel thing to say, and it has defined her self-image ever since.

A wiser man once said that women see themselves in one of three ways: beautiful, nurturing or clever. Obviously a woman can be all three, but generally one characteristic will dominate. In your grandmothers' day, when asked whether they would rather have a clever daughter or a beautiful one, most women would have replied beautiful; nowadays, the opposite is true. Which begs the question: if women now truly value brains over beauty, why the existence of a multi-billion-pound cosmetic industry that sucks every ounce of confidence out of any vaguely

ordinary-looking woman and exhorts her to be reed thin, wrinkle-free and unnaturally swishy-haired? Either someone is lying or there are some raging double standards going on out there.

It's easy to blame the media, the culture, the magazines, Hollywood, Hugh Hefner, Barbie – but the enduring obsession with the way we look may stem from something far more fundamental: human nature. Research insists that big eyes, regular features, shiny hair, soft skin and a shapely figure are all outward signs of health and fecundity: it's more natural selection than aesthetic judgement. Fortunately, humans are also creatures of intellect, which enables them to override their more bestial responses. Art, literature, some of the more enlightened newspapers – they all encourage you to see beyond outward appearance to the more important things. It does not have to be all models and film stars – women's lives and minds are enriched with the examples of Catherine the Great, Virginia Woolf and Andrea Dworkin – but for all this, there is still something about beauty which can undo the bravest and most rational female.

Beautiful women are used to people paying attention when they open their mouths. They enter a room, and all eyes are on them. They smile at a waiter and their every whim is met. At dinner, the male side of the table hangs on their every word. Even the sanest women occasionally dream of a piece of *that* action. Imagine, just for once, having the kind of face that could launch a thousand ships, or at the very least a medium-sized tugboat. Imagine the simple, feral pleasure of being the hottest hottie in a whole room of hotties. That, dear reader, is the dream of the cream: buy this particular unguent and you – yes you, sleep-deprived middle-aged mother of two – can look like this slip of a model-cum-actress that we have hired on a lucrative three-year contract to gaze alluringly into the camera while airbrushes miraculously smooth away every wrinkle and pimple on her already perfect face.

Put like that, the whole thing is absurd. No self-respecting female seriously believes that a tub of water-based emollient can make a devastating difference. But every woman knows that it can make a *bit* of a difference. So you swallow the lie, even though it's an insult to your intelligence; you part with the cash and you slap on the cream, all the time keeping your fingers tightly crossed that maybe, just maybe, it will Release your Inner Radiance.

If you stop to consider it, being truly beautiful may be as much pain as pleasure. Beauty can be all-consuming, a monstrous exercise in time-suckage. Never having to sing for your supper can stunt a person's intellectual growth; constantly being the centre of attention may lead to solipsism and brattishness. But most cruel of all is the threat of the inevitable. The man at the start of this chapter was rude, but he was right: the more beautiful a woman is, the more she has to lose from the passage of time. As the ability to turn heads or inspire awe ebbs away, the ageing beauty experiences a form of bereavement every bit as real as the writer whose memory begins to fail. And if she has neglected to take out any sort of insurance policy in the shape of a personality, a career or a family, life can seem very empty indeed.

All rational women know this, but there is a dark part of them that still dreams of having that crazy beauty, even just for a day. And that is what the multi-million-pound beauty industry is based on: the culture-induced insecurity of the ordinary woman.

COSMETIC SURGERY.

Despite what the small ads would have you believe, there is no such thing as painless plastic surgery. You cannot radically alter a person's appearance without causing some kind of physical trauma, and physical trauma tends to hurt. Cosmetic surgery is not a frivolous trip to a beauty parlour: it is some serious intervention.

Plastic surgery used to be restricted to film stars, eccentric members of the aristocracy or very, very thin old ladies living in Monte Carlo. In those days it was recognised that nose jobs and facelifts and breast enlargements were serious undertakings, requiring crazy sums of disposable income, and a lengthy period of recovery in a remote and exclusive Swiss mountain clinic. Above all, no one talked about it. You waited until the children were away at boarding school, packed the husband off to his club, and melted away discreetly for a few weeks. Upon your return, you accepted compliments gracefully; when friends remarked on how well rested you looked, you put it down to the marvellous mountain air and special restorative dandelion tea. You never, ever, not even when you could barely shut your eyes, and your skin was stretched tight as a mummy's over your crumbling cheekbones, admitted to having had 'work' done.

Nowadays, the culture of plastic surgery is more open and more mundane. People go and do it in their lunch break. Cosmetic surgery has been democratised. Celebrities shamelessly parade their fake bosoms in front of the cameras; actresses openly re-sculpt their bodies, posing for photo-shoots in clothing that a normal 17-year-old would have trouble pulling off; superannuated stars of stage and screen have fat sucked out of their bottoms and pumped into their lips (we know; why, *why*?). The female form is pummelled and re-shaped and moulded like so much plasticine. There are 14-year-olds who look like 28-year-olds, 30-year-olds who look like 17-year-olds and 60-year-olds who look like Lord Voldemort. The women are in the grip of an epidemic of face and body fascism never before seen in the history of human existence.

The forty-something generation of women could well be the last not to alter their appearance through surgical intervention. They may come to be seen as freaks. 'Look,' people will say, stopping to point and stare in the street, 'That woman hasn't had any Botox at all. Her lips – they're completely normal. What's *wrong* with her?' Plastic surgery refusniks will be invited on to national television to explain their stubborn Luddite tendencies, a caption running beneath them saying: Joan – refuses to have a facelift even though her family have begged her to and her children are embarrassed to be seen in public with her. Or: Stella – has turned her back on laser resurfacing.

The term 'anti-ageing' is one of the more nonsensical of the modern age. It's like saying anti-breathing, or anti-the-planet-turning-on-its-axis. The implication is that you can somehow stop your cells from slowing down, prevent your body from changing with age. 'If I could turn back time,' Cher once sang, and then proceeded to have a damned good go at it. But here's the thing: you *can't*. However much you re-sculpt yourself, you are always going to age, minute by minute, hour by hour, year by year. It's the death and taxes deal. The question is: do you want the most enduring part of you to be your personality, your sense of humour, your sharp wit, your kind heart, or a pair of inflatable silicone bags filled with salt water that will linger in your grave once the rest of you has been eaten by a convocation of worms?

For a woman who is genuinely tormented by some physical freak, plastic surgery may be a rational choice. Bad, irresponsible, unnecessary plastic surgery, however, isn't – and there is a lot of it about. The regulations for cosmetic procedures in Britain are barely more exacting than those covering manicurists. A poorly qualified chancer with a weekend diploma in liposuction will brashly advertise the benefits of his or her ministrations, but will suddenly remember a pressing appointment the second you probe deeper. A serious cosmetic surgeon, on the other hand, will not be shy about the fact that he is going to fillet the skin on your face away from the muscle, re-attach it a few millimetres further up before stapling it all back together behind your ears. He will be honest about the fact that you will look like you have been in a multiple pile-up on the M4, that you may have to eat through a straw and that there will, inevitably, be some unsightly seepage.

The main question you have to ask yourself is this: is it really going to make you happy? You know it probably isn't strictly *necessary*, but a deep feeling of inadequacy brought about by loathing your appearance can be horribly real and debilitating. Such a feeling may seem absurd to others, it may be the result of a warped culture that places far too much emphasis on female beauty, there may be any number of logical, sane arguments against it, but if you find yourself staring miserably in the looking glass, paralysed by your own reflection, perhaps surgery may be the thing for you. We would never wish to judge, but we do urge you to remember that there is no silver scalpel to cure a sense of self-loathing. There is the danger of displacement: is it *really* your nose that you hate, or is that just emblematic of a deeper malaise which no army of surgeons can cure?

Because full-blown surgery is so serious, so invasive, and still so expensive, a new kind of cosmetic intervention has raced to the top of the charts. Botox and fillers and sand-blasters, collagen and lasers and chemical peels are seen as a less nuclear option, but, in some ways, the latter may be preferable to the former. It is not just that there is some evidence to

suggest that Botox seeps into the brain, which is never a good place for a poison, it is because Botox appears so much quicker, easier and safer. Whilst surgery remains the preserve of relatively few professionals and their rich clients, it remains a minority pursuit. Botox is far cheaper, more accessible, anyone can do it – not well, of course, for that you really do require a professional (they say that the best people are dentists, since they have such an intimate understanding of facial anatomy). Ersatz clinics have sprung up everywhere offering the stuff, often administered by someone who was until a few weeks previously doing nothing more medical than a facial scrub. The result is that in certain affluent postcodes the sight of bowling-ball foreheads (that shiny, polished look that skin takes on when it has been pumped full of fillers), frozen smiles and eyebrows that hover half an inch above their natural station in life is becoming depressingly commonplace.

The real tragedy is that these women all think they look fabulous. Precisely because the effects of Botox are so incremental, they are blind to the extent to which they look freakish. It creeps up on them, in the way that fat creeps up on the middle-aged, in tiny, barely noticeable stages. Have a brow lift, and the change is palpable; go for a little Botox here, a little there; a filler here, a filler there, and before you know it you can no longer register any other emotion except mild surprise.

These are not necessarily cases of bad practice, either. Flick through the pages of any glossy magazine and you will see any number of stars – many of them A-list – who have fallen into the Botox trap, despite the fact that they have unfettered access to the best people. One of the worst cases we ever saw was the receptionist at a famous Harley Street clinic, who had Botoxed her forehead into oblivion. She looked like a cross between a mannequin and a Klingon.

ACCEPTANCE, AND WHY IT CAN BE HARD.

If you sat down and worked out how many minutes, hours, days and months of your life have so far been wasted worrying about the fact that you don't look like Audrey Hepburn in *Roman Holiday* or Debbie Harry in her Blondie days, or Eva Herzegova in those Wonderbra ads, you might very well find that you could have mastered ancient Greek, or written the definitive dissertation on early Renaissance painting, or perhaps even found a cure for the common cold. It begins early, this eternal dissatisfaction. A girl child starting school will define female classmates by how pretty they are; soon, they will start commenting on their own appearance. They will identify the slightest non-conformist feature, often because they have been pointed out to them by other children. It is heartbreaking to have to comfort a teary five-year-old who has just been told their ears are 'flappy'; but sadly it is only the beginning.

Looking good is not, as it should be, an art and a pleasure; it has become an obligation, a duty even, yet another hurdle to jump in the already exhausting race to be a successful modern female. If a man is successful, no one cares if his hair is a mess. If a woman is successful, particularly in the public arena, her appearance will be dissected down to the minutest detail. She will find herself hemmed in by the weight of public expectation. She lives in terror of being told, often by middle-aged men with the dress sense of Jeremy Clarkson, that she has Let Herself Go.

This can lead to some very messy public breakdowns. Perhaps the most terrifying example of modern times is the case of the pop singer Britney Spears, who began her descent into madness by shaving her hair off in public. Newspapers and the increasingly vitriolic blogosphere seemed to regard her actions as mildly amusing. The last thing on editors' minds was the mental condition of a young girl who was displaying behaviour alarmingly close to that exhibited by rape victims; but Spears's very public disintegration was merely an amplification of the kind of self-loathing that, at one point or another, affects so many women.

All of which goes a long way to explain why women get excited about a new lipstick or face cream, especially when endorsed by a famous beauty or actress whose appearance inspires emulation. The beauty industry's bedrock is the assumption that all women look less good than they want to, and it does its best to fan that flame until it turns into a brushfire, without any sense of shame.

WHY BEING A LIBERATED FEMALE DOES NOT MEAN YOU HAVE TO CULTIVATE YOUR UNDERARM HAIR, DESPITE THE IDIOT STEREOTYPE.

All right-thinking post-feminists know that emancipation and exfoliation are not mutually exclusive. You may shave your legs and still be a radical. Looking nice is not a betrayal of the sisters. Believing that prettiness is the only defining mark of a woman *is*.

POTS OF MONEY; OR, WHY PERFECTLY RATIONAL WOMEN WILL PART WITH QUITE ASTONISHING AMOUNTS OF CASH FOR SOMETHING THEY KNOW CAN'T REALLY MAKE THAT MUCH OF A DIFFERENCE.

This is best illustrated by a little story, taken from life.

You're pregnant with your second child, you've got the first one howling at your hip, you haven't brushed your hair for two days, and wham – you bump into an ex-boyfriend. He has his arm slung casually over the shoulder of some slip of a thing, all skinny jeans and stilettos. They have clearly spent the morning in bed, or in pursuit of some equally hedonistic activity, such as reading books without anyone throwing up on them, or finishing a sentence. You, on the other hand, haven't slept properly for a year, and are having difficulties remembering the rudiments of the English language.

You brace yourself. He thinks about it for a split second too long, before your face registers. She regards you with a mixture of indifference and horror, as though you were a bag lady, or a member of an eccentric sect. There is a perfunctory exchange of personal information. He is unmarried, no children, doing well for himself. Mercifully, it is over soon:

Slip Of A Thing is bored, an emotion that she communicates by pouting her glossy lips and twirling a manicured finger in her expensive hair. You say goodbye, promise to stay in touch. They amble off down the road. You can almost hear him saying it: 'Really, babe, she never looked like that when I was going out with her.' You can just hear the echo of a disbelieving laugh.

And then suddenly, unaccountably, because you know he wasn't any good for you and you're actually not that unhappy, you feel utterly deflated. You catch a dispiriting glimpse of yourself in a shop window. And before you know it, you've wheeled into Space NK and you're talking to a nice lady with eyelash extensions while your child slowly, deliberately, demolishes the shampoo section.

You want something for under the eyes, a cream to get rid of wrinkles, maybe some mascara, a definitive shade of rouge and a lipstick, definitely a lipstick. Nothing gives you a lift like a nice new lipstick, does it? You don't even ask for prices. Twenty minutes later and you leave, almost £100 lighter and clutching a bag of nonsense which, somehow, fleetingly, makes you feel a whole lot better. There is still hope, even if it comes in a bag.

This is the magic of comfort make-up. It is the cosmetic equivalent of chicken soup with dumplings. Who cares if none of it works, and you know that perfectly well? For a moment, you have bought the fairy tale, that sheer fuck-you glamour which can be bought from a shop. We have absolutely nothing against comfort cosmetics. The effects work for at least half a day, before you fall back to your usual, rational self, and there is nothing criminal about a new lipstick. It's definitely better than hard drugs.

FIGHTING BACK: THE MYTH.

Beauty is a universal fact, and a human invention. Despite the vaunted golden mean, where ratios between eyes and chin can be reduced to equations in the pursuit of the ideal face, and an insistence that resemblance to babies is the most reliable indicator of attractiveness, ideas of beauty have not only varied hugely between cultures and periods in history, but also between individuals. Everyone knows about the eye of the beholder, and how unreliable it is.

Cleopatra, one of the great female icons of outrageous beauty, immortalised by Shakespeare in all her infinite variety, was not in fact the black-haired siren that moderns imagine. The raven bob and the cut-glass features came about through the movies, when she was played first by Theda Bara and then Elizabeth Taylor, all smouldering eyes and white skin. In fact, contemporary busts of her show a slightly fat little face, with a tiny grumpy mouth. (Google it; it will make you laugh.) The famous hair was much more likely a dull shade of red, styled in odd little bubbles all over her head.

You don't even have to go that far in time or place to find ideals of beauty radically at odds with those of the current era. Bette Davis, with her odd nose and bulbous eyes, was the most ragingly successful leading lady in the Hollywood of the 1930s and 40s. Now she would be reduced to character roles only, as a more bland and uniform idea of glamour has conquered the visual zeitgeist. There is something oddly interchangeable about many of today's film beauties. Can you tell the difference between Charlize Theron and Ashley Judd? Theron, interestingly, rebelled against her own beauty, getting uglied up for her most critically acclaimed part, that of murderer Aileen Wuornos, as if desperate to show that she was more than just a pretty face.

And here, of course, is the complication of beauty. Like money, everyone wants it. It is held up as the gold standard. If only you could be beautiful, all your daily problems would be solved. But the beautiful themselves are often oddly haunted by their own genetic quirk. It is easily forgotten that great beauty is very rare. Because of the parade of television programmes where even lab technicians and coroners are played by unusually attractive actresses, modern women fall into the trap of believing that beauty is quite common. You only have to walk down the street to see that most people are what one might kindly term average-looking. In reality, beauty is, literally, odd. Great beauties can feel themselves to be freaks, they are so unlike the normal population. Other women may stare at them in frank envy, or even fear; men gaze at them with a desire which is predicated not on their interesting mind or wild sense of humour, but simply on a random combination of physical attributes.

Beauties quite often describe themselves as lonely; they can find themselves confused by their looks and what they represent. We know one woman who was so beautiful when she was younger that people would stop and stare in the street, not in a lascivious way, but out of sheer acknowledgement. She wanted so much to be admired for what she saw as her real self – good mind, erratic sense of humour, creative sense – that she refused to use any beauty products at all, except for the odd lick of Vaseline, until she was into her late thirties. Her face, unprotected by SPFs, unadorned by expensive make-up, weathered into the normal but attractive range, and only then could she relax. It was then, ironically, that she felt people were taking her at face value in the metaphorical rather than literal sense.

Assumptions are automatically made about beauties – that they are somehow better, cleverer, even more moral, than ordinary women. The beauty herself then feels that she has to live up to unrealistic expectations. The primal scream of the Elephant Man – I *am* a human being – is also the secret cry of the great beauty. Poor Marilyn Monroe felt so trapped and diminished by her status as a sex symbol that she used to carry a copy of *Ulysses* with her onto the film set, as if to prove that she was more than just a walking aphrodisiac.

Beauties also get regarded as public property, and they must live up to their billing, even when going out to get a cup of coffee. There is an arbitrary and frightening hysteria in the populist media when a film star or rock icon is seen showing the slightest flaw. In the week of writing, pictures of Demi Moore were splayed over the tabloid press because she had dared to go outside looking a little pale. To our eyes, she appeared exactly as a forty-five-year-old mother of three with great bone structure might be expected to – pretty rather than full-wattage, red-carpet glamorous – but the writers screamed foul. 'Age takes its toll despite a fortune on plastic surgery' yelled the headline, in a frenzy of Schadenfreude. Her skin, apparently, looked dull and tired; 'her drooping jowls only added to her haggard look'. There is an almost psychotic cruelty in this, an absolute abdication of any kind of reason or sympathy.

One picture is taken of a film star looking fairly normal, and you would have thought from the reaction that she had taken to running over kittens or performing eugenics or selling crack to teenagers. In the same paper, on the same day, Kate Moss was also accused of looking haggard, with 'scraggy' hair. Her knees had committed the ultimate crime of appearing knobbly. Just as if that were not enough beauty-bashing, there were pictures of Courteney Cox looking 'skinny and strained'. From this, it was extrapolated that her career was on the skids and her marriage in trouble.

Cox is an interesting case of how beauty gets in the way. She is almost exclusively featured in the press on account of her looks; *Friends* has become so much a part of the vernacular that it is hard to remember that it broke ground in becoming the most successful sitcom of all time. Not only that, but Cox was the standout turn, by a country mile. She was playing against some talented actors, so the bar was high, but she cleared it without blinking with her perfect comic timing and the wonderful edge of hysteria that she brought to the part. In her best moments, she was right up there with the glory girls of Hollywood's golden era, those magical comediennes like Carole Lombard and Lucille Ball. But all the tabloids are not interested in her professional accomplishments, no no, not when they can get a photograph of her looking *haggard*.

The horrible irony is that the publications which so love to bash the beauties are the very ones which run constant articles about how you too can become one. They offer endless rehashed advice on how to drop two dress sizes before lunch, which plastic surgery you should have before you are fifty, which new magical cream will transport you to the prairies of pulchritude. They hold up beauty as an ideal to which all women should aspire, even as they are tearing down the women who do in fact possess it. We are amazed that the entire female population does not just give up and go and lie down in a darkened room. We think that the entire female population should instead rise up and point out that it is more than just a pretty face.

THE NARROWING OF BEAUTY.

Beauty has become an oddly constrained thing, a matter of blonde hair and blonde faces and small, regular features. No one talks much of the *jolie laide* any more, the kind of eccentric Diana Vreeland face that is so ugly it carries a beauty of its own. It is as if some secret memo has been sent out which instructs that women like Anjelica Huston, with her forthright features, or Lauren Hutton, with her gappy teeth, are not allowed any more. It is hard to imagine now that Glenda Jackson was considered beautiful in the seventies, with her small eyes and big teeth, or that Maria Callas's blatant nose and hooded eyes were a wild example of high diva beauty in the 1960s. The airbrush school of beauty has insinuated itself into the collective consciousness, and everyone must look the same. It is all about smallness, tightness, smoothness – it is, above all, about youth.

It's not just that beauty has become depressingly skin deep, it's that the skin must all look the same. There is a paucity of imagination when it comes to beauty which is deeply demoralising. It is two-dimensional and shallow: join the dots, tick all the correct boxes before you are allowed to proceed.

It is exemplified by the horribly termed *makeover*. Making over is such big bucks now that there are entire cable channels dedicated to it. We recently saw an article in a magazine about three women ('real people', as the fashion insiders like to call them) getting made over. There were the Before and After pictures – showing a trajectory from ordinary females to ones who had been plastered in make-up, had their hair titivated, been guyed up in the latest trends. We were convinced it was a spoof, and kept looking fruitlessly for the punchline, because every single one of the women looked twenty times more attractive in the *before* pictures. There they were, relaxed, smiling, authentic, until some crazed stylist got hold of them and left them looking artificial and posed, with slightly stretched and nervy smiles.

The most beautiful woman we know in life, rather than on the screen, would not pass any single one of the current beauty tests. She is hitting fifty, with the lines on her face to show it. She has smallish eyes, freckled

skin, and mildly imperfect teeth. She is not tall, or thin. Her hair is a little frizzy. She does not even have especially fine bones, let alone the kind of cheekbones that you could balance a tray on, or the carved jawline that is now indicated for any attempt at beauty. Yet, in our eyes, she is utterly, ragingly gorgeous. She is French, and she does have that *bien dans sa peau* thing going on, but it is something more than that. The beauty comes in a hundred indefinable ways — an easy laugh, a light in her eyes that hints of secrets and memories, a kindness that pours out of her like starlight. But if the magazines saw her, they would put her in the Before picture, and send out a stylist SOS.

We say: sod 'em. Beauty, in life as in art, comes in a thousand different guises. You can't reduce it down to before and after. Open your eyes, and you will see it everywhere, even in your very own bathroom mirror.

THE FALSE PROMISE OF BEAUTY.

Beauty is being sold now with more frenzied determination than almost any other attribute. No other marketing campaigns come close. Beauty is hawked about the public square as if it is the answer to the Universal Why.

There is nothing wrong with beauty itself. A lovely face adds to the general aesthetic. There is a keen pleasure in watching a coltish teenager who is young enough to be quite unconscious of how outrageously pretty she is, or one of those wonderful old women who still has her glorious bone structure and has not allowed her face to be carved up by the surgeon's knife. Equally, there is nothing vain or shallow in wanting to make the best of what you were born with. There can be something vital and celebratory about putting on a great dress and dyeing your hair crazy colours and turning your mouth into a defiant slash of vermilion. It is perfectly rational to soothe your skin with a delicious cream so that your face does not start flaking off when you are sixty; but when a certain type of culturally prescribed beauty becomes an imperative and a trap, then everyone is in dark trouble. Beauty has been given a weight of meaning that it cannot carry; it buckles under the heft of false promise and phoney expectation. The underlying theme of all the advertising and selling, the editorials and photographs, the pushing of the cosmetics and the potions, is that beauty is not only within your grasp, if you get injected and lasered and lifted enough, but, more fatally, that it will *cure everything*. The dangerous fantasy is that beauties are somehow different, so nothing can touch them. If you go out and get yourself a perfect aquiline nose, then all the magical things of which you dream will come true. The prince will come, the rain will not fall, the job will not fail: all manner of things will be well.

Let's say, for the sake of argument, that you buy the beauty myth. You don't care what the grumpy feminists say; they are just snide spoilsports, coming to rain on your parade. You damn well *will* spend thousands of your hard-earned pounds on that new face. You will get the pouting collagen lips. You will have the drooping eyelids snipped away. You will have your nose broken and reset. You will get a persuasive doctor to slice into your cheeks and pull the skin tight. You will have deadly poison inserted into your forehead, to remove all the creases. You will get your fragile skin pummelled by lasers and sand-blasted until all marks of living are removed. You do not bloody want the face you deserve, you want the face you see staring perfectly down at you from the billboards.

And that's fine, because the women who came before you fought for you to be free, and you won't be told what you can and cannot do. It is your choice and it's what you want, and it's your money and that's what you are going to spend it on.

The question is: then what? You are still the exact same person. You cannot get your mind or your heart or your ideas lasered or lifted. After the initial thrill of seeing a flawless face staring back at you from the glass, where do you go? You have been sold a taunting pack of false expectations, and buyer's remorse may set in when you find that you still have all the identical hopes and fears and night terrors that were there before you submitted to the knife. They can suck out your cellulite, but they can't suck out your demons, because everyone has those. They can't liposuct the human condition.

When the real tests in life come, as they will, does your new perfect face make the difference? Tragedy hits the beautiful and the plain; there is no discrimination. When the big sorrows come, will you be consoled by the fact that you have a gorgeous new nose? Your perfect face will not help you when your husband is fired, or you get an unexpected tax demand, or your child gets bullied at school. You will not achieve a better job or a nicer house or a happier dog just because you look fabulous. The best you can hope for is a few compliments and people speculating where you got your work done or what facialist you are visiting.

There are good reasons for human beings to feel inadequate. Acts of cruelty, carelessness, malice, dishonesty, are proper matters for regret; but to castigate yourself for not coming up to some randomly dictated idea of beauty is to fall for the lie that a pretty face can transform your life.

To love well and be loved in return, in all the manifest and various forms that love takes, is probably the highest human achievement. No one worth loving is going to care a lick that you look five years younger than your actual age, or have no wrinkles. The ones who love you properly will not give a damn that age is leaving its traces on your face,

because to them it is your dear face, the one they know as well as their own. What they care about is that you make them laugh so much that their stomach aches with it, and that they can call you up when they are caught in melancholy, and that you make the best chicken soup this side of Brooklyn. Those are the things which are the true beauty, the one that lasts, the one that *means* something. They are the only beauty that actually matters.

BUT WHY, CONVERSELY, YOU DO NOT HAVE TO TURN INTO A PURITAN.

A gratuitous, slightly too expensive beauty product can be a simple pleasure. Just because you occasionally allow yourself a delicious pot of Spiezia balm, or an unnecessary bottle of Darphin face oil, or a soothing serum from the lovely bearded Dr Andrew Weil, does *not* mean that you have also bought, wholesale, the entire beauty myth. We ourselves are suckers for some good product, in a rather girlish, sybaritic manner. It does not all have to be cold cream and charcoal biscuits, certainly not in our house.

It is just a matter of understanding that a product is only a product. It will not change your life. It will hardly even change your face. It will not prevent wrinkles from appearing; the only thing that would stop lines is never, ever smiling or frowning again. But it will make your skin feel supple and cared for, and sometimes may even represent a potent dose of self-love. It is a treat, not a panacea. That's all. Know the difference, and you will never feel like a victim ever again.

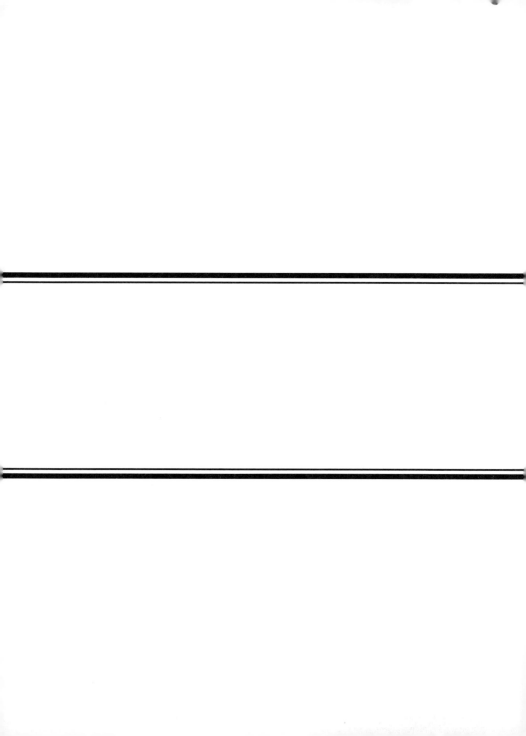

SEX

—

CHAPTER FOURTEEN

Ah, sex. At last, you are saying. We are certainly saying. Despite what certain unreconstructed back-to-the-1950s moralisers might have to say about it, it really can be all things to all women. It can comfort and reassure; it can make you feel as if you are queen of the world; it can make you laugh, it can make you gasp. It can remind you that you are human. It can be profound and quiet and intense; it can be antic and funny. It can be an act of defiance, or even, once you get really good at it, a form of showing off. It is perfectly absurd, when you deconstruct it into its constituent parts, and yet it is entirely wonderful.

It is also the one most uncomplicated area where women really do beat the men hands down. The penis is all very well (and we do think it *is* very well) and men have been waving it around in a literal and metaphorical way for centuries, but when it comes to pure pleasure the clitoris wins every time, with its millions of nerve endings all packed into one tiny convenient little space, ready to give you hours of outrageous pleasure.

The male orgasm is a linear straightforward matter, catch and release, but the *female* orgasm, ah, the female orgasm – we are talking many grades of complexity and feeling. There are the quick shallow ones, and the little tingling ones; the ones that come fast and almost shockingly, the ones that build for ages before sending you into orbit like a speeding rocket. There are the ones that are so powerful that it is as if you are falling off a cliff, with a feeling of swooning vertigo, and the ones that take you over so completely that you do not know where you are or what your name is. There are the ones that are tightly focused on the clitoral area, and the ones that spread over your entire body and go on reverberating for several minutes afterwards, as if every atom in your body is vibrating with pleasure. There are the deep emotional ones that make you want to cry, or the rolling superficial ones that make you laugh.

And, of course, the greatest advantage a woman has is that once her orgasm is over, she does not need to lie still and recuperate as a man does, but is ready to go all over again. One racy female we know is quite unblushing in admitting that her record is three in seven and a half minutes (we rather love it that she went to the trouble to count).

When you think of all this wonder, free, easily available, with no need for any special equipment or expensive qualifications – all you need is a willing body and an open mind and an accommodating gentleman – it is inexplicably strange that so many people have insisted on seeing only the dark side of sex. Religions, moralists, family values fanatics, schoolmasters, entire social systems, have persisted in regarding sex as something dangerous and dirty, most especially when it comes to the ladies. The old double standard can still, even now, be found, insisting that men who put it about are studs while women who do the same are sluts. In the richest and most powerful nation of the First World, there are bizarre ceremonies where young women *pledge their virginity* to their fathers, in some twisted imitation of the marriage service, promising not to have sex until they are wives.

It seems profoundly sad to make joyless and dangerous something that is so essentially joyful. With bodies clearly and carefully designed for sexual pleasure, it is wilfully perverse to turn sex into a sin. Rather like those mothers brought up in the war for whom wasted food is a crime, we believe that to squander all that tremendous potential for fun and delight is the real sin.

SINGLE SEX.

Single sex, when you are of a certain age, can be one of the great unalloyed pleasures of your adult life. You no longer have the unblemished smooth body of youth, but you have the age and experience to know that none of that really matters. All you need is some good lighting and a little exfoliation to keep the skin smooth. What you do have, which is much more important than a magazine body, is a certain confidence. You are no longer young and foolish enough to be pressured into absurd Kama Sutra positions to prove a point or to impress someone. You know that trussing yourself up in ridiculous underwear is really not worth the candle; suspenders and basques and garter belts are not necessarily going to illuminate the experience. You understand that swinging from the chandeliers or breaking the bed are not defining marks of sexual success. You are, crucially, quite comfortable with saying no, as in: No, thank you so much, rubber is really not my thing. You are also brave enough to say yes, as in: Yes, do it there, for some considerable time, if you don't mind.

You are quite capable of taking a gentleman home with you, should the mood take you, and then kindly giving him back in the morning. You know that, despite what some of the myths insist, you can have utterly fabulous sex with someone you like very much, but are not necessarily in love with. You also know enough not to let yourself get led astray by perfectly marvellous sex and believe that it is enough to base an entire relationship on, although we do admit that sometimes the sex can be so blinding that it takes a few days to work that one out.

COMFORT SEX.

Comfort sex, like comfort eating, should not be confused with the cheap fast-food variety. You do not have to be in love to have comfort sex, but in ideal circumstances it should contain an element of like.

The need for comfort sex often comes in times of sadness or exhaustion or high tension, when you want to turn off churning emotions, or racing thoughts, or juddering worries, and feel a good warm body next to yours. It is about simplicity in a time of complication. This is why it is important to choose your partner in comfort sex wisely. Best of all is someone you already know and like, preferably with whom you have done it before, because then no explanations are necessary. If you choose a man who is not known to you, it is advisable to explain quite clearly what it is you want from him, so that he does not go all lovelorn on you the next morning and start making plans for holidays in Rome when in fact you have got exactly what you wanted and really just need to get back to work. You do not want to get into the business of hurting people's feelings. We know one woman who once propositioned a man by saying she would like to take him home and use him for sex and would he mind. It turned out that he did not mind at all.

Once the niceties are observed, you get to have a night, or even two, of wonderful physical pleasure, and when you are in a time of great stress that can be almost medicinal. The act of orgasm releases tension in the muscles and floods the body with endorphins; it can act as an analgesic, and is so much better for you than gin or paracetamol. But beyond this, there is a very clever thing that you can do when you are past your twenties and you understand a little of how the world works. It is that as well as doing sex for one night with no strings attached, you can do intimacy for one night. It is this that stops comfort sex from being soulless sex. When you both know what it is you are doing it for and what it is you want, there is a tremendous liberation in that: there is no imagined future; this is not the beginning of something important; it is what it is. This allows you both to exchange revealing information, dreams and hopes and fears, as well as doing the wild thing. We think that comfort sex without a bit of chatting is slightly sad; you might as well stay at home and do it on your own.

INADVISABLE SEX.

We really believe that hardly any sex is inadvisable, except perhaps when very, very drunk (you almost always regret it in the morning) or, you know, in an alleyway or something. We are not much for dogging or group sex, but each to each. We think there is only one golden rule. (We tend not to go in for immutable rules; we have lived too long in our very own glass house to start throwing any stones.) But our golden rule is fixed and we are not shy about stating it clearly. It is: never, ever have the sex with a married man.

There it is, bald and unadorned. There are no riders. We do not mean: unless you really really love him, or except when his wife truly does not understand him (she never does), or in the cases when you absolutely cannot help yourself. You can always help yourself. This is the marvellous thing about clambering out of the primordial soup and developing the human attribute of free will. You are a modern woman in a modern country; you are not living in Sudan; you have choices.

This is practically the only area where the moralist in us raises her head like a bird dog, sniffs the wind, and decides it is time to bark. Married men belong to *someone else*. They have taken vows. Sleeping with them is an act of betrayal and disloyalty and untruth. It is also a grievous act against the sisterhood. We know one woman who takes this rule very seriously; she once started an affair with a man who had been separated for two years, feeling that this was allowed. He was living apart from his wife, lawyers had been consulted, there was no doubt that his marriage was over. And yet she still got a terrifying email from the wife saying: I hear you are *fucking* my husband. If this level of rage is engendered by sleeping with a separated man, just imagine what would result from dallying with a properly married one.

Morality aside, there are practical objections. If you are ever tempted by a married man, thinking it perhaps a little glamorous, life on the edge – *you* are not tied by bourgeois regulations, you are a free spirit and you obey the call of true love, we suggest you listen to Nina Simone singing *The Other Woman*. The burden of the song is that the other woman is scenting herself and arranging flowers and doing her hair and *waiting* for the man to come around. (The shrinks, less lyrically, would nod their wise old heads and observe that she has just given all her power away.) The other woman, Nina sings, sadly, with the perfect note of truth, spends her life alone.

You cannot call him when you want; the sexy secretive glory of a snatched *cinq à sept* wears off very quickly when you find yourself wanting to be able to spend the night with him; weekends and national

holidays are off limits, so you get no date for a Saturday night and no one to dance with on New Year's Eve. You begin to live in a hinterland of deception and subterfuge. Instead of walking out proudly in the light, you find yourself slinking around in the shadows.

Most crucially, however much he swears he loves you, he is lying to someone he also once swore he loved. If he can do it once, chances are that he will do it again. Once you are no longer in the white heat of sexual abandon and into the low hum of daily married life, there will come a moment when you notice him noticing other women, and you will, sure as eggs is eggs, begin to wonder. It has become a cliché that when a man marries his mistress he creates a vacancy, and it is a cliché for a reason.

MARITAL SEX.

Despite what the fairy tales say, despite the many manuals featuring hirsute gentlemen and their liberated lady wives indulging in gentle yet sensual marital activity, despite the heart-warming personal stories of couples who still preserve their passion even though they have a collective age of 157 and three mechanical hips between them, the joke about marital sex is still the old line: Does he *bother* you much?

The short answer, inevitably, is no. Which in itself is interesting, not just because of what it implies, but also because in this age of psychobabble talk shows, where people will quite happily go on television and discuss almost anything, from penis extensions to incest, it appears that ordinary marital sex is still a taboo. Apart from the occasional anonymous appearance in the problem pages, it is virtually ignored by the newspapers and magazines; it is not even something that women talk about much among themselves.

The women do not discuss married sex for two reasons: loyalty and pride. The first because, well, he's your husband and you love him and you don't want to hurt him by implying that your sexual relations are anything less than cataclysmically exciting; and the second because, like the great conspiracy of silence surrounding babies, it's much easier if everyone just takes the line that it's all brilliantly satisfying and generally fantastic. And, in fact, it is nobody's business but your very own.

On paper, it all seems like a great idea. After years on the sexual front line you can finally look forward to meaningful, fulfilling sex with a person who loves you and who won't mind unduly if you only do your bikini line in summer. (Does anyone sane actually do it at any other time? Apart from working girls and swimwear models?) You have a life companion, someone to share your best and worst moments, a person who is all yours and who is on your side. The sex is going to be easy, giving, boundless and, crucially, always available.

And so it is – at least for the first idyllic year. But unless you have no worries, no problems and no obligations, the everyday business of life starts to press in, and, partly because you know the sex is a done deal, you start to put it to one side. As your life together takes off – bigger house, bigger bills, bigger jobs – the one area in your life which can genuinely provide you with release and reaffirmation becomes the last thing you want to do at the end of the day.

For many couples it starts in earnest with babies. Not at the moment of birth, although that comes with its own set of difficulties, but at the very moment of conception, or even in the hours prior to it. There are few things less conducive to an exciting sex life than trying-for-a-baby sex. The very expression makes us feel slightly faint, conjuring up as it does visions of thermometers, folic acid and relentless scheduling. When it comes to erotica, semantics do matter. You really don't want the term *trying* anywhere near your nether region.

When all the trying does eventually result in pregnancy, the process of de-eroticisation begins in earnest. There is the shock of the first internal examination (just pop your pants off and hop up on the bed, will you dear? To which we would quite like to say: *pop* your own pants off). There is the frankly feral finale. There may be stitches, haemorrhoids, prolapses and any number of unpleasant and potentially humiliating side-effects. Your breasts, once so integral to the pursuit of pleasure, are suddenly swollen and bloated with milk, encased in unflattering bras and permanently in danger of leakage. Procreation, which cannot happen without sex, is itself deeply unsexy.

Your poor body has taken an almighty bashing. Even if your partner is genuinely unfazed by the extra folds of flesh on your stomach, the stretch marks and any distressing internal transformations that may have occurred, you, in all likelihood, will be. Unless you are one of those fabled creatures who bounces back after birth (we don't believe these women exist in the wild; they are only possible in our modern world thanks to a unique combination of personal trainer, rabid dieting and Photoshop), your womanly self-regard will be at rock bottom. You have just brought forth another member of the human race (growing an entire human in your very own stomach is really one of the great unsung wonders of the world), but your sense of self may be severely dented. Overnight, you will have been transformed from independent woman to lactating baby slave, whose sole purpose is to protect a very small, very fragile and often very frightening little new person for whom you are now entirely and inescapably responsible.

And so when, at your baby's six-week check-up, the nurse snaps off her plastic examination gloves and asks you, in that special cheery voice

that the medical profession reserves for the very sick, the very old and the very shattered, 'Have you thought about contraception?' you will feel as well disposed towards her as the inhabitants of the Danube shortly after Attila the Hun laid waste to their villages and built his court on the bones of their loved ones. Angry, upset, and quite possibly resentful.

It is then that you enter phase two of marital sex paranoia, because if the nurse is asking you about contraception, the implication must be that all mothers of six-week-old babies are at it like crazed rabbits. Since you are barely able to get out of bed, let alone leap into it in a frenzy of coital passion, the further implication must be that there is something wrong with you. It is then that the really bad stuff starts going on in your head: the not having of the sex becomes a worry. It becomes another opportunity for failure; it becomes an obligation rather than a pleasure; it becomes a *chore*.

Meanwhile your partner, who has been making his own mental adjustments to the new arrival, is looking forward to the resumption of normal service. By now he may well have a similar air to that of a small puppy watching its owner eating a fillet steak: enthusiastically hopeful, mildly soulful, possibly willing even to perform tricks.

There is no perfect way out of this situation, but there is an infallible cure for it: just do it. Dive in. Forget your stomach, your hair, your exhaustion, just crack open a bottle of wine and get on with it. You may be twice – or indeed half – the woman you once were but he is still the man he always was, and somehow you are going to put this thing back together again. It's not about you not fulfilling your marital duties, or anything as Jurassic as that; it's about reconnecting as a couple. Which is essential if you are going to stay married.

Once you're over that first hump, so to speak, it is surprising how quickly you get back into things. Until, of course, it happens all over again …

WHY THERE IS NO EXCUSE FOR BAD SEX.

Oh, all right, perhaps we have two golden rules. This is the second. Because, you know, there really *is* no excuse. This is not the fifties, no woman should have to put up with it. There are manuals and magazines and all the information out there on the interweb, and people can talk about it now, which they could not then, and the societal assumption that ladies were not really supposed to enjoy it unless they were hardly better than hookers has died a magnificent and overdue death.

Good sex, like good cooking, is not the province of a few lucky, talented individuals. It does not require an unreasonably high IQ or a cordon bleu course. It is just a matter of a little care and attention. You should not confuse it with the bells and whistles school that the pornographers love. Good sex can be quick sex, or simple sex (very much like food, again). There is no requirement for 78 positions and any special accoutrements. A little elementary biology and some enthusiasm are all that are required.

In our experience, most men are quite intoxicated by the idea of giving vast amounts of pleasure. It makes them feel madly manly and potent. They just need a little guidance in the early days, and they are off. The guidance is not because they might be ignorant, but simply because what works for one woman will do nothing for another. So some polite suggestions, and a round of applause when he hits the bullseye are fairly essential. Once you are used to each other, subtlety can be an alluring part of sex, but at the start you may find that being bluntly overt is more useful. Yes, there, yes, that, yes please – leave him in no doubt and you will have a lifetime of pleasure. Possibly the sexiest words a man can hear when he is in bed are: Don't Stop.

Should you, by some odd chance, find yourself in bed with someone who seems to have no idea what he is doing, who assumes that five minutes of unimaginative thrusting will do it, or, even worse, twenty minutes of relentless pounding, while you lie there and plan your spring wardrobe, you have two choices. You can write him off and move on to someone more accommodating, or you can have the delicate conversation. We use the word delicate advisedly, because in sexual matters the male ego is at its most fragile, and if bruised, can turn nasty. But sometimes, however gentle and patient you are, the message does not get through. We know one woman who had to explain a few anatomical home truths to a clueless man; she felt so liberated and modern that she could actually have this conversation that she practically drew him diagrams. That night, she skipped up to the bedroom, anticipating a night of wild exploration, only to find him already asleep. She left the next day. There are occasions when losses have to be ruthlessly cut, and that was one of them.

As for your side of it, we do not imagine for a moment that you are anything other than an absolute vixen and would not presume to offer anything so demeaning as sexual tips. This is another of the lovely advantages of getting to a certain age and having been around the block a few times. We suspect that you have been on the receiving end of a few rounds of applause of your very own. But occasionally, even the most sophisticated and experienced woman can be subject to sudden attacks of sexual doubt. This is particularly true if you have come out of a long relationship, or are single and have not done the wild thing in a while – is it really like riding a bicycle or will you find that you have actually forgotten what to do with your hands?

We can report with some authority that it is exactly like riding a bicycle and you do not forget at all. It is one of the few things in life that

does not bear much thinking about. Sex is not an intellectual activity. The danger is, after a spell of drought, that your brain takes over something which should be instinctual and elemental. Not only do you wonder whether you will remember how, but other horrid doubts set up shop in your head and start chattering about your less-than-perfect body and how you are not as bendy as you once were and your eyes get a little squinty first thing in the morning. You can get to the dangerous stage of starting to believe that after years of bitching about bad sex, and laughing at those men who practise it, you might be the one actually doing it.

We contend that it is physically impossible to do bad sex as long as you maintain an open mind, as much abandon as you can muster, enthusiasm, and good manners (it is very bad form to laugh and point). It is helpful to remember that he will absolutely categorically *not* be noticing your little bit of cellulite because he will be far too busy marvelling at your wonderfully smooth skin and the fact that you actually have breasts. So have a cocktail, tear your clothes off, and go crazy. We guarantee that after the first three minutes, all doubts will have run for the border, where they will have to look for some other poor soul to torment.

WHETHER IT IS POSSIBLE OR EVEN DESIRABLE TO INDULGE IN SEX IN THE WAY THAT MEN DO, WITHOUT STRINGS.

It is certainly and wonderfully true that in the liberated noughties, women can, and do, take their pleasure where they can. They can do a one-night stand, and walk away the next morning with their head held high and a little John Wayne swagger in their step. Certain women have even parlayed this ability into entire careers, writing blogs and books and columns on the subject. Pure lust, after years in the dark, has finally stepped out into the sunshine.

But it does seem that there are some fundamental differences between men and women when it comes to sex. Men are evolutionarily designed to have sex with as many and various women as possible; in this way, their genes win the Darwinian battle and go on to conquer the world. The idea of fidelity is biologically unnatural. As humans gathered themselves into societies, and worked out ideas about the family, and the most efficient and comfortable circumstance for bringing up children, the construct of two people pledging themselves to each other was born. But the basic urges of the male could not be denied so easily.

This is why the mistress and the prostitute are such emblematic figures throughout history. Kings and emperors kept mistresses and elevated ladies of the street to perfumed consorts: Nell Gwynn is as much a part of the national consciousness as Queen Victoria. Polygamy has been practised by groups as diverse as Siamese royalty to Salt Lake

City Mormons. The harem is not such a very distant memory. The only famous woman who came anywhere close to such arrangements was Catherine the Great, with her penchant for young guardsmen, although her tally of lovers has been vastly exaggerated – it was probably closer to twelve than the rumoured hundreds, and the thing with the horse was a vicious libel, almost certainly propagated by the French.

So a societal expectation was born to accommodate the male sex drive: it was considered unremarkable for men to need extra-curricular entertainment, while the women sat at home, having the babies. A more pernicious myth grew up alongside this: the reason that women did not run around in the way that men did was because the ladies did not really like sex very much, nor should they. For men it was an expected pleasure; for women, it was simply a necessary mechanism for breeding. The reason that women like Cleopatra and Catherine the Great are so notorious and fenced about with rumour and innuendo is that they were considered entirely unnatural in their sensuality. This falsity was not seriously challenged until the end of the 1960s, and that was only in the more modernised parts of the world: the rumour still holds in many parts of the Middle East and Asia, the more Catholic areas of South America, and in the Bible Belt of North America.

A curious overlap happened as this nasty fable was in its death throes. This was the growth of the idea that fidelity should be actual, rather than a mere lip service. Although various churches and temples had preached constancy for centuries, the hypocrisy of the pious saw to it that there was always unofficial acceptance of the bit on the side. The most vivid example of this is Henry VIII's sexual incontinence while rejoicing in his position as supreme ruler of the Church of England. It is only in our own generation that the custom of a man keeping a mistress has come to seem impossibly seedy and old-fashioned. The idea of heads of state and captains of industry and artistic geniuses maintaining an accommodating lady in a convenient flat in Maida Vale is as antediluvian as keeping a fleet of footmen. Men still are, of course, unfaithful, but in a much more furtive manner.

The science of sex is in its very early days: the brain is still largely a dark continent. There are neurologists who insist that the famous male sex drive is all to do with the amygdala and the hypothalamus. They are currently having a stand-up drag-out fight with the behaviourists who say that sexual attitudes and preferences are entirely to do with societal expectation and customs: witness, for example, the lovely sexually liberated ladies of Tahiti who struck Fletcher Christian and his crew as such a charming contrast to the starched British maidens that the sailors never went home again. The evolutionary psychologists bring out their own theories of hunting and gathering. Statistics are hurled about like custard pies. Just to confuse everyone, newspapers run sensationalist headlines, framing the latest academic findings to suit their own agendas. Every new scholarly paper is greeted with acres of contradictory anecdotal evidence.

The old ideas of Jung and the new ideas of the biologists can lead to confusions of their own. Not every man will have a pure male brain, nor be all animus. There is a subtle difference between being a woman, and having feminine attributes. Hormones have an undeniable effect on behaviour, but not every human gets an exactly calibrated set. It does seem that men do have more sex, think about it more, and are more likely to do it with people whose names they did not quite catch. Men are more prone to be thrilled by even the most amateurish pornography, and can easily disassociate sex from love. It is still unclear whether this is a result of differences in the brain, or cultural attitudes, nature or nurture, and the fighting between the different schools of thought rages on like mad radio static.

If it is true that men can go out and have sex with the same emotional detachment that they bring to eating a sandwich, and we are certainly not sure that this *is* true of all men, then can women, in these thrilling days of equality and anything goes, do that too? Our initial, instinctive reaction to this question is: probably not. Women do seem more inclined to link sex with love, and a series of one-night stands can leave a faint hangover of futility. Despite the new theories of the biologists that women will be unfaithful because they are subconsciously looking for the best genes for their offspring, there is still the rock hard fact that the male prostitute is vanishingly rare, while men of all classes and cultures still routinely pay for sex. Women have great power as consumers: entire marketing departments are devoted exclusively to them. If there was a demand for the male hooker, surely he would be out there by now?

There is still the notion of shame that hangs around sex, when it comes to women. They are far less likely to admit to masturbating than men are, and will not boast about their number of sexual partners, or blatantly bask in their powers of seduction. Even in these enlightened days, there are no male equivalents for the words slut or slapper, which, despite the dark fears of the anti-PC lobby, are still in unremarkable usage. It could be that women, despite their liberation, have internalised the message that it is not quite nice to go out and find sexual pleasure where they will.

All this means that it probably is more difficult for a woman to have sex without strings than it is for a man. But it may quite easily be that many of these ideas do not always obtain. It could be nothing to do with your gender. If you love sex, know better than to confuse it with romantic love, are adventurous and bold, and refuse to fall for the trap of false expectations, you have everything you need to just go and get it. It could be that this has little to do with your chromosomes, and everything to do with your very own character. All humans are the products of their biological make-up and their environment: the hundred billion neurones firing off in your brain, the snaking story of your DNA, and the narrative woven by your culture all combine to make you what you are. But you do not have to be a slave to any of those things; you can question assumptions and challenge entrenched ideas. Which is a very long way of saying that if you want to have the sex, maybe you just should, whatever anyone else has to say about it.

MOVIE SEX.

There are elements of the culture which are so commonplace and blatant that they get taken entirely for granted. The fact that you can watch two strangers performing sexual intercourse in your own front room is, once you stop to think about it, ragingly odd. Yet every time you watch a film with a sex scene in it, this is what you are doing. (It is also quite strange that people like watching murder, evisceration and blunt force trauma for entertainment at nine in the evening, but then this is a human tradition that goes back to public hangings.)

We are not Mary Whitehouse manqués, tutting furiously about decency and the end of days, but it does seem remarkably peculiar that in any movie featuring a man and a woman, whether it be about political corruption, alien invasion, global warming or family crisis, there will almost certainly be a moment where all their clothes fall off and there is a certain amount of moaning and writhing.

Some people might think this a good thing. Your grandmothers would never have seen anyone having sex, possibly not even themselves, since they mostly did it in the dark. Shining a light on the mystery might have helped remove taboos – come on in, the water is fine. But there are dangers to movie sex. There is almost never any foreplay. Kiss, kiss, shove it straight in, momentary sighing and arching of the back, instant orgasm. This may lead to a skewed idea of what is actually involved, in real life. There is rarely any laughter, which is a crucial component of good sex, especially when it doesn't go quite right. It is all very earnest and seamless, with a great deal of meaningful gazing. The movie sex clichés are mildly annoying: the hand clutching at the bedclothes to indicate ecstasy, the *ripping* of the shirt as shorthand for 'I must have you now or I shall explode', the silent closing of the eyes to denote erotic fulfilment. No one ever says: No, no, not there, or, Is it in yet?

Films are not life, everyone knows that, but the danger is that, in the movies, sex is the province of the fabulously beautiful. It's all Angelina Jolies, all the time. In films, no one who is old, fat, plain or spotty has sex. It is confined to the utterly gorgeous, with perfect bodies, smooth skin, lustrous hair and taut muscle tone. Because no one ever remarks on these oddities, the risk is that the subconscious concludes that the normal woman, with her rounded belly and her little bit of cellulite and her bad hair days, is not really allowed to have sex at all, or at least should follow her grandmother's example, and do it with the lights off.

Should you ever find yourself anywhere close to falling into this trap, remember what short, skinny, odd-looking Woody Allen had to say about it: 'Is sex dirty? Only if you're doing it right.'

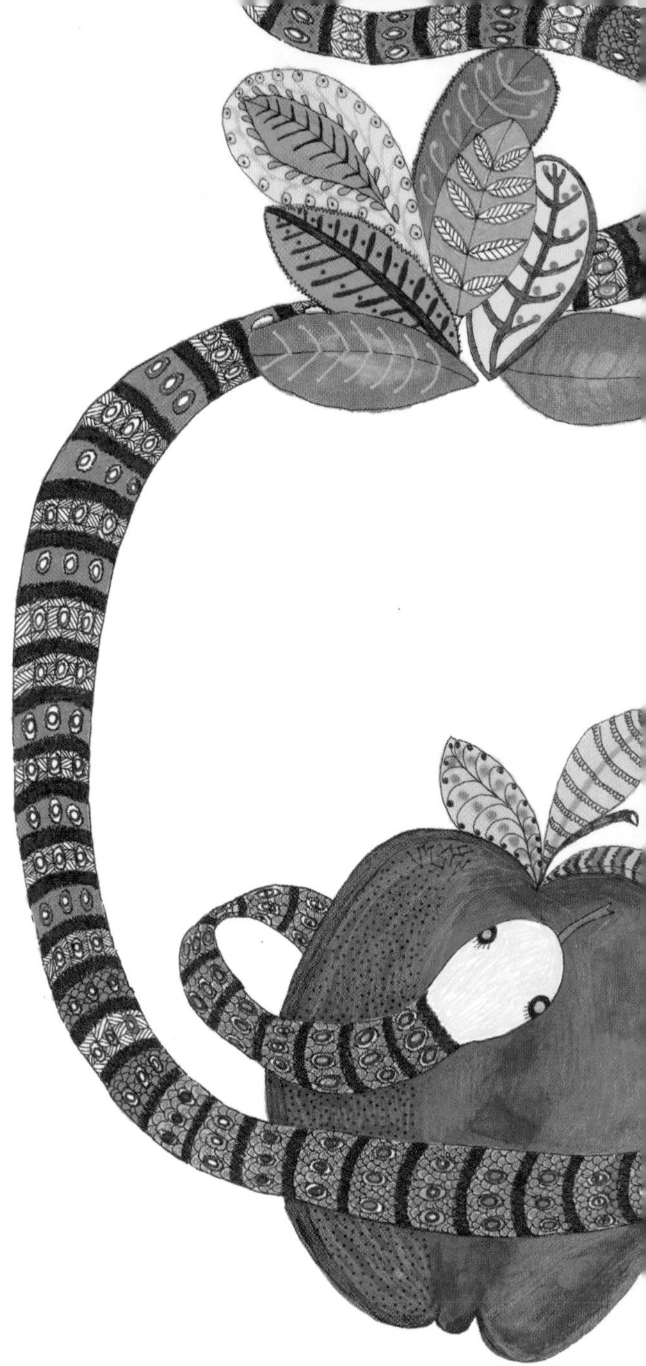

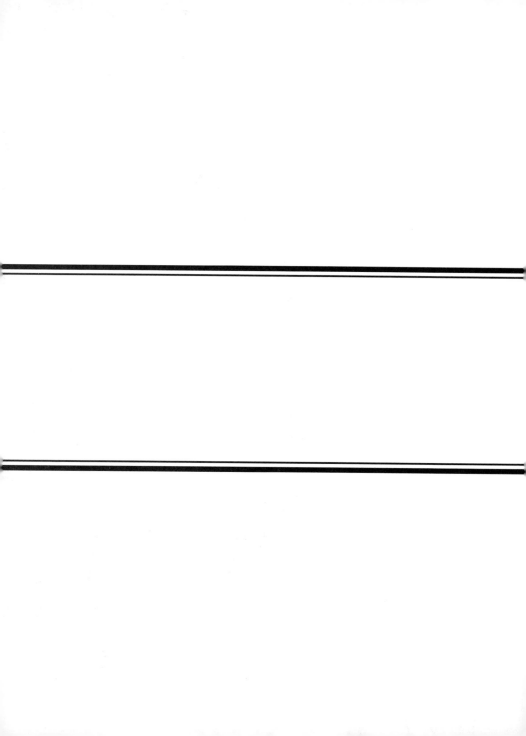

THE PRACTICAL CHAPTER

–

CHAPTER FIFTEEN

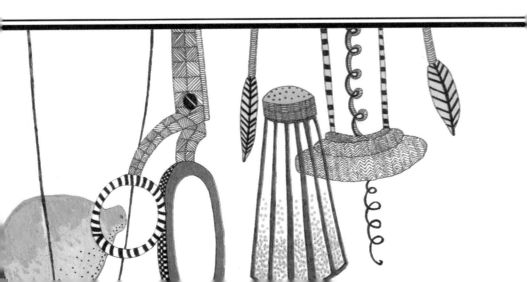

THINGS TO COOK.

This is just a small selection of recipes we love, almost all of which you can fit on the back of a credit card. Most of them are our own inventions, although some are inspired by, and adapted from, our favourite cookery books.

A NOTE ON INGREDIENTS.

You will notice that we make liberal use of olive oil and garlic in almost everything we cook. We do not apologise for this, although it may make some of the recipes sound a little repetitive. We also cook almost nothing without sea salt: we like Maldon the best, although we understand this is open to debate.

For cooking, it is best to use a standard virgin olive oil. For dressing or drizzling purposes, get the best extra virgin you can afford. It really does make a difference.

Marigold Swiss Vegetable bouillon powder, should you not have heard of it, is such a miracle that we can't remember what we did before it was invented. You can find it, in its little green pot with the distinctive orange lid, in every supermarket and most good local shops. You simply mix up one heaped teaspoon to a regular cup of hot water and it is as if you have actual chicken stock. We find it indispensable for soups and stews, and even add it to salad dressing. It also gives a lovely flavour to any boiled vegetable – especially potatoes and winter root vegetables; simply add it to the cooking water instead of salt. We would like to make it clear that we have no idea who the Marigold people are, are not sponsored by them, related to them, bribed by them, or anything sinister. It's just truly wonderful stuff.

A tip on chillies: when using fresh chillies, bear in mind that the heat is in the seeds. If you want something very spicy, keep most of the seeds; if you just want a suggestion of heat, discard them.

ULTIMATE HEALTH-GIVING GREEN SUMMER SOUP.

This is not only a delicious cooling treat, but a very useful tonic to have in your fridge – we quite often just drink it out of a glass to make sure we are getting our five-a-day. Heaven in a cup.

In a liquidiser, put a cucumber, cubed, a handful of watercress, the juice of half a lemon, I peeled garlic clove, a tablespoon of Marigold bouillon powder, a generous gloop of good olive oil, 2 tablespoons of natural yoghurt, and a pinch of dried chilli. Add a couple of ice cubes, and $\frac{1}{3}$ of a litre of water. Blitz. Check for seasoning. You can add a little more water if it is too thick.

Enough for 4.

THE ONLY
TOMATO SALAD.

We firmly believe that all you need for a tomato salad is olive oil and salt; no nonsense with balsamic vinegar or fancy dressings. The number of tomatoes you use depends on how many people you are feeding, and their appetites.

Slice the tomatoes and then anoint them with your very best sea salt. Let the tomatoes sit for at least an hour. The salt will draw out all their lovely juices. Then you just add a good drizzle of quality olive oil, a little twist of black pepper, and possibly a scattering of basil, or finely chopped parsley, or a snip of chives.

SIMPLE BUT PERFECT
PATATE AL FORNO.

Peel your potatoes, allowing one large one for each person. We have an irrational love of red Desirée, but anything not too waxy will do. Cut into rough cubes. Rinse under a cold tap and throw into a baking tray. Drench in olive oil and scatter with sea salt and a little freshly ground pepper. Bake at 180°C/350°F/Gas Mark 4 for approximately 35–40 minutes, turning once or twice.

If you're feeling fancy you can add a few cloves of whole garlic; some oregano, rosemary or thyme; some chilli paste (this makes them a bit like *patatas bravas*, so then you might want to whip up a little tomato sauce to dip them in); a handful of pancetta.

DINNER-PARTY CHICKEN.

This is a variation on a brilliant Jamie Oliver recipe. It is perfect for when people are coming over because you can throw it in the oven and it cooks itself. It goes really well with the *patate al forno*.

For 4:

Preheat the oven to 170°C/325°F/Gas Mark 3. Arrange four chicken thighs and four breasts in a deep-sided baking tray. Split and peel six garlic cloves, and poke them underneath the meat. Cut as many tomatoes as you fancy into quarters, or halves, depending on size (use lots – cherry are ideal, but this recipe is great for using up old ones from the bottom of the fridge) and then scatter about ⅓ of them on top of the chicken and around the tray. Tear up a big bunch of basil, including stalks, and stuff into every remaining nook and cranny. Pour over about ½ bottle of wine, drizzle in the olive oil and season with salt and black pepper.

Roast for about 1 hour and 20 minutes. Check every now and again to make sure the liquid hasn't dried up, and if it's looking low, top up with more wine. Don't cover the skin with liquid, though: what makes this so delicious is the combination of moist meat and crispy skin. When you're ready to go, lift the chicken pieces out of the pan using a big slotted spoon, so that the liquid stays behind, and arrange in a dish with the tomatoes, which will be all lovely and slow-roasted by now. Put the jus in a jug and serve on the side.

DELICIOUS AND SIMPLE SQUID WITH TOMATOES AND GARLIC.

This is a lovely easy supper, best suited for 1 or 2.

Cut up 3 fat tomatoes into rough cubes, and finely chop 3 garlic cloves and a red chilli. Soften the garlic for a couple of minutes in a little olive oil, over a low heat; add the tomatoes, turn up the heat to medium, and cook for about 5 minutes. Add a dash of lemon juice and a good pinch of sea salt. Put into a bowl.

Meanwhile, slit open a squid tube, score it gently all over in a criss-cross pattern, making sure not to cut right through the flesh. (Helpful tip: make sure the squid is absolutely dry: if necessary, pat it with kitchen paper to remove any moisture.) Cut into pieces about an inch square.

Take a big frying pan, add a gloop of olive oil, and put it over a high heat. When the pan is hot, throw in the squid, and cook it very quickly, for literally 2 minutes, stirring a bit. The squid will curl up. Remove with a slotted spoon and add to the tomatoes. Throw over a scattering of chopped green parsley. Have a taste – you may need to add a dash more lemon and salt.

AUBERGINES WITH GARLIC AND WILTED GREENS.

This is adapted from a Nigel Slater recipe. It is perfect as a vegetarian supper for a Sunday night, or a wonderful side dish with lamb or chicken.

Will serve 2 as a main course, or 4 as a side dish.

Chop up one large or two small aubergines into smallish cubes. Fry in a big sauté pan with some olive oil over a medium heat, along with a couple of cloves of finely chopped garlic. Keep it all moving or the garlic will burn. After 3 or 4 minutes, add ½ cupful of chicken stock or made-up Marigold bouillon, and let the aubergines simmer. The liquid will reduce, so you may need to add a little more. Cook for 10 minutes or so, by which time all the stock should have been drawn into the vegetables, and you will be left with a soft silky mess. The aubergines should be outrageously tender: no al dente here. You can add a little dried chilli if you want a bit of heat.

Finally, throw in a handful of rocket or watercress leaves, and stir until they have just wilted in the heat.

COMPLETE CHEAT'S TOM YUM SOUP.

This is so easy and such a cheat that we sometimes feel mildly guilty even making it.

This recipe serves 2.

Finely chop 3 cloves of garlic and 1 red chilli. Bring enough chicken stock or Marigold bouillon for two generous bowls to the boil. Add the garlic and chilli and simmer for a couple of minutes. Stir in a good tablespoon of Thai red curry paste – we like Blue Dragon. (They do have an actual Tom Yum paste, but we think there is something not quite right about it, and have found it is the curry paste that gets the exact flavour we want.) Throw in the juice of 1 lime and 2 handfuls of raw tiger prawns. These will cook very quickly, so you only need to simmer them for 2 minutes. You can also used cooked king prawns if you want; they're not quite as good, but perfectly acceptable. If you do use them, cook them for 1 minute only. Taste. You may want to add a little more lime juice – the citrus flavour should be quite strong – or even a pinch of dried chilli for more spice, and possibly a little sea salt for flavour.

Serve in deep white bowls with a generous scattering of coriander. You can add a little chopped mint as well, if you like; it is not at all correct, but it tastes lovely.

That's it. It will be almost like being in a proper Thai restaurant. Your friends will be amazed. For extra deliciousness, you can add some very finely sliced strips of red pepper and a few straw mushrooms at the beginning, but it is just as lovely without.

IRISH STEW.

Don't listen to anyone who tells you that Irish stew should be a brown stew, and talks about dredging with flour or browning or any other heresies. Irish stew is a *white* stew. There are purists who argue that the addition of carrots is an abomination, but we have no strong feelings about this. Carrots will give a slightly softer sweeter flavour, so it is up to individual taste.

This version is the traditional one, as taught to us by our mothers. Serves 4.

Take 8 small lamb chops, or 4 lamb steaks cut into largish chunks. Slice 4 big waxy potatoes, quite thickly. Slice 1 large onion, finely. If desired, slice 1 large carrot. Take a big heavy pot (Le Creuset is best), and make a layer of each ingredient, starting with the onions, seasoning with sea salt and black pepper as you go. Cover the lot with chicken stock. Bring to a very low simmer, so that the water is barely moving. This is important: any hint of a boil will turn the meat tough.

Cook on top of the stove for a minimum of 3 hours, preferably 4 or 5. You may need to remove the scum that comes to the surface. (Do not be alarmed by this, it is a normal by-product of the simmering meat.) Check occasionally to see if you need to add a little more stock. The liquid should just cover the dry ingredients.

In the final 15 minutes, add 2 handfuls of pearl barley, which you cook separately by bringing to the boil in some lightly salted water, for about 45 minutes.

You can make this dish the day before and reheat it, as the flavours will have developed more by the second day. It is the perfect winter supper, giving you tender melting meat, and a delicious thin broth. We like to serve it in big bowls with a spoon and fork for eating, and a generous sprinkling of chopped parsley – the regular kind, flatleaf is too strong – and some soda bread.

For a spring version of this, leave out the pearl barley, and instead add 2 handfuls of frozen petits pois for the last 5 minutes of cooking, which gives a delightful light fresh stew, perfect for a windy April day.

SPAGHETTI WITH BACON, CHILLI AND ROCKET.

This is a little invention of our own. The colours of this dish are particularly pleasing: the yellow of the spaghetti, the deep green of the leaves, the pinkish brown of the bacon and the sharp red flecks of the chillies make it a thing of beauty.

Serves 4.

Cook two good handfuls of spaghetti in plenty of salted water, as usual. The Italians say that spaghetti should be cooked in water as salty as the Mediterranean; it is also important to make sure it is at a good rolling boil before you add the pasta.

Meanwhile, chop 6 rashers of streaky bacon and fry them in olive oil until browned and slightly crispy. Set aside. Using the same pan, so as not to waste the bacon flavours in the oil, turn the heat right down, and very gently fry 4 finely chopped garlic cloves with a good pinch of dried chilli for 3 minutes; add 2 handfuls of rinsed rocket leaves, turn the heat up to medium, and swish about with the garlic until the leaves are wilted. This also takes only a couple of minutes. Add to the bacon in a big bowl.

Drain the spaghetti and pour on top of the other ingredients. Mix it all up, and check for seasoning. Because of the saltiness of the bacon, you will probably not need to add any extra salt. You might like to drizzle over a little good grassy olive oil, as a final *je ne sais quoi*.

SMOKED MACKEREL PÂTÉ.

This is so easy it's almost embarrassing. It is especially nice served with toasted white sourdough bread, or as a dinner party starter with a green salad.

Serves 4 (greedy) people.

In a medium-sized mixing bowl, bash up some boneless smoked mackerel fillet (of the type that comes vacuum packed) with a fork, adding a glug of olive oil. Snip 1 or 2 anchovies (in brine) into little bits and add to the fillets, followed by a spoonful of capers, if you want. (If you don't like capers, chopped black olives can work well too.) Add ½ pot of fromage frais and the same of half-fat crème fraiche (around 300g in total) and stir, all the time mashing up the fish: you want it roughly to the same consistency as lumpy hummus. Give it a good squeeze of lemon, add some chopped parsley and season with freshly ground pepper. Cover with cling film and chill until ready to serve.

FOR THE TIMES YOU ARE TIRED AND HUNGRY AND CAN HARDLY BE BOTHERED TO COOK.

These are ideas, more than recipes.

HALLOUMI.

A rubbery, salty cheese you either love or hate, which is delicious lightly dredged in flour and fried in olive oil for a couple of minutes each side, until golden, and served with sliced tomatoes and a scattering of flatleaf parsley or rocket leaves.

COD'S ROE.

You can do a similar thing with the cod's roe that you find in little green tins – a perfect storecupboard staple. Drain the roe, dredge in fine polenta, and fry in olive oil over a medium heat for 3 minutes each side. Dress with plenty of lemon juice and black pepper and a pinch of sea salt. Some people like this on toast for a Sunday night treat. Again, plain tomatoes are a perfect accompaniment, or a little green salad.

CHICKPEA MASH.

This is one of our favourite comfort foods, and only takes 5 minutes. Take a tin of cooked chickpeas, rinse thoroughly in cold water, and drain. In a small pan, bring 3 cups of water to the boil with a tablespoon of Marigold bouillon powder, a clove of garlic and a pinch of saffron; boil the chickpeas for 3 or 4 minutes. Remove with a slotted spoon so that you capture all the slender saffron strands. Do not throw away the stock.

Put the chickpeas into the Magimix with a glug of olive oil, a pinch of sea salt, a dash of lemon juice, and, if you like, a pinch of dried chilli (you can see we are on a bit of a chilli kick at the moment, ever since we heard of its serotonin-boosting properties). Blitz until you have a rough paste. If it is a little stiff, add some of the cooking liquid. You want the consistency to be loose, but not sloppy.

This is lovely on its own for a quiet supper with perhaps some sourdough toast, or, if you have the energy for grilling, quite outrageously delicious with a lamb chop.

It is also good cold, with tortilla chips or pita bread.

SALT AND SPICE PRAWNS.
This is another 5-minute wonder.

Take as many raw peeled king prawns as you want, dredge in a mixture of plain flour and fine polenta flour, cook for 3 minutes in very hot groundnut oil, with a good pinch of dried chilli. Serve with a generous sprinkling of sea salt and a dash of lemon juice and eat with a green salad.

If you have the time and inclination, you can do a Chinese version. Before cooking the prawns, fry 1 chopped garlic clove, 2 sliced spring onions, and 1 finely sliced red chilli per serving very, very gently in a little sesame oil. The garlic should not brown. Set aside. Cook the prawns as above, minus the dried chilli, and then toss them in the spring onion and garlic mixture, adding the salt, but leaving out the lemon. You can eat these on their own, or with some egg noodles, or white rice.

PRAWNS WITH GARLIC AND PARSLEY.

Another incredibly quick and comforting supper. Very gently fry 6 chopped garlic cloves in butter until tender; add a handful of chopped parsley and a handful of breadcrumbs. Put in a big bowl, then flash-fry a double handful of king prawns in olive oil – this takes 2 minutes. Add to the garlic and breadcrumb mixture and mix up. Perfect for 2, with a little watercress salad on the side.

WILTED GREENS WITH FRIED BACON AND GARLIC.

Yet another 5-minute wonder. For two people: fry up four rashers of bacon, chopped, turn down the heat and add a few sliced cloves of garlic (go gently, you do not want the garlic to brown), and cook for a further couple of minutes. You can throw in a sliced chilli if you want some spice. Rinse a quadruple handful of green leaves – spinach, watercress and rocket is a lovely combination – and add to the pan. Turn up the heat and stir with a wooden spoon – the delicate leaves will wilt in a matter of moments. Dress with some good olive oil.

PEAS WITH FETA AND MINT.

A classic spring dish. Cook some baby peas, and while they are still hot, stir in plenty of finely chopped mint, and a handful of feta crumbled into little cubes, and a dash of olive oil. If you are feeling energetic, you can add some broad beans.

FISH SOUP.

For many years of our young lives, we were afraid of fish soup, regarding it as something you could only cook well if you were born in Marseilles. Finally, we drove off our piscine demons, and invented our very own version, which is so foolproof that you can make it whether you were born in Market Harborough or Musselburgh.

This will do well for 4.

Finely chop 1 small onion, 1 red chilli and 4 cloves of garlic, and, in a deep sauté pan, fry very gently for a few minutes in olive oil. Add a pinch of saffron, and 6 fat tomatoes, roughly chopped. Fry for another minute over a low heat. Add 4 cups of fish stock (bought is fine, although if you have any prawn shells and fishbones, you can easily make your own by boiling them up for 10 minutes with a bay leaf and a stick of celery, and a tablespoon of Marigold bouillon powder. Bring to a simmer, and leave to cook for a good hour, really, the longer the better. It will reduce, so you will need to add more stock, or water, at intervals.

Once all the flavours have deepened, and you have a wonderful red broth, add the juice of $\frac{1}{2}$ lemon, and a handful each of raw peeled king prawns, squid sliced into rings, and monkfish cut into chunks. You can substitute any other firm white fish, but nothing flaky, as this breaks up into the soup and muddies the broth. Bring back to a low simmer and cook for no more than 2 minutes. Check for seasoning; you might need a good pinch of sea salt.

And there is your perfect fish soup, entirely inauthentic, nothing to do with Marseilles, but absolutely delicious for all that. Serve it with chopped parsley. If you want something a little more substantial, more like a fish stew, simply add some lovely yellow waxy potatoes, cooked separately and cut into inch-square chunks.

Sadly, it does not bear reheating, as the prawns will go tough and the monkfish woolly.

A SLOW, YELLOW
PEA SOUP.

This takes time, but is absurdly simple.

This will do for 4 as a first course, or 2 as a supper on its own.

Take 1 very finely chopped onion, 2 chopped cloves of garlic, a pinch of saffron, and 2 heaped cups of split yellow peas, cover with water, add a good pinch of sea salt or a teaspoon of Marigold bouillon powder, according to taste, bring to a mild simmer, and cook for 1½ hours. The split peas have a tendency to stick, so you need to stir them regularly, and add more water if they are absorbing all the liquid.

At the end you will have a thick, scented, yellow soup. Check for seasoning, and serve in shallow bowls, with a drizzle of olive oil and a good go of black pepper. We sometimes fry up thinly sliced bacon rashers until crispy and add a spoonful to the finished soup.

A FAST GREEN PEA SOUP

Serves 4 people.

Take 6 big handfuls of frozen petits pois, 3 cups of water, a clove of garlic, and 2 teaspoons of Marigold powder; bring to the boil and cook for 3 minutes. Put into the liquidiser with a glug of olive oil, 2 or 3 leaves of mint, a pinch of dried chilli, if you fancy it, and blitz until smooth.

That's it. Really.

AN ELEGANT MOZZARELLA SALAD.

This salad is a perfect marriage of textures and tastes, and looks incredibly pretty on the plate. Big white plates are best, to show off all the different colours to their best advantage.

Serves 4.

Take 2 fat balls of buffalo mozzarella (this is important; the bog-standard stuff is too rubbery for this particular salad) and tear them up into biggish pieces. Place in the centre of your 4 plates. Cook a cupful of puy lentils in chicken stock if you are being fancy, or plain salted water if you are not. Drain, and let them stand until they are just warm. Scatter them over the cheese.

Surround this with rocket leaves and red peppers, sliced as finely as you can contrive. If you feel like it, you can add a few cherry tomatoes. Drizzle with olive oil, a good pinch of sea salt, and a very little black pepper.

WHITE CHOCOLATE POTS WITH BLACKBERRIES.

We are not much for pudding, usually offering people squares of Green & Black chocolate, or cheese and watercress salad at the end of dinner, but if we ever feel a bit swanky, this is our failsafe. It was adapted from the famous Ivy recipe of frozen berries with white chocolate sauce.

This will do for 4 or 6, depending on the size of your cups or ramekins. It is very rich, so you do not need much. It should ideally be eaten with a delicate teaspoon.

Melt a bar of good white chocolate; add ¼ litre of double cream, and stir very gently over a low heat until thoroughly integrated. You should really do this with a double boiler, or with a glass bowl over a pot of boiling water, but we quite often just do it very gently with a non-stick pan and a wooden spoon.

Decant the mixture into little white ramekins and put into the fridge for at least 3 hours. (It can also look fabulously pretty in delicate espresso cups, if you are having a grand dinner party.)

When you are ready to serve it, just add 3 or 4 lovely fresh blackberries on the top. The black of the fruit looks glorious against the white vanilla, and the slight sourness of the berries cuts the thick sweetness of the pots. Strawberries are too sweet, although we sometimes add a raspberry.

Interesting note: We once had a disaster with this, when we were having 9 people for lunch. We took our eye off the chocolate and it caught and burnt, because we were naughtily not using a double boiler. It was a Sunday and there was no time to go out and get anything else. But when we tasted it, it was in fact delicious: the burning had produced a wonderful caramel effect. So we put the lot into little cups, and added great dollops of whipped cream, and called it Burnt Vanilla Pots, and it went down a storm. This proves for us one of the great lessons of cooking: sometimes a complete rout will turn out to be a marvellous new recipe.

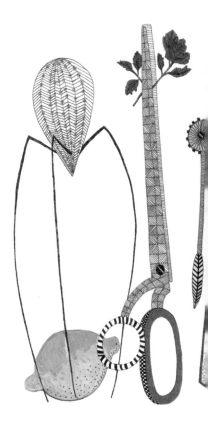

OTHER USEFUL PRACTICAL THINGS – NOT TO DO WITH FOOD.

HOW NOT TO MAKE ASSUMPTIONS.

You will never be able to eradicate this habit entirely, since it seems that humans are hard-wired to sum people up in the first seven seconds of meeting. Almost certainly the ancestral past required humans to be incredibly quick to recognise friend or foe, real or phoney, because in those good old days it was literally a matter of survival.

But assumptions are cheap and lazy; they confine the mind rather than broaden the horizon. There is civilisation now; there is literature and poetry and the study of psychology. The mind can be trained not to extrapolate too much from the trap of first impressions.

The best way to avoid assumptions is to keep in mind those you have made in the past that turned out to be catastrophically wrong. Our own favourite took place on the top deck of a lovely old Routemaster bus, chugging slowly down Piccadilly in Christmas traffic.

In the seat next to us was a woman with a weathered face and a smoker's voice, and a little boy of about seven, with a severe skinhead haircut. Hardly even thinking about it, we assumed, from his hair, from his strong London accent, from his sports shoes and his age, that he was a tough little tyke. Suddenly, he pointed out of the window. '*Look*,' he said to his mother, in tones of awed wonder.

We looked ourselves, wondering what he could be pointing at – a huge Hummer, a flashy Ferrari, a man with only one leg? The bus had stopped outside Fortnum & Mason, one of the grandest, most sophisticated shops in London, catering to the exclusive rich. Its Christmas window display was one of delicate, expensive items – Sèvres china, Waterford glass, cashmere gloves, many pointless baubles, the kind of thing entirely geared to catch the eye of hedge fund babies and Russian princesses.

'Look,' said the little skinhead boy, gesturing at the window, his voice falling soft and low. 'Lots of *beautiful* things.'

There was not a toy or a truck in sight in this window display, no athletic equipment or shiny gadgets guaranteed to appeal to small boys of any class. And yet he was bewitched.

We read ourselves a small lecture and smiled the rest of the way home. Now whenever we are tempted to make an assumption too far, we remember that child.

HOW NOT TO GO MAD.

Do not always believe everything you read. Some of it certainly will not be true.

HOW NOT TO GO MAD, PART TWO.

There are going to be moments when no one gets it. You try and explain in words of one syllable, and they look at you as if you have special needs. They just don't understand your desire to be alone, your rejection of the expected, your secret dreams: they disregard your darkest fears, your most obvious shining hopes. Sometimes strangers or acquaintances do this, and it is fairly easy to brush off. You can call on your age and experience and know that not everyone will get it. It's a minor communication problem, a matter of different perspectives. You might feel a small bruise, because even after twenty years in the adult world, it can sometimes be a shock to find that not everyone sees that world as you do.

The real killer is when the people you love the most don't get it. If you are anything like we are, you like to romanticise your friendships. Of course you do – with the old and the dear ones, you have years of history together. You are getting to that age when looking back on your youthful selves and all you have come through together is one of the greatest and most alluring comforts known to woman. So when the oldest and the most known don't get it, it can be like a kick to the stomach.

You have defences for the slights of strangers, but a small misunderstanding from an old friend cuts into you like a steel stiletto. You were all fine and grown up and suddenly you are falling apart, and no amount of perspective police can make any difference, and you feel as if you are losing your reason.

The only solution to this one is to understand that sometimes there is *no one in the entire world* who gets it. This is the human state, and there is no pill for it. It is part of the deal. You can get furious, and tearful, and disappointed, and that is fine. You know your own remedies: red wine, plain chocolate, dancing about hysterically in the kitchen at eleven at night, with the songs of the mid-seventies' Stones very, very loud. It's a reality check, and maybe everyone, no matter how secretly romantic, needs those.

You can take it. It's life, Jim, just exactly as we know it.

HOW NOT TO GO MAD, PART THREE.

Never try to change a man. You know this, but sometimes it is necessary to be reminded. You can polish him up a little, buy him a sharp suit, make gentle hints about getting rid of that fringe, but you can never change him in any fundamental way. Love him just the way he is, otherwise you are setting yourself up for the heartbreak of dashed expectations.

We don't really know why women so love to think they can transform men. There are no double-blind studies on this one. Who knows? Maybe we ladies just like a project.

HOW TO MAKE YOUR BED.

A little trick our mothers taught us is to make the bed before you get out of it. Instead of throwing off the blankets and jumping up in the morning, lie there for a moment and pull the sheets up from within, then slide out of the side, so that you leave the bed virtually made. Then it is just a matter of tucking in the edges and smoothing the top. It sounds absurd, but it really is much easier this way. It makes us happy each morning, anyway.

HOW TO SAVE MONEY AND NOT FEEL TRAPPED BY THE BEAUTY INDUSTRY, ALL AT THE SAME TIME.

There are some easy and cheap ways to make your own beauty products, if you have ten minutes and a liquidiser.

You can make your very own perfect exfoliating scrubs by putting a handful of sea salt and a bunch of thyme or rosemary and two cups of olive oil in a blender and blitzing the whole thing.

A perfect cleanser can be composed of a cup of avocado oil with five drops each of lavender and camomile essential oil. Massage it into your face at night and then remove with a flannel and some warm water.

A combination of avocado and groundnut oil, with whatever essential oil you prefer added, makes a lovely body moisturiser. We like bergamot, lime and lavender, or rosemary with a dash of jasmine.

Bath oil is fabulously expensive, and the really good ones are a heavenly and subtle treat. But you can just as easily concoct your own with any good base oil you like – sunflower, groundnut, whatever – and again, some essential oils. Rosemary is good to wake up with in the morning, lavender calming before going to bed at night, rose frankly sybaritic, and frankincense exotically strong medicine.

Making your own shampoos, soaps and candles is possible, but time-consuming, and involves a lot of surfing the interweb for recipes and special ingredients. But a mashed-up avocado on the hair or some coconut oil do work wonderfully as conditioners.

HOW NOT TO EAT LOTS OF CHOCOLATE LATE AT NIGHT.

For some reason, it has taken us almost forty years to master this one, and even now we're not sure we've quite managed it. You know how it is: you've been good all day, you've eaten your five fruits and colourful vegetables, you've drunk the water, you've avoided caffeine and crisps. You've eaten your nutritionally complete supper and now you're just settling down to watch a nice bit of television, or read a book, or wander about on the internet and something, somewhere, in the darkest recesses of the most primitive corner of your brain, starts up the mantra: cho-co-late; cho-co-late. It's like some ancient drum-beat, an irresistible siren call. Before you know it, you're surrounded by empty wrappers, and you can't even remember how. Or why. All you know is how much, and it's a lot, enough to awaken the serpent of self-loathing, who more often than not just takes one look at the carnage and says, in a hissy voice: Oh, what the hell, you might as well scoff the lot. Which is how you can end up eating an entire bar of Green & Black's Almond milk chocolate in one sitting, or a whole tub of Cadbury's Celebrations.

Rule number one: count to ten before you reach for the box, bar or tin. It's a very simple technique, but it works. Then select no more than three chocolates, and put them on a small plate. This is the equivalent of pouring a glass of wine instead of slugging it straight from the bottle. Do not, at this stage, start throwing them in your mouth: eating standing up is a recipe for disaster, since you will almost certainly be able to consume at least two before making it back to the sofa.

Now put the remaining chocolate away. Do not take it with you.

Eat your chocolate slowly and consciously. Savour it. It helps also if the chocolate you keep in the house is only of the highest grade. Cheap chocolates are much easier to scoff than expensive ones, not just because of the straightforward economic implications, but also because the latter are much richer. Embrace the warm, smug feeling of being in control.

OR, CONVERSELY, HOW TO EAT YOUR CHOCOLATE WITH PRIDE.

If you, like us, sometimes do eat a whole bar, for the very hell of it, just because you are an autonomous human, and you can do what you like, it is important to resist the temptation to beat yourself up afterwards. You have not been out selling dodgy sub-prime mortgages to people who cannot afford them; you have not single-handedly blown a hole in the ozone layer. Put in an emergency call to the perspective police at once. They will kindly remind you that failing to exhibit self-control does not mean that you are an evil person. If they are feeling chatty, they might go on a bit about how there are people out there with perfect self-discipline who are actually not very nice at all, and insist on controlling their environment to such a degree that they never get laid.

HOW TO DEAL WITH A BORE.

There are some people who seem to regard talking exclusively about themselves and their own roaringly dull concerns as a life's work. We used to regard bores with pity, thinking dullness was something innate, like being born with brown eyes or no sense of taste. Now we think it is in fact an act of narcissistic aggression. The true mark of a bore is someone who has absolutely no interest in anything except themselves. You say something innocuous about dialectic materialism, and they say: 'Funnily enough, I once met a girl in 1973 in Colchester who could not abide shellfish. No,' they say, 'I tell a lie, it wasn't 1973, because in 1973 I was living in Acton, in the days before it was colonised by yuppies.' At this point you have no choice but to sit back and watch them go, even though you would quite like to point out that no one has used the word 'yuppie' since 1987.

The key to not dying of sheer dullness is to regard these people as some kind of sociological experiment. Imagine you are a scientist, observing some rare species in the wild. You are an anthropologist, tracking the arcane rituals of a forgotten tribe. See how long it is before they actually ask *you* a question. You can even time them, with furtive glances at the second hand on your watch. At this point, the whole thing becomes quite diverting, and the feeling of having pins stuck in your eyes lessens.

HOW TO JUDGE CHARACTER.

If you want to know if someone is genuinely nice, take them for dinner in a restaurant. The way a person treats waiters is one of the quickest and most infallible methods of judging whether he or she is a warm-hearted, generous human being or a sociopathic bigot – although 'Hello, my name is Robert Mugabe' can also be a clue. But in normal social situations, the restaurant thing can be very helpful.

HOW NOT TO PANIC IN SOCIAL SITUATIONS.

Social phobia stems from the fear of being shown up. Either you're wearing last year's kitten heel when everyone else is in wedges; or they've all just come back from Marrakesh while you've been to Wales in a caravan; they've got better jobs, bigger houses, more perfect children, smaller bottoms. It's a wonder you dare go out at all.

In such circumstances, there is only one sensible course of action. Tell the truth. If someone says to you, 'Have you seen the latest Mamet play, isn't it simply marvellous?' and you never, ever go to the theatre, either because you can't afford it or because you loathe it, just be honest. Don't try to pretend that you have even the slightest idea what this person is talking about. Say so, unapologetically. What's the worst that can happen? If the person is well brought-up, they will change the subject. If they're not, you don't really want to be talking to them anyway.

Besides, no one is ever as confident as they look. If you're at a large party, here's what you do if you walk in and see no one, absolutely no one, you recognise. Take a deep breath, pick up a drink and proceed to a quiet area of the room. Assume an air of detached confidence, and just observe. Enjoy seeing all the people coming and going, air-kissing and gesticulating. Think to yourself: I am a Social Observer, not a Social Outcast. Drink your drink, grab a few passing canapés (one of the advantages of this technique is that if you are on the sidelines, you always get more food, because waiters hate braving the scrum). Sooner or later, we guarantee, the one person at this ghastly gathering whom you do know, and who does like you, will spot you and make a beeline in your direction. This is because you look calm and confident, even though you may believe that you are completely terrified inside.

That's the theory, anyway. Sometimes it does not work. A sick, tense feeling builds up in your stomach. The waiters start looking at you with pity. This is what taxis are for. Exercise your human right to get in one and let it take you home.

A useful maxim for avoiding social tiger traps is General Montgomery's idea that time spent in reconnaissance is seldom wasted. We know a woman who sat down next to a charming but perfectly unassuming gentleman at a dinner party one evening. There was obligatory small talk, before the conversation turned to more serious matters, including the print media. She had a bit of experience, and a few strong views, and they argued amiably. After a while, realising that he obviously knew a bit on the subject too, she asked him what it was he actually did. Rather sheepishly, he confessed to being in publishing too. What area, she pressed him. Newspapers, it transpired. In what capacity? 'Well …' He paused, clearly casting around for the right word. 'I sort of, well, I own them,' he said, with a slight tone of apology in his voice. She had spent an hour and a half telling a leading publishing baron how to run his newspapers. So remember: if you're not sure, check.

HOW TO DEAL WITH BEING IN THE WRONG.

Admit it, at once. Make no excuses, or even explanations. Move quietly away from the rationalisation box: there is nothing in there for you. You may, if you are very good, say something like: I don't know *what* came over me. You almost certainly did not.

Apologise, freely, with great grace. Resolve, to yourself, or to the other person, that you will never make the same mistake again.

Remember, when you get home, with the trail of shame still smouldering after you, that being in the wrong is a finite state, not a general one. Taking a mistaken turn and ending up there once does not mean that you must live there forever. Your inner Sat-nav screwed up, that's all. It does not mean that you are a worthless person and that you must go into the garden and eat worms for the rest of your natural born life.

HOW NOT TO TAKE YOURSELF TOO SERIOUSLY.

The work you love, the relationship you cherish, the children you adore: all those deserve a profound degree of seriousness, but you are just a person, and every human carries an intrinsic absurdity.

One of the things we never quite understand is why the word irrational is used as a derogatory term, when it seems that the default position of most people is the irrational. This is why they read horoscopes and do the lottery and believe in aliens. Even the most learned secularist will have moments of whimsy or fantasy or sheer raw insanity, from time to time. There is no reason that you should be the only person on earth who is immune. So when you find yourself doing a little tap dance in the kitchen and singing along to *My Funny Valentine* when you should be

solemnly cleaning the Frigidaire, remember that this is just what people do. Celebrate your inner idiot; it will make you very happy. It is also why people love you the most.

HOW TO GET WAX OUT OF THE CARPET.

Take a piece of brown paper, the kind using for wrapping up parcels, and a warm iron, and iron the wax. It will lift off like magic.

HOW TO HAVE A HAPPY DOG.

Train it. It's a bore, and will involve buying many of those dog-whispery books, and keeping treats in the pocket of every garment you own, so that you can reward the canine when it sits on command. We even know one woman who sent herself and her dogs to a special dog boarding school on the Isle of Mull.

Once you establish yourself as the pack leader (I am the alpha dog and you are my bitches, as one of us likes to say) your dogs will be happy, and so will you. Dogs need to know who is in charge: if they think it is them, they grow panicky and neurotic. Indulging them is not kindness, it makes them sad and fretful. And you will be calm in the knowledge that you can take them anywhere and they will not disgrace themselves.

Feed them good dry food so their breath does not smell, give them plenty of exercise, let them chase a rabbit or two on high days and holidays, and resist the temptation to dress them up in any kind of garment, which is a form of cruelty all of its own.

HOW TO DO YOUR TAX RETURNS WITHOUT CRYING.

Get an accountant. The fees you pay will be worth it in the tax and trouble you save. Keep all relevant pieces of paper in a special tax box. Although you should beware of rodents. A woman we know managed, for the first time in her adult life, to do the whole tax box thing; she was so proud of herself when January came that she practically did a little dance. Then she opened the box to find that a mouse had got in there, and shredded every single receipt and made them all into a nice little mousy nest. And the dog really did eat my homework.

When the time comes to sort out all the relevant bills and other horrors to send off to the kind operative, put some very loud music on, and keep a bottle of good red ready for emergencies. Then just do it.

Or you could just *become* an accountant yourself, in which case tax returns are more fascinating to you than the letters of Lord Chesterfield, and you have no fear.

HOW TO DEAL WITH RAGE.

Women are not allowed to be angry. No, no, because ladies are all sugar and spice, and must do the empathy and the kindness and the smiling otherwise the world will spin off its axis. Entire books have been written about women and anger, because it is such a fraught subject.

We say: forget this particular tired assumption. You are a human, sometimes you get crazy furious, and there is nothing strange or unnatural about that.

What you may need to work out about your rage is: what is it *really* about? If you find yourself cutting up a white van at the lights, or being randomly rude to a hapless shop assistant, chances are that you are not in fact cross about bad drivers or sloppy service. It is the old equation of being angry at Object A, and taking it out on Object B. It may be as well to go home and figure out whether you have a few unresolved abandonment issues, and what it actually was that set them off.

The other second great rule about anger, which one of us still has great difficulty with, even after years on the bloody couch, is: it does *not* mean the end of everything. You can love someone madly, and still be enraged by them. We know one lovely little five-year-old girl who has already worked this out, while we are still struggling with it, at the age of forty-one. Fury and love are not mutually exclusive.

And finally: careful where you put it. You might have entirely righteous, empirically justified anger towards someone; you can be emphatically in the right; and yet, throwing the rage at the person may be fatally destructive. If done incontinently, it can mean the fracturing of friendships and the stretching of marriage to the point of breaking. You need to work out when to express anger, and when to take it away and deal with it yourself. Making someone hurt and defensive to no sane purpose only ends up with you feeling regretful and foolish.

Our own way of dealing with this is to write an unfettered, incandescently angry letter, with no edits. Then we put it away for twenty-four hours. Quite often we find that once the fury is out, the trick is done; we can once again think clearly, and no longer have the sense of a clenched fist in our stomach. The letter need never be sent, the other person will never know, all is calm again. If not, get to the post office before someone closes it down.

HOW TO TALK YOURSELF OUT OF A BAD MOOD.

We heard an interesting programme on the radio the other day about the notion of good character, and how it has come to be seen as old-fashioned or somehow patronising, when it should be more relevant than ever. As women, we realised that we are sometimes too fearful of past values, and we had to read ourselves a little lecture about babies and bathwater.

So now, when we wake up in an absolute stinker of a mood, as all humans sometimes will, we remind ourselves about the importance of character. It is not clever or kind to indulge every single mood you have at the exact moment you have it. Every woman knows the horror of a person who can spread a bad mood through the house like smoke, so that everything is contaminated with it. There is no excuse for it. All sentient adults can reason themselves into some semblance of good humour.

It's not that every day has to be sunshine. Sometimes we actively recommend taking your inner bitch out for a test drive; it can be marvellously refreshing. But random bad moods, for no good reason, are debilitating and depressing for you and anyone within spitting distance. So call in the perspective police, turn the music up loud, *laugh* yourself out of it (we find internal teasing particularly effective), shout at the radio, cuss and swear, until it is past. Indulge it for a moment, and then kick it out. You can leave it in the bathroom, where it belongs. It does not have to follow you around for the whole day.

HOW TO HAVE THE CONVERSATION.

You know the one. It's the awkward one, where uncomfortable truths must be expressed, or your own vulnerabilities, which you take such care to cover, are let out in public. It's the one where you have to *ask* for something, and you hate to ask, because the answer might be no. It's the one where you risk looking like a fool.

You run it in your head. The inexplicable rule of this is that, in your own finely honed cerebellum, The Conversation always goes incredibly badly. The person doesn't get it; they laugh or mock or wilfully misunderstand. They get angry and actually shout. They accuse you of unnatural thoughts. You will certainly have to contemplate leaving the country, in order to deal with the shame.

The lovely truth is that, in reality, The Conversation almost always goes so well it is as if you have taken a course. Halfway through, you start shouting with relieved laughter. The other person, especially if it is your best friend, almost certainly knows half of it before you start, and by the end you are saying, in unison: *why* did we not do this before? Ah, ah, the air is clear, no one had to emigrate, the mutual affection is stronger than ever.

Just do it. There really is a reason that everyone goes on about the importance of communication. You will feel so much happier afterwards. And if not, well, fuck it. It's not death by suffocation.

Sarah would like to thank:

MICHAEL AND THE MITTENS, FOR THEIR ETERNAL
LOVE AND PATIENCE.

Tania would like to thank:

EVERYONE ON THE COMPOUND, FOR THEIR
UNDYING ENTHUSIASM, AND TERENCE BLACKER,
FOR HIS WISE COUNSEL.

And we both would like to thank:

CLARE AND EUGENIE FOR CURBING OUR
EXCESSES, MARTA MUNOZ FOR GIVING US THE
PICTURES, AND GINGER ROGERS, FOR INSPIRING
THE TITLE.